Medals and Ribbons of the U.S. Navy

An Ilustrated History and Guide

Press

Colonel Frank C. Foster

Hardcover Edition ISBN — 978-1-884452-78-9
Softcover Edition ISBN - 978-1-884452-79-6
eBook Edition ISBN — 978-1-884452-91-8

Library of Congress Control Number: 2021935184

Copyright © 2025 by MOA Press

All rights reserved. No part of this publication may be reproduced, stored in retrieval systems or transmitted by any means, electronic, mechanical or by photocopying, recording or by any information storage and retrieval system without permission from the publishers, except for the inclusion of brief quotations in a review.

Edited by Mrs. Linda Brailsford Foster

Published by MOA Press (Medals of America Press)

114 Southchase Blvd.
Fountain Inn, SC 29644
www.moapress.com
www.usmedals.com

325 Rocky Slope Road
Suite 234
Greenville SC 29607
www.moapress.com

About the Author

COLONEL
Frank Foster

COLONEL FRANK C. FOSTER (USA Ret.), obtained his BS from The Citadel, MBA from the University of Georgia and is a graduate of the Army's Command and General Staff College and War College. He saw service as a Battery Commander in Germany and served in Vietnam with the 173rd Airborne Brigade and USARV General Staff. In the Adjutant General's Corps, he served as the Adjutant General of the Central Army Group, the 4th Infantry Division and was the Commandant and Chief of the Army's Adjutant General's Corps from 1986 to 1990. His military service provided him a unique understanding of the Armed Forces Awards System. He currently operates Medals of America Press and is the author of *The Decorations, Medals, Badges and Insignia of the United States Army*, *The Medals and Ribbons of the United States Air Force* and coauthor of *The Decorations and Medals of the Republic of Vietnam* and *Marine Awards and Insignia* along with numerous other publications. He and his wife Linda, who was decorated with the Army Commander's Medal in 1990 for service to the Army, live in Greenville, South Carolina.

Grateful Acknowledgements

The author wish to express his deepest appreciation to the following individuals for their invaluable contributions. Without their unselfish efforts, this book would have ended as an unfilled dream.

The entire Medals of America team with special thanks to:

- Mrs. Linda Foster for the splendid job in editing this book.
- Medals of America, Fountain Inn, SC for providing all the medals, badges, insignia and display cases.
- Col. (Ret.) Charles Mugno, Director of the Institute of Heraldry.
- Mr. John Sylvester, for Vietnamese awards.
- Major Peter Morgan for great insignia advice.
- Dr.. Steve Himes and Mrs. Terri Himes for their techinical assistance in getting the book on different production platforms.
- Mr. Bryan Scott Johnson for his references on Medals of the Revolution and readiness to lend a helping hand.
- Mr. Tyke Supenchick for splendid editing and expert advice on U.S. Navy awards and insignia as well as excellent art work.
- Mr. Clinton Foster for the generous use of his fine photographs of early numbered U.S. Military Medals.
- Mr. Augusto Meneses, Design Director of ADDMedia Creatives for his most excellent work in preparing this book.

Introduction

Twenty plus years ago, Jim Thonpson, a former Marine and I sat down at a table in Red Top Farm, Fountain Inn, South Carolina to draft the first edition of our *Complete Guide to United States Navy Medals, Badges and Insignia*. After several editions and 30,000 copies it is time to replace and expand the book. If any justification is required, you need only to note that the United States Armed Forces have produced over 100 new military awards in 70 plus years since the unification of the Armed Forces in 1947, or an average of over one new award per year. What is also remarkable since 1947 the majority of the new awards have been ribbon only awards. To put it in prospective of the over 100 new military awards since 1947, 57 of them have been ribbon only awards. While the establishment of so many awards is a clear indication of the many missions and roles thrust upon the Armed Forces since the United States assumed its mantle of world leadership it also reflects the importance of medals and ribbons to an all volunteer force .

This book is enlarged by over 30 pages and encompasses not only the award changes made over the past 20 years, but now covers all significant military medals back to the start of the Republic in 1776. As before, it is designed to be a definitive illustrated reference and guide covering United States decorations, medals and ribbons for veterans, their families, active duty and reserve personnel. It is also meant as a single source for the military decorations and medals of each service. Some of the material is derived from the latest military awards and uniform manuals and other authoritative sources, although my personal opinions usually slip in from time to time.

Owing to the complimentary reviews enjoyed by earlier books, I expanded the original format and substantially upgraded readability (hopefully). There are new sections on the history of military medals, how to determine a veteran's medals and how to display veterans medals and ribbons so as to make the subject a little clearer.

The book also tries to reflect the growing appreciation throughout our country for the sacrifice and effort our veterans have endured to earn these awards. This awareness is coupled with the desire of families and veterans to display the honors their grateful country has awarded them. I have kept the best of the earlier editions and enhanced them with new material on the wear, display and variations of our military awards.

I hope that you will be pleased by the level of detail and features in this book that cover the entire spectrum of United States Military awards. Some of the new sections are:

A. The color device and ribbon attachment pages that reflect a complete history and their correct wear.
B. Complete order of precedence charts for the wear of multi-service ribbons developed in response to veterans who have served in more than one Service branch.
C. Detailed ribbon charts which show award precedence for each of the six Services spanning the period from World War II to the Global War on Terrorism.

Finally, in what has become a trademark, the new *Inherent Resolve Campaign Medal* is presented after the Iraq Campaign Medal.

And then there's that ugly word; MISTEAKS. Every book in print, probably dating back to the Gutenberg Bible, no matter how often edited, brilliantly-conceived or well-intentioned, is bound to possess its share of errors and mispelled words. We have worked hard to make this an error free book. If any errors are detected, please accept my apologies, let me know through our publisher and be assured they will be corrected in future editions. In this spirit, I will start the ball rolling by pointing out that the words "MISTEAKS" and "mispelled" in the second sentence of this paragraph are both misspelled.

As the famous Charleston artist John Doyle once said: 'It takes two people to paint a picture, one to paint and one to tell the painter when to stop." This book may have gotten a little carried away in some areas, but hopefully not. I hope that this new edition will provide you the insights and information to honor the veteran in your family.

Your suggestions to improve future editions are always appreciated. Cheers!

Col. Frank C. Foster
(USA, Ret.)
Greenville, SC

Medals and Ribbons of the U.S. Navy

Introduction	3
The Beginning of Military Awards	5
History of United States Navy Awards	6
Navy Medals, Ribbons & Devices Wear Guide	28
Armed Forces Ribbon Chart Displays	30
How to Determine Veteran's Military Medals	52
Issue of U.S. Medals to Veterans, Retirees and Their Families	54
World War II to Iraq Military Service Medals	58
Examples of Navy Awards Displays 1941-2012	63
U.S. Merchant Marine Medals	75
Wear of Medals and Ribbons by Veterans	76
Early U.S. Military Medals 1782 to 1939	78
The Pyramid of Honor	84
U.S. Military Awards 1939 to Present	85
The Medals of Honor	86
U.S. Navy Decorations, Service Medals Unit Awards & Service Ribbons	91
Foreign Military Decorations	155
WW II Foreign Campaign Medals	160
United Nations and NATO Medals	162
Post WW II Foreign Campaign Medals	165
USN Marksmanship Awards	170
Commeorative Medals	173
Bibliography	176
Abbreviations for Navy Awards	177
Index	178

The Beginning of Military Awards

While the beginning of military awards can be traced to the ancient Egyptians and the Greeks it was the Roman Legions who first organized an award system honoring their soldiers for bravery and service. Once recognized, Roman soldiers wore these decorations in battle, parades and displayed them in their homes after their military service. If an entire Roman legion was cited for valor a decoration was added to the Legion's eagle standard. The symbols from the Roman standard pictured can be seen in the decorations and awards of Napoleon, United States Navy insignia as early as 1812 and the Third Reich to name a few. So, as we begin the history of United States decorations and awards it is clear our early designs of the eagle, lightning, victory wreaths of laurel and oak came from ancient Roman Legions.

After the fall of Rome, the custom of awarding medals for military service probably owes its origin to the badges used within the armies of England after the decline of armor and before the introduction of distinctive uniforms. The badges themselves of course grew out of the coats of arms which emblazon retainer's liveries. There are a number of instances of record where commanders rewarded men on the battlefield by giving them badges struck in some valuable metal or perhaps embossed with precious stones. Heroes, who were decorated in this way removed the ordinary metal insignia from their coats or hats and wore instead the much prized emblem. This was probably the beginning of medal granting and wearing as it is in the Armed Forces of today.

It was Queen Elizabeth I who introduced the custom of bestowing medals as rewards for naval and military service based on her fleet's defeat of the Spanish Armada in 1588. The most famous is known as the Armada Medal medal and bore the profile of Queen Elizabeth in an elaborate quilted dress with neck ruff and diadem. The reverse of the medal shows a tiny island surrounded by a storm beaten sea while a bay tree stands unaffected by the wind. The inscription in Latin translates," Not even in danger affect it". The design provided is with a loop for suspension around the wear'ers neck and influenced medals for the coming centuries. While Queen Elizabeth was the first to award an English war medal she presented them sparingly and only to naval personnel.

Armada Medal

Medals of America Press 5

A Brief History of United States Military Awards

Benjamin Franklin, the U.S. Ambassador to France commissioned Benjamin Duvivier, Chief Engraver of the Paris Mint to produced the first medal in 1781 to honor General Washington for the Seige of Boston.

Revolutionary War 1775-1782. *"Few inventions could be more happily calculated to diffuse the knowledge and preserve the memory of illustrious characters and splendid events, than medals."* These words written in 1787 by General Washington's aide expressed the feelings of the Continental Congress in March 1776 when they instituted the tradition of awarding medals as the highest distinction of national appreciation for our military heroes.

General Washington's success in driving the British from Boston in 1776, General Horatio Gates' victory at Saratoga in 1777, the storming of the British Forts at Stony Point and Paulus Hook in 1779, and General Greene's Southern victories in 1781 all led to the final British surrender at Yorktown in 1781. These were great milestones in the United States' War of Independence. The people and Congress were very proud of their heroes and wished to bestow a sign of national recognition especially upon those officers who had distinguished themselves in battle.

As a result, Congress voted to award gold medals to outstanding military leaders. The first approved medal honored George Washington and similar medals were bestowed upon other victors such as General Horatio Gates and Captain John Paul Jones for his naval victory over the HMS Serapis in 1779.

Since Benjamin Franklin, the U.S. Ambassador to France at the time, had access to the best of the French Royal engravers, it was only natural for this country to turn to France for help in the actual production of our first military medals. Under Franklin's leadership the Chief Engraver of the Paris Mint produced the first medal in 1784. However, following Franklin's departure from France, the development of the other medals for American heroes was extremely slow until Col. David Humphreys and, later, Thomas Jefferson became involved. It was not until March, 1790, that President Washington received his gold medal and silver copies of all the medals approved by Congress over 10 years earlier.

While these large table top presentation medals were not designed to be worn on the military uniform many thought otherwise since General Horatio Gates' portrait shows his medal hanging from a neck ribbon. Thomas Jefferson wanted these medals, of which he was very proud, to be known and preserved throughout the world. He planned to present sets of these medals to heads of state, foreign dignitaries and every college in the United States. Jefferson clearly saw medals as the best way to preserve the memory, valor and distinction of America's soldiers and sailors.

President Thomas Jefferson clearly saw medals as the best way to preserve the memory, valor and distinction of America's soldiers and sailors.

The Battle of Flamborough Head

On 23 September 1779, off the east coast of England, a four ship Continental Navy squadron comprising the 40 gun ship USS Bonhomme Richard, a 36 gun and 32 gun frigate, and a 12 gun Brig, encountered a 41 British merchant ship convoy arriving from the Baltics laden with precious commodities. The merchants were guarded by two British warships, HMS Serapis of 44 guns and a smaller ship of 20 guns. At the conclusion of the battle both British ships struck their colors.

The stories of the battle are as important as the actually event. The battle saw Captain John Paul Jones in command of USS Bonhomme Richard, a French merchant ship refitted for battle. Jones locked his ship on the HMS Serapis since his ship was no match for the 50 gun British frigate. Pounded by the heavier British frigate and with his ship taking on water, burning, and despite heavy casualties the legend of Captain Jones yelling out "I have not yet begun to fight," to his sailors and "I will sink before I strike," to the British Captain set the tone and standard for American Naval valor. While a bloody and mutually destructive fight, the victory of the USS Bonhomme Richard against the powerful Royal Navy gave the United States Navy its earliest traditions of heroism and victory.

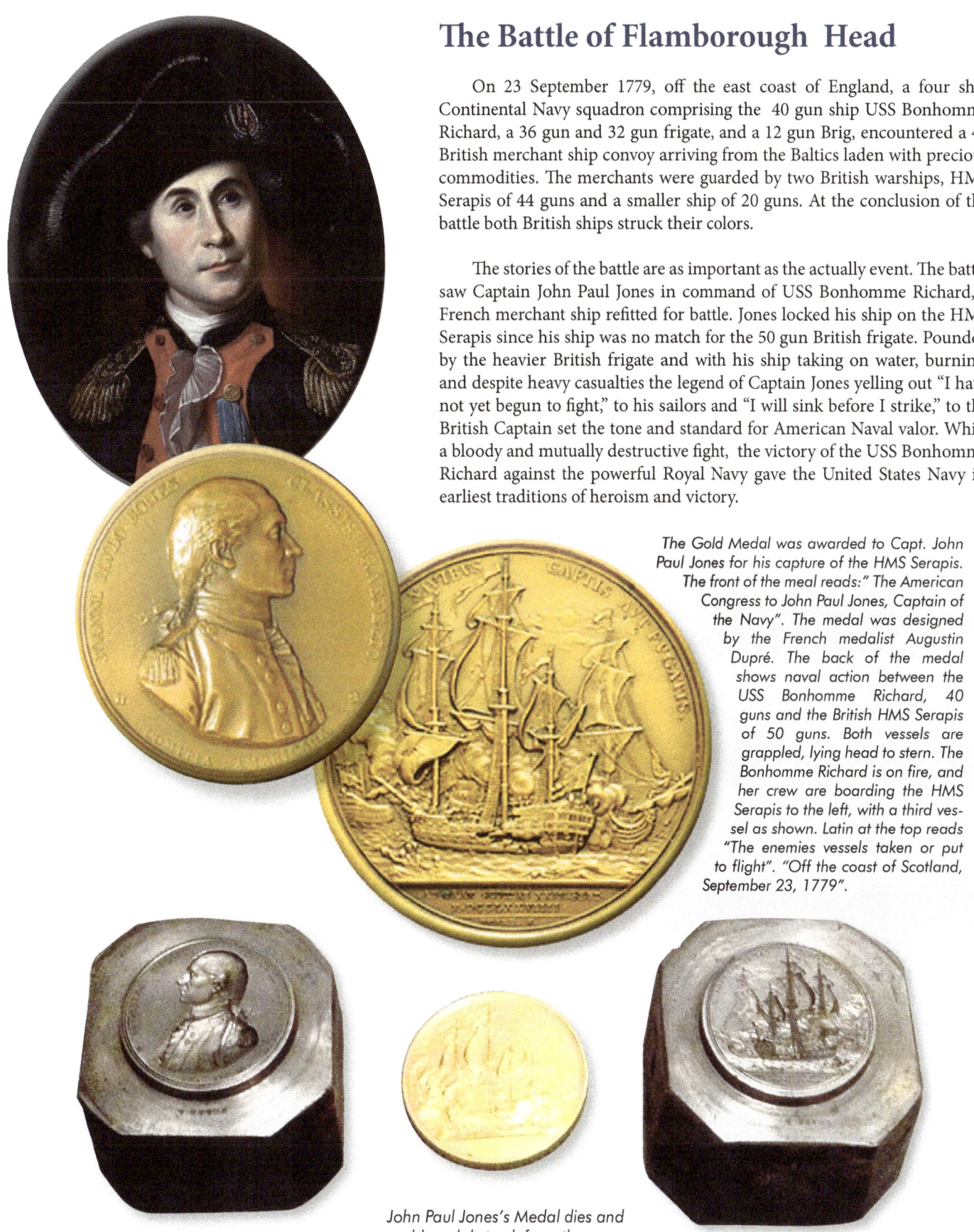

The Gold Medal was awarded to Capt. John Paul Jones for his capture of the HMS Serapis. The front of the meal reads:" The American Congress to John Paul Jones, Captain of the Navy". The medal was designed by the French medalist Augustin Dupré. The back of the medal shows naval action between the USS Bonhomme Richard, 40 guns and the British HMS Serapis of 50 guns. Both vessels are grappled, lying head to stern. The Bonhomme Richard is on fire, and her crew are boarding the HMS Serapis to the left, with a third vessel as shown. Latin at the top reads "The enemies vessels taken or put to flight". "Off the coast of Scotland, September 23, 1779".

John Paul Jones's Medal dies and a gold medal struck from them.

In a letter Thomas Jefferson wrote to M. Dupre, Engraver of Medals and Medallist of the French Royal Academy of Painting and Sculpture, dated Feb.13,1789, he sends the "devices" (designs) "for the medals for General Morgan and Rear-Admiral Paul Jones… " *to Dupre for "the success of the dies up to the striking of three hundred and fifty of each medal in gold, silver or bronze… The hand engraved dies of medal by the French medalist Augustin Dupré as well as gold and bronze examples are shown above.*

Medals of America Press **7**

Quasi-War with France 1798-1801

With independence won, the last ship of the Continental Navy was sold in 1785, and the Nation soon experienced the consequences of neglecting sea power. The actions of Mediterranean pirates caused Congress in 1794 to provide a Navy for the protection of commerce. Subsequently, depredations by the privateers of Revolutionary France against the expanding merchant shipping of the United States led to an undeclared Quasi- War with France was fought entirely at sea.

The new U.S. Navy 's Captain Thomas Truxtun's insistence on the high standards of crew training led the frigate Constellation to two complete victories over French men-of-war L'Insurgente and La Vengeance. U.S. naval squadrons, operating principally in West Indian waters, sought out and attacked enemy privateers until France agreed to an honorable settlement.

Captain Thomas Truxtun's Gold Medal

Barbary Wars 1801-1805, 1815

The Barbary States of North Africa demanded tribute money, seized American ships, and held crews for ransom or sold them into slavery. The United States sent naval squadrons into the Mediterranean. Under Commodores Richard Dale and Edward Preble, the Navy blockaded the enemy coast, bombarded his shore fortresses, and engaged in close, bitterly contested gunboat actions.

Lieutenant Stephen Decatur's exploit in destroying the captured frigate USS Philadelphia, and Captain Richard Somers attempt with the fire-ship USS Intrepid to blow up enemy vessels in Tripoli harbor, set valorous examples for the young naval service. Gradual withdrawal of the U.S. Navy led the Barbary powers to renew their age-old piratical practices. Following the War of 1812 two naval squadrons under Commodores Decatur and Bainbridge returned to the Mediterranean. Diplomacy backed by resolute force soon brought the rulers of Barbary to terms and gained wide spread respect for the new American nation.

Uniforms - The first uniform instructions for the United States Navy were issued by the Secretary of War on 27 August 1791. This first set of instructions provided for a distinctive dress for officers who would command ships of the Federal Navy. The instructions didn't specify a uniform for enlisted personnel, but the usual dress for seamen was made up of a short jacket, shirt, vest, long trousers and a black crowned hat. The bell bottom trousers were introduced in 1817 and allowed men to roll them above the knee when washing down the decks. These first trousers had seven buttons until the early 1800's, when they had 15. *(The 13 buttons common during World War II are said to be for the 13 original colonies, but there is no basis in fact for this.)* The short jacket, or jumper, had a "tar" flap which was intended to protect it from the grease or powder normally used by seamen to hold their hair in place.

Neckerchiefs, or bandannas, were originally used as sweat bands and collar closures. The predominant color was black, which was less likely to show dirt.

Captain Oliver Hazard Perry and Captain Jesse D. Elliott. In recognition of the "decisive and glorious victory gained on Lake Erie" by Captain Oliver Hazard Perry and Captain Jesse D. Elliott, on September 10, 1813. Approved January 6, 1814

The War of 1812 (1812-1815)

During the first 50 years of the United States, military awards and decorations were extremely few compared to today. Generally only high ranking officer were honored for heroic efforts and victory. Congress had 3 ceremonial accolades reserved for senior officers of victorious battles. All of these awards had to approved by congress. The most prestigious award was a "Congressional Gold Medal" minted and engraved for a specific action or event. Next, was the "Ceremonial Sword," custom made to recognize a spectacular achievement. However, the most common reward for a highly distinguished officer was a "Letter of Thanks" from the congress.

British impressment of American sailors into the Royal Navy, interception of neutral ships and blockades of the United States during British hostilities with France led the United States to declare war against Great Britain in 1812. The War of 1812 saw widespread introduction of the American bald eagle as the national symbol on flags, hats, breastplates and belt buckles. The Congress retained the custom of commissioning large presentation medals to victorious commanding

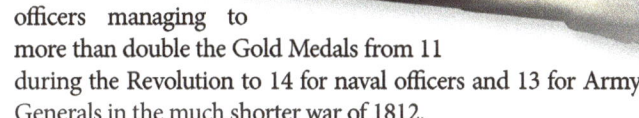

officers managing to more than double the Gold Medals from 11 during the Revolution to 14 for naval officers and 13 for Army Generals in the much shorter war of 1812.

A number of naval officers were voted medals, swords and other honors by Congress for victories. The Navy won several courageous victories in ship-to-ship actions; the most memorable of which was that by Captain Isaac Hull in USS Constitution *(Old Ironsides)* over HMS Guerriere. Commodore Oliver Hazard Perry's victory in the Battle of Lake Erie placed the Northwest Territory firmly in American control and boosted American morale. Another fleet victory by Commodore Thomas Macdonough on Lake Champlain turned back a British invasion from Canada.

Commodore Daniel Patterson's small naval squadron in New Orleans delayed and harassed the advancing British with ship gunfire allowing General Andrew Jackson to prepare his defenses and win victory in New Orleans..

Nation Building 1816-1843 – Engagements between pirates and American ships occurred repeatedly around Cuba, Puerto Rico, Santo Domingo and Yucatan. Over three thousand pirate attacks on merchantmen were reported between 1815 and 1823. In 1815, the Second Barbary War was declared against the United States by the Barbary States, but not reciprocated by the United States Congress. However, Congress did authorize a large fleet under Captain Stephen Decatur to attack Algiers and obtain indemnities. Here, as in the past, victories were noted by congressional or by local medallions or commemorative swords.

Medals of America Press

African Slave Trade Patrol 1820-1861

Slave trade was declared by Congress in 1819 to be piracy, and as such, punishable by death. The Patrol, which from time to time included the USS Constitution, USS Constellation, USS Saratoga and USS Yorktown, patroled the waters off West Africa, South America, and the Cuban coast, capturing more than 100 suspected slavers before the Civil War.

The Mexican War (1844-48) and the Beginning of Change

With the admission of the Texas Republic into the United States, tensions between Mexico and the United States led to war. The Navy's squadrons blockaded Mexico's east and west coasts, seized many ports and conducted operations to land army troops. Commodore M. C. Perry, led a brilliant one day amphibious landing of 12,000 Army troops on the beaches of Veracruz which opened the door to the capture of Mexico City.

During the time of the Mexican War and thereafter the Federal Government still showed a great reluctance to strike medals for soldiers and sailors but continued the award of Congressional Gold Medals. However, various states such as South Carolina and New York showed no such resistance. For example, the state of South Carolina struck 1000 Silver Medals for members of the Volunteer Palmetto Regiment who served in the Mexican War. Each large silver medal was engraved with the name of the Soldier and individually presented to the Soldier or next of kin. Officers received Gold Medals. Some cities such as Charleston, South Carolina also commissioned medals specifically for their local company. It is interesting to note that the South Carolina medals were designed for table top display but veterans immediately took to drilling small holes in the top of the medal and wearing them as watch fobs or hanging them from their coat lapel on patriotic occasions.

This was the turning point where Congressional Gold Medals no longer became the only military award for valor and victorious service but focused on persons who performed an achievement which had an impact on America history long after the achievement. So here we leave Congressional Medals and begin to focus on military medals as we know them today.

South Carolina struck 1000 Silver Medals for members of the Volunteer Palmetto Regiment

USS Mississippi, a paddle frigate, was the first ship of the United States Navy to bear that name. She was named for the Mississippi River. Her keel was laid down by the Philadelphia Navy Yard in 1839; built under the personal supervision of Commodore Matthew Perry. Mississippi joined the West Indian Squadron in 1845 as flagship for Commodore Perry. During the Mexican–American War, she took part in expeditions against Alvarado, Tampico, Pánuco, and Laguna de Términos, all successful in tightening American control of the Mexican coastline.

10 Medals and Ribbons of the U.S. Navy

Civil War (1861-1865)

Army

Navy

Civil War Medals of Honor

Navy Civil War Campaign Medal reverses

Army Civil War Campaign Medal

The Civil War saw the first United States military decorations. The Navy Medal of Honor arose from a public resolution signed into law by President Lincoln on 21 December 1861. It authorized the preparation of 200 Medals of Honor to promote the efficiency of the Navy. It was followed by a joint resolution of Congress on the same day which approved the design and defined requirement eligibility of the potential recipients. The Army Medal of Honor was established by a joint resolution of Congress, July 12, 1862 with an effective date of April 15, 1861. The Medal of Honor was originally only to be presented to enlisted men for heroic service in the United States Army. However, as the war continued the award of a Medal of Honor was extended to include Army officers.

In 1905 President Roosevelt authorized campaign medals retroactive to the Civil War. The Civil War Campaign Medal (Army) was issued for any federal army service between April 15, 1861 and April 9, 1865 (with extended service in the state of Texas through August 20, 1866). The Navy and Marine Corps were also authorized Civil War Campaign Medals, with each service having a different design on the reverse of the medal. Very few Marine Corps medals were ever issued making it one of the rarest of all American campaign medals. The original Army campaign medal had a red, white and blue ribbon which was changed in 1913 to match the Navy and Marine Corps Civil War Medal blue and gray ribbon design.

The Civil War Campaign Medal is considered the first campaign service medal of the United States Armed Forces. The decoration is now authorized members of the United States but not the Confederate States Armed Forces who had served in the American Civil War between 1861 and 1865. *The blue and gray ribbon denotes the respective uniform colors of the U.S. and Confederate troops.*

The Navy Good Conduct Badge of 1869

Navy Good Conduct Badge of 1869

The Navy Good Conduct Medal dating back to 1869 is the third-oldest continuously presented award after the Army Medal of Honor and the Navy Medal of Honor. While there have been four versions of the Navy Good Conduct Medal, the first was issued from 1870 to 1884. The medal was not worn on the uniform but presented as a badge during discharge. This of course makes the Navy Good Conduct Medal the earliest of any of the Services' Good Conduct Medals. The Marine Corps issued their Good Conduct Medal in 1896, the Coast Guard in 1923 and the Army in 1941.

The 1869 medal was a Maltese cross made of nickel, with the words "FIDELITY - ZEAL - OBEDIENCE" in a circle and "U.S.N." in the center of the disc. The reverse was blank except for the engraved name of the recipient. The cross hung from a small one-half inch wide red, white, and blue ribbon. Sailors called it the "Nickel Cross". It was redesigned in 1880 along the lines of the current medallion.

Spanish American War (1898 -1899)

It was not until the turn of the 20th Century that a host of medals were authorized to commemorate the events surrounding the Spanish-American War. This was future President Theodore Roosevelt's "Bully Little War" that produced seven distinct medals for only four months of military action. Supply had finally caught up with demand.

The first of these was the medal to commemorate the victory of the naval forces under the command of Commodore Dewey over the Spanish fleet at Manila Bay. This award was notable as it was the first such medal in U.S. history to be awarded to all officers and enlisted personnel present during a specific military expedition. It is also one of the handsomest American medals ever designed.

When Roosevelt, an ardent supporter of the military, ultimately reached the White House, he took it upon himself to legislate for the creation of medals to honor all those who had served in America's previous conflicts. Thus, by 1908 the U.S. had authorized campaign medals, some retroactive, for the Civil War, Indian Wars, War with Spain, Philippine Insurrection and China Relief Expedition of 1900-01. While the Army, Navy and Marine Corps used the same ribbons, different medals were struck. Concurrently the custom of wearing service ribbons on the tunic was adopted during this same time frame (using different orders of precedence for each service). Thus, the different Armed Services managed to establish the principle of independence in the creation and wearing of awards that is virtually unchanged today.

Admiral Dewey wearing his Campaign Medal known as the Manila Bay ("Dewey") Medal.

USS Olympia, a protected cruiser was commissioned in 1895 and became famous as the flagship of Commodore George Dewey at the Battle of Manila Bay during the Spanish–American War in 1898. The bronze to the left was presented by the City of Olympia and is now mounted between the two main guns on the foredeck.

West Indies Naval Campaign (Sampson) Medal (Navy)

West Indies Campaign Medal Navy and Marines

Spanish Campaign Medal Navy, Marines

Specially Meritorious Medal, Navy

Medals of America Press 13

Military Society Medals (1865-1913)

Society of the Cincinnatus

Aztec Club of 1847

General Society of the War of 1812

Grand Army of the Republic Society Medal

Military Order of the Loyal Legion

Military Order of the Dragon 1900

Up until the Spanish American War no Army or Navy in the world was so little decorated as the United States. The simplicity of uniforms were set off by no medals or ribbons. After the Civil War, Congress under pressure from veteran's organizations permitted officers and enlisted men to wear their Corps and Division badge. For nearly twenty years, the Medal of Honor remained the sole American military award of any kind. Although the Navy had authorized the first Good Conduct Badge in 1869, clearly the officers and enlisted personnel of the Army and Navy wanted to have medals like their counterparts around the world.

Their solution was to have Congress approve the wearing of the military society medals such as the Aztec Club which consisted of officers who served in Mexico in 1847, the Grand Army of the Republic, the Loyal Legion, Army and Navy Union of the United States of America, and the Military Order of the Dragon, commemorating the China Relief Expedition were just a few. The point was the professional officer corps wanted an awards system to recognize service and if the government was not going to create one they would. The post Civil War Congress contained a large number of veterans so approval to wear these society medals on uniforms was not difficult. In regard to military society medals a subject that often comes up is a question of wearing certain military society medals on military uniforms. Title X of United States code, section 1123 (a) states:

"A member of the Army, Navy, Air Force or Marine Corps who is a member of a military society originally composed of men who served in the Armed Forces of the United States during the Revolutionary War, the War of 1812, the Mexican War, the Civil War, the Spanish-American War, the Philippine Insurrection, or the Chinese Relief Expedition may wear, on certain occasions of ceremony, the distinctive badges adopted by that society."

Basically this can be interpreted that a member of the Armed Forces who is a member of one of the societies listed can wear these medals on their uniform. The Society of the Cincinnatus, the General Society of the War of 1812, the Aztec Club, the Military Order of the Loyol Legion of the United States, the Naval order of the United States and the medals of the Veterans of Foreign Wars since the original founders of the VFW were veterans of the Spanish American war, the Philippine Insurrection and the Chinese Relief Expedition of 1900.

While there may be an occasion when one would wear Society medals or ribbons on their active duty uniform it is seldom to my knowledge actually done. However, the occasion does occur, that veterans wearing miniature medals on formal occasions could wear their society medals after (at the end) of their military decorations and service medals.

Veteran's Medals such as this jeweled Grand Army of the Republic Society Medal could equal the jeweled orders of Europe.

Philippines, China and Central America (1900-1917)

Philippine Campaign Medal (Navy)

China Relief Expedition Medal (Navy)

Cuban Pacification Medal (Navy)

Nicaraguan Campaign (Navy)

Mexican Service Medal (Navy)

Haitian Campaign Medal (Navy)

Dominican Campaign (Navy)

By the time the final peace treaty with Spain was ratified in March 1899, the Philippine Insurrection had already broken out and the majority of regular army and volunteer troops were in the Philippines fighting against insurrectionists, Philippine nationalists and Muslim fundamentalists, a conflict which raged from 1899 to 1913. Between 1900 and the 1930s, American Soldiers, Sailors and Marines were dispatched to such areas as China in 1900, Cuba in 1906, Mexico in 1911, Nicaragua in 1912, Haiti in 1915, and the Dominican Republic in 1916, to quell rebellions and deal with civil unrest. As was their earlier custom, the Army and the Navy designed and authorized their own medals to commemorate these events. The Marine Corps, although under the overall command of the Navy, preserved their uniqueness by using the Navy medals with the special Marine Corps design on the reverse.

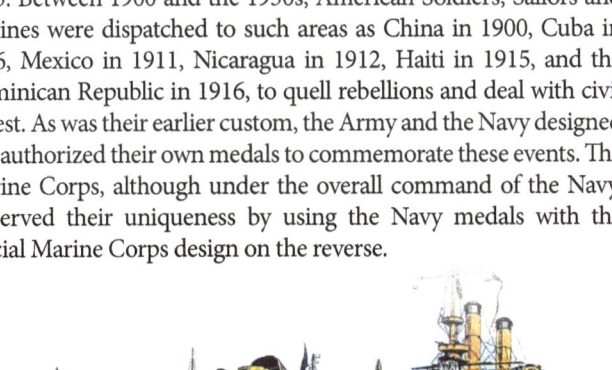

In 1905, the Navy's version of the Philippine Campaign Medal was issued with no devices authorized and was originally suspended from a red and yellow ribbon but on August 12, 1913, the Navy changed the ribbon color to match the Army's version of the award. The Navy was also covering the West Indies, Caribbean and projecting its power as far as China. In 1900, when fanatical Chinese called "Boxers", a rough English translation of the "Righteous Fists of Fire Society," attacked American nationals and other foreigners in the International Legations in Peking, China, the United States sent more than 5,000 Soldiers and a battalion of Marines to join a multinational relief force.

The final action just prior to World War I was the Mexican Campaign which took place between the years 1911 and 1917. Large-scale military activities by well-armed revolutionaries, caused the United States to mount a Punitive Expedition into Mexico to bring peace to the region. In the largest naval activity since the Spanish-American War, Navy and Marine Corps personnel took part in major battles along Mexico's Caribbean coast. The Army Mexican Service Medal was awarded to approximately 15,000 Soldiers and the Navy version was awarded to 16,000 Sailors and 2,500 Marines. As was common practice by now, the medal designs were all different, but the ribbons were identical. Early versions of the Campaign medals were issued with serial numbers stamped on the bottom rim of the medal or engraved on the reverse side with the date of service. This practice was discontinued on later replacement medals.

World War I (1917-1918)

Navy Cross

Navy Distinguished Service Medal

At the time of the U.S. entry into World War I, the Medal of Honor, Certificate of Merit and Navy/Marine Corps Good Conduct Medals still represented America's entire inventory of personal decorations. This presented the twin dangers that the Medal of Honor might be cheapened by being awarded too often and that other deeds of valor might go unrecognized. By 1918, popular agitation forced the authorization of two new awards, the Army's Distinguished Service Cross and Distinguished Service Medal, created by Executive Order in 1918. In the same year, the traditional U.S. refusal to permit the Armed Forces to accept foreign decorations was rescinded, allowing military personnel to accept awards from the grateful Allied governments. In 1919, the Navy created the Navy Cross and its own Distinguished Service Medal for Navy and Marine Corps personnel.

The issuance of the World War I Victory Medal established another precedent, that of wearing clasps with the names of individual battles on the suspension ribbon of a general campaign medal. This was an ongoing practice in many countries, most notably Britain and France, since the 19th century. When the ribbon bar alone was worn, each clasp was represented by a small (3/16" diameter) bronze star. Fourteen such clasps were adopted along with five clasps to denote service in specific countries. However, the latter were issued only if no campaign clasp was earned. Only one service clasp could be issued to any individual and they were not represented by a small bronze star on the ribbon bar. It is a final irony that the British, who were the greatest proponents of the practice, never issued a single bar with their own version of the Victory Medal.

During this period, the Army introduced the Citation Star which was established by Congress on July 9, 1918. This award, a 3/16 inch diameter silver star device, was originally authorized to be worn on the World War I Victory Medal to denote those who had been cited for extreme heroism or valor. The device, which evolved into the Silver Star Medal in 1932, was soon made retroactive as an attachment to the Army service medals for the Civil War, Indian, Spanish, China and Mexican Campaigns. Although the Citation Star was strictly a U.S. Army device, an identical ribbon attachment designated the Navy Commendation Star, was authorized for wear on the World War I Victory Medal by Navy and Marine Corps personnel who had received a Letter of Commendation from the Secretary of the Navy. However, the two awards were not considered equivalent and the Navy version was not upgradable in subsequent years to the Silver Star Medal. Bronze oak leaf clusters were also introduced to indicate a second award of the Medal of Honor or other decoration in lieu of a second medal.

World War I Victory Medal with Campaign Clasps

With Silver Star

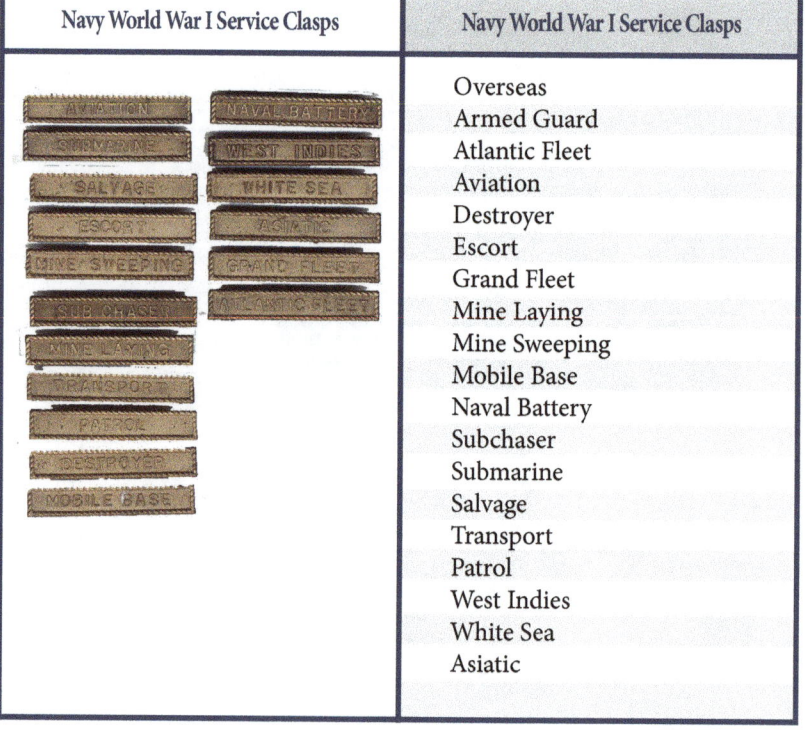

Navy World War I Service Clasps	Navy World War I Service Clasps
	Overseas
	Armed Guard
	Atlantic Fleet
	Aviation
	Destroyer
	Escort
	Grand Fleet
	Mine Laying
	Mine Sweeping
	Mobile Base
	Naval Battery
	Subchaser
	Submarine
	Salvage
	Transport
	Patrol
	West Indies
	White Sea
	Asiatic

World War I Navy Uniforms

World War I Commemorative Medals

Upon the return of troops to the United States after World War I, many county, state and federal organizations rushed to produce Commemorative medals to honor their returning soldiers. The quality of medal design and strike was quite good and the local commemorative medals were highly prized by veterans and their families. Almost a thousand different WW I Commemorative Medals were presented to their returning veterans by city, county, state and fraternal organizations. A beautiful example is South Carolina's Greenville County Medal shown to the right with other examples.

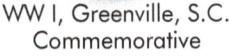

WW I, Greenville, S.C. Commemorative

Medals of America Press

World War II (1941-1945)

American Defense Service Medal

American Campaign Medal

On September 8, 1939, in response to the growing threat of involvement in World War II, the President proclaimed a National Emergency in order to increase the size of U.S. military forces. For the first time, a peacetime service award, the American Defense Service Medal, was authorized for wear by those personnel who served during this period of National Emergency prior to the attack on Pearl Harbor on December 7, 1941.

America's participation in World War II saw a significant increase in both personal decorations and campaign medals. Since U.S. forces were serving all over the world, a campaign medal was designed for each major *(and carefully defined)* area. The three medals for the American, Asiatic-Pacific and European-African-Middle Eastern Campaigns encompassed the globe. However, the World War I practice of using campaign bars was discarded in favor of 3/16" bronze stars that could denote each designated military campaign from a major invasion to a submarine war patrol.

European African Middle Eastern Campaign Medal

Asiatic-Pacific Campaign Medal

The war also saw the large scale award of foreign medals and decorations to American servicemen. The Philippine Government, for one, authorized awards to commemorate the Defense and Liberation of their island country. The first foreign award designed strictly for units, the Philippine Presidential Unit Citation, patterned after a similar American award, was also approved for wear by American forces. In the European Theater, France and Belgium made many presentations of their War Crosses *(Croix de Guerre)* to U.S. military personnel.

WW II Victory Medal

Navy Occupation Service Medal

The end of World War II saw the introduction of two counterparts of previous World War I awards, the Victory and Occupation Medals. This time, no bars or clasps were authorized for the Victory Medal, but bars were issued with the Occupation Medal to denote the recipient's area of service. The Prisoner of War Medal and the Philippine Independence Medal are other examples of medals approved after the war.

Prisoner of War Medal

Philippine Defense Medal

Philippine Liberation Medal

Philippine Independence Medal

18 Medals and Ribbons of the U.S. Navy

World War II Campaign Areas

The United States Navy grew rapidly as it faced a three front war on the seas from 1941–45. It achieved notable sucess in the Pacific Theater, with its "island hopping" campaign. The Navy fought six great battles against the Imperial Japanese Navy: Pearl Harbor, Battle of the Coral Sea, the Battle of Midway, the Battle of the Philippine Sea, the Battle of Leyte Gulf, and the Battle of Okinawa.

By the war's end in 1945, the Navy had added nearly 1,200 major combatant ships, including twenty-seven aircraft carriers, eight "fast" battleships, and ten prewar "old" battleships totaling over 70% of the world's total numbers and total tonnage of naval vessels of 1,000 tons or greater. From 7 December 1941 through 31 December 1946 the Navy grew to 4,183,466 personnel *(390,037 officers and 3,793,429 enlisted)*.

Officers 1941 Full Dress · Dress Blues · Aviation · Dress whites

Chief Petty Officers 1941 · Aviation · Crackerjack Dress Blues and Whites

| American Campaign Medal | European African Middle Eastern Campaign Medal | Asiaitic-Pacific Campaign Medal | Victory Medal | Occupation Medal | Philippine Liberation Medal |

Where were the World War II Navy Veterans's Medals at the End of World War II ?

Ribbon bars were generally all a veteran Sailor recieved at the end of the war.

During World War II, generally only decorations such as the Navy Cross, Silver Star, Distinguished Flying Cross and Purple Heart were manufactured. Brass was restricted to the manufacture of munitions so campaign medals were issued as ribbon bars. *In fact most of the campaign medals were not actually minted until several years after the war.* By then many Sailors had been discharged from the Navy and returned to civilian life. Unless the veteran sailor went through the process of writing the government and asked for their medals, many World War II veterans never received their actual campaign medals. In fact a number World War II awards were not approved until several years after the war. The World War II Occupation Medals were not approved until mid-1946 by which time many of the personnel authorized such awards had left the Armed Forces. The Prisoner of War Medal and the Philippine Independence Medal are other examples of medals approved after the war.

This Sailor's World War II discharge to the right shows the rating he held in box 21 (WT3/c) Water Tender 3rd Class and the ships he served on. In July 1942 the Navy discontinued the procurement and issuance of Good Conduct medals for the duration of World War II to conserve metal and offset the increased clerical work. Notations of eligibility were made in service jackets for later issue however, the Navy required 3 years service for a Good Conduct Medal and his discharge shows 2 years, 5 months and 9 days active service so he did not qualify for a Good Conduct Medal. However, his European African Middle Eastern Theater Campaign Medal should show at least 1 battle/campaign star as you can not earn the medal without being in at least one campaign. This sailor is authorized the 4 medals shown plus 1 star on his European African Middle Eastern Theater Campaign Medal. He may also be authorized the Philippine Liberation Medal.

Medals and Ribbons of the U.S. Navy

The "crackerjack" uniform above is a good example of what was available for veterans to wear home. His Presidential Unit Citation, Good Conduct Medal and two campaign ribbons (American Theater and Asiatic Pacfic Campaigns) along with his Victory ribbon.

That is the reason you seldom see WW II veterans wearing their medals or displaying them. Not that they weren't proud of their service for they were very, but you can not wear medals you do not receive.

While the WW II Petty Officer's medal display above includes personal decorations of the Distinguished Flying Cross and Air Medal. Almost all Navy Veterans of the Pacific Theater would have the five medals on the bottom representing the Navy Good Conduct Medal, The American Campaign Medal, the Asiatic Pacfic Campaign, The Victory Medal and the Philippine Liberation Medal.

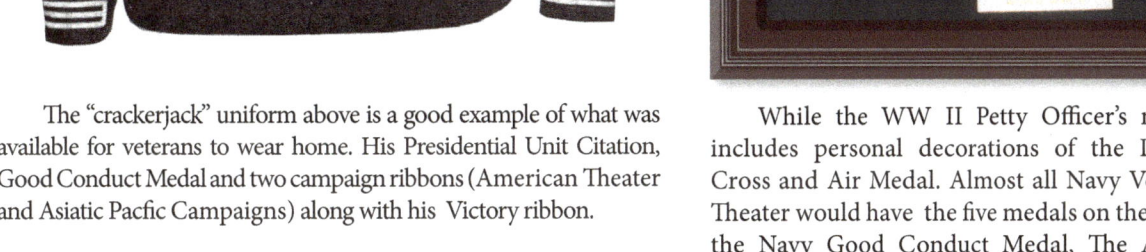

Post World War II and The Cold War

When the Iron Curtain descended over Europe, the Cold War became a major geographical and political threat and the United States Navy undertook new roles. Beginning in 1946, the Cold War lasted more than 40 years with tension and intense competition between the West under the leadership of the United States, and the East led by the Soviet Union and its satellites. From the mid-1940s to the early 1990s, both sides tried to gain advantage using weapons development, military coalitions, espionage, invasions, propaganda and competitive technology, including the famous "space race". The Cold War produced massive defense spending on conventional forces and nuclear arms and multiple proxy wars but no actual combat between the USA and USSR. However, American Sailors were actively engaged in Lebanon, the Dominican Republic, Grenada, Beirut, Libya and Panama just to name a few Cold War crisis. Tens of thousands of Sailors served during the Cold War often in tense and dangerous situations during this period.

In 1998, Congress authorized the Secretary of Defense to award a Cold War Victory Medal to all veterans of the Cold War. However, to date the Secretary of Defense has only authorized a Cold War Recognition Certificate to all members of the Armed Forces and qualified federal government civilian personnel who served during the Cold War, September 2, 1945 to December 26, 1991.

The Department of Defense has stated that it will not create a Cold War Service Medal; however, commemorative medals are minted by private vendors for veteran's displays. The Army runs the Cold War Recognition Certificate program and Cold War veterans can write to the address below for a certificate. Response can take more than a month. Write:

U.S. Army Human Resources Cmd
Cold War Recognition Program
ATTN: AHRC-PDP-A Dept 480
1600 Spearhead Division Ave.
Fort Knox, Ky 40122-540

Cold War Victory Commemorative Medal

22 Medals and Ribbons of the U.S. Navy

The Korean War (1950-1954)

Republic of Korea Presidential Unit Citation

National Defense Service Medal

Korean Service Medal

UN Korean Service Medal

ROK War Service Medal

Korea Defense Service Medal

The North Korean invasion of South Korea in June 1950 saw deployment of the Navy as a major deterrent to counter the Communist aggression during the bitter three-year fight to reestablish the independence of South Korea. The Korean Conflict, fought under the United Nations banner, saw the creation of two new medals for service. The first was the Korean Service Medal, which continued the practice of using 3/16" bronze stars on the ribbon to denote major campaigns. The second, the National Defense Service Medal, was established to recognize the contribution of all military personnel to national defense during a period of armed hostility. Some outstanding units were also awarded the Republic of Korea Presidential Unit Citation and all participants were awarded the United Nations Service Medal.

In the 1950s, the Republic of Korea (ROK) asked the United States Government for approval to present the Korean War Service Medal to the U.S.personel who served in the Korean conflict, but the award was turned down by the U.S. Government. However as the 50th Anniversary of the Korean War approached, veterans groups placed more pressure on their congressional representatives and in 1999 the medal was approved for Korean War veterans. The late approval results in the Korean War Service Medal's order of precedence being after the Kuwait Liberation Medal instead of the normal chronological order for foreign awards.

The Korea Defense Service Medal (KDSM) was instituted in 2003 and made retroactive to 1954. The medal is awarded to members of the Armed Forces who have served in the Republic of Korea or adjacent waters since the Korean War to uphold the armistice between South and North Korea. A service member must have at least thirty consecutive days service in the Korean theater to qualify for the KDSM. The medal is also granted for 60 non-consecutive days of service for reservists on annual training in Korea. All Korean War veterans who served 30 days in Korea after 27 July 1954 are eligible for the Korea Defense Service Medal.

The period of the Korean War saw the standardization of service ribbons for the Navy and Marine Corps to a smaller size of 3/8 inch high by 1 3/8 inch wide. This had long been the service ribbons size used by the Army and the Air Force. Prior to the standardization the Navy and Marine Corps used ribbons 1/2 inch high by 1 3/8 inches wide.

Medals of America Press

The Vietnam War (1965-1973)

National Defense Service Medal — Armed Forces Expeditionary Medal — Vietnam Service Medal — RVN Campaign Medal — RVN Gallantry Cross Unit Citation

The first American advisors in the Republic of South Vietnam were awarded the new Armed Forces Expeditionary Medal which was created in 1961 to cover campaigns for which no specific medal was instituted.

However, as the U.S. involvement in the Vietnamese conflict grew, a unique award, the Vietnam Service Medal was authorized, thus giving previous Navy recipients of the Expeditionary Medal the option of which medal to accept. The Government also authorized the acceptance of the Republic of Vietnam Campaign Medal for six months service in-country, or in the surrounding waters or the air after 1960. Towards the end of the war a blanket general order authorized the RVN Gallantry Cross Unit Citation for all military personnel who served in Vietnam.

The most notable change in medal policy occurred during the Vietnam War when the Department of Defense authorized the large scale acceptance of South Vietnamese awards. The South Vietnamese Armed Forces had a comprehensive awards system built to reflect their past as a former French colony. Since a large number of American military advisors and special forces worked with the South Vietnamese Armed Forces for more than 15 years, *(many serving multiple tours)* numerous medals for valor and service were presented to U.S. personnel. Some of the most awarded were the Vietnamese Cross of Gallantry *(for valor)*, the Civil Actions Medal and the Armed Forces Honor Medal *(meritorious service)*. The last two medals are unusual since they were in two different degrees; first class for officers and second class for enlisted personnel.

All foreign medals awarded to members of the U.S. Armed Forces were either furnished by the foreign government or purchased by the recipient since the United States government does not provide foreign medals to members of the Armed Forces.

After Vietnam, many new decorations, medals and ribbons came into being as the Department of Defense and the individual services developed a complete awards structure to reward performance from the newest enlistee to the most senior Joint Staff officer. Some of the awards, such as the Overseas Service Ribbon have no medal but recognize unique service.

The termination of the Vietnamese War and the following military drawdown saw the number of Sailors on active duty drop. However, during the Reagan era American defense buildup, the Navy expanded its structure and training, while supporting such special operations as Operation Urgent Fury in Grenada and Operation Just Cause, the invasion of Panama in 1989. The amazing abilities of the U.S. Navy to go anywhere at any time was one of the significant contributors to the collapse of the Soviet Union and the end of the Cold War.

Vietnamese Navy Cross of Gallantry (for valor)

Vietnamese Navy Meritorious Service

Vietnamese Navy Sea Service

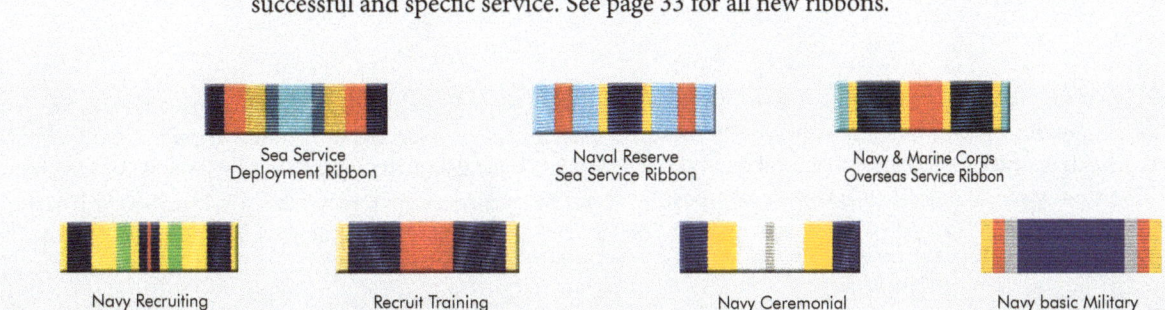

Following the Vietnam War, starting in the 1980s, the Navy established a number of new ribbons only awards to recognize successful and specfic service. See page 33 for all new ribbons.

Sea Service Deployment Ribbon

Naval Reserve Sea Service Ribbon

Navy & Marine Corps Overseas Service Ribbon

Navy Recruiting Service Ribbon

Recruit Training Service Ribbon (Obsolete)

Navy Ceremonial Duty Ribbon

Navy basic Military Training Honor Graduate Ribbon

Gulf War (Desert Shield / Desert Storm) Medals *(1991 to 1995)*

National Defense Service Medal

Southwest Asia Service Medal

Saudi Arabian Medal for the Liberation of Kuwait

Kuwait Medal for the Liberation of Kuwait.

The end of the Cold War did not mean the end of the Navy's mission of worldwide deterrent. Operations Desert Shield, Desert Storm in early 1991 saw the amazing ability of the Naval forces to steam halfway around the world and smash the invading forces of Saddam Hussein. The awesome effect of Naval power allowed the rapid liberation of Kuwait and struck awe and shock into the enemies of our country.

The conflict in the Persian Gulf saw the reinstitution of the National Defense Service Medal (this time it also covered the Reserves) and the creation of the Southwest Asia Service Medal for the personnel in Iraq, Kuwait, Saudi Arabia, Oman, Bahrain, Qatar and United Arab Emirates. Between January 17, 1991 and November 30, 1995, service members who performed duty "in support of" the Persian Gulf War are eligible to receive the Southwest Asia Service Medal if duty was performed in either Israel, Egypt, Turkey, Syria or Jordan.

The Department of Defense also approved the wear of the Saudi Arabian Medal for the Liberation of Kuwait and later the Department of Defense also authorized the Kuwait Medal for the Liberation of Kuwait.

NATO Medals *(1998 to Present)*

Former Yugoslavia

Kosovo

NATO Article 5 Medal

NATO Non Article 5 Medal

NATO ISAF Medal

During the 1990's many Sailors were awarded the NATO (North Atlantic Treaty Organization) Medal for service under NATO command or in direct support of NATO operations. The idea is somewhat similar to the U.S. Joint Service awards which are used to reward joint staff service outside of a service member's normal branch of service (i.e. Army, Navy, Air Force, Marine Corps, Space Force or Coast Guard). U.S. Forces use service stars to indicate additional awards of the NATO Medal.

For U.S. Forces, the NATO medals authorized for wear include the NATO Medal for Former Yugoslavia, the NATO Medal for Kosovo Service, both of the Article 5 Medals, the Non-Article 5 Medals for the Balkans and Afghanistan International Security and Assistance Force (ISAF), The NATO Meritorious Service Medal, the Macedonia NATO Medal and the Non-Article 5 Medal for service in the Global War on Terror. There are now currently ten versions of the NATO Medal.

The Global War on Terrorism, The Liberation of Afghanistan and Iraq

National Defense Service Medal

Afghanistan Campaign Medal

Iraq Campaign Medal

Inherent Resovle Campaign Medal

Global War on Terrorism Expeditionary Medal

Global War on Terrorism Service Medal

The cruel and cowardly terrorist hijacking and attack on the World Trade Center led to a vigorous series of counter attacks on terrorists and their supporters. To recognize these efforts, the National Defense Service Medal was reauthorized in 2001 and two new awards, the Global War on Terrorism Expeditionary and Service Medals were created. A White House spokesman said the medals recognize the "sacrifices and contributions" military members make in the global war on terror.

Following the liberation of Afghanistan, an Afghanistan Campaign Medal was created on November 29, 2004 retroactive to October 24, 2001 to acknowledge service there. A similar medal, known as the Iraq Campaign Medal, was authorized for service during the same period within the borders of Iraq and it is retroactive to March 19, 2003. These medals replace the Global War on Terrorism Expeditionary Medal for service in Afghanistan and Iraq and military personnel cannot receive both for the same period of service. In March 2016 the President approved a new Inherent Resolve Campaign Medal for members of the Armed Forces assigned to fight against Islamic terror organizations.

Navy decorations, service medals and ribbons provide a unique and handsome way for our nation to honor sailors for valor and faithful service but also have another very important purpose. Displaying awards on the Navy uniform can tell a commander, fellow members of the Armed Forces and veterans the level of experience and performance of the wearer. When a commander reviews his officers, petty officers and non-rated; it takes only a minute to recognize their backgrounds and performance based on their ribbons. From the individual service members viewpoint, military awards recognize devotion to duty, performance, valor and service in a way no other manner can accomplish. The medals and ribbons of the United State Navy reflect how our country recognizes hundreds of years of unbroken dedicated service and valor by members of the Navy going back to the birth of the Republic.

Wearing Navy Awards, Order of Precedence and Attachments

The United States Navy awards system has evolved into a highly structured program often called the "Pyramid of Honor." The system is designed to reward services ranging from heroism on the battlefield to superior performance of non combat duties and even includes the completion of entry level Navy training.

After World War II and Korea, the Navy has generally embraced Napoleon's concept of liberally awarding medals and ribbons to enhance morale and esprit de corps. Over the years an expanded and specifically-tailored awards program became generally very popular in the all-volunteer Navy and has played a significant part in improving morale, job performance, recruitment and reenlistments among junior officers and enlisted personnel.

The various ways of wearing decorations and awards by active duty, reserve and veterans are shown on the following pages. These awards paint a wonderful portrait of the Navy's men and women whose dedication to the ideals of freedom represent the rich United States Naval military heritage.

Ribbon Chart Showing the Complete History of U.S. Military Awards

This one of a kind chart on pages 30-31, reads left to right and shows the ribbon for every United States military award since 1861 with many of the variations used. The chart is a colorful walk through our Military awards history.

Navy Order of Precedence Ribbon Chart

On page 33 the current correct order of precedence for Navy ribbons is shown going back to World War II. Authorized attachments for each ribbon are displayed below the ribbon and a reference bar on the right side of the page provides guides to a detailed graphic.

Next is the Navy Order of Precedence Chart for Multi service awards. Veterans who have service in multiple branches of the Armed Forces can determine their military ribbon order of precedence beginning on page 34.

Navy Ribbon Devices *(Appurtenances)* start on page 36 and all Navy ribbon devices are shown as correctly mounted to ribbons and medals. All Navy ribbon devices are shown in alphabetical order starting with the Gold Airplane. For those who desire even more detail charts for proper placement of Navy Ribbon Devices *(Appurtenances)* start on pages 40.

Wearing Military Ribbons, Miniature Medals and Full Size Medals on Navy Uniforms.

Starting on page 43 are examples along with a brief description of Naval regulations governing current wear.

(USN photo)

Variations of a United States Military Medal

Full Size Medal
Used in display cases and mounted for wear by active duty and Reserve Naval personnel

Full Size Anodized Medals (Gold plated) Used in display cases and mounted for wear by Washington Naval Ceremonial Guard.

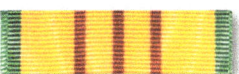

Regulation Ribbon Bar

Enamel Lapel Pin

Miniature Medals are made in brass or Anodized (Gold plated). Miniature Medals are generally only mounted for wear.

Mini Ribbon*, these are the width of Miniature Medal.

Enamel Hat Pin*

Enamel Hat Pins* & Mini Ribbons* are an unofficial item requested by Veterans for wear on unofficial clothing.

US Navy Regulations Medals mounted for wear.

Navy Ribbons are mounted three to a row for wear.

US Navy Regular Brass Miniature Medals mounted for wear.

Medals of America Press

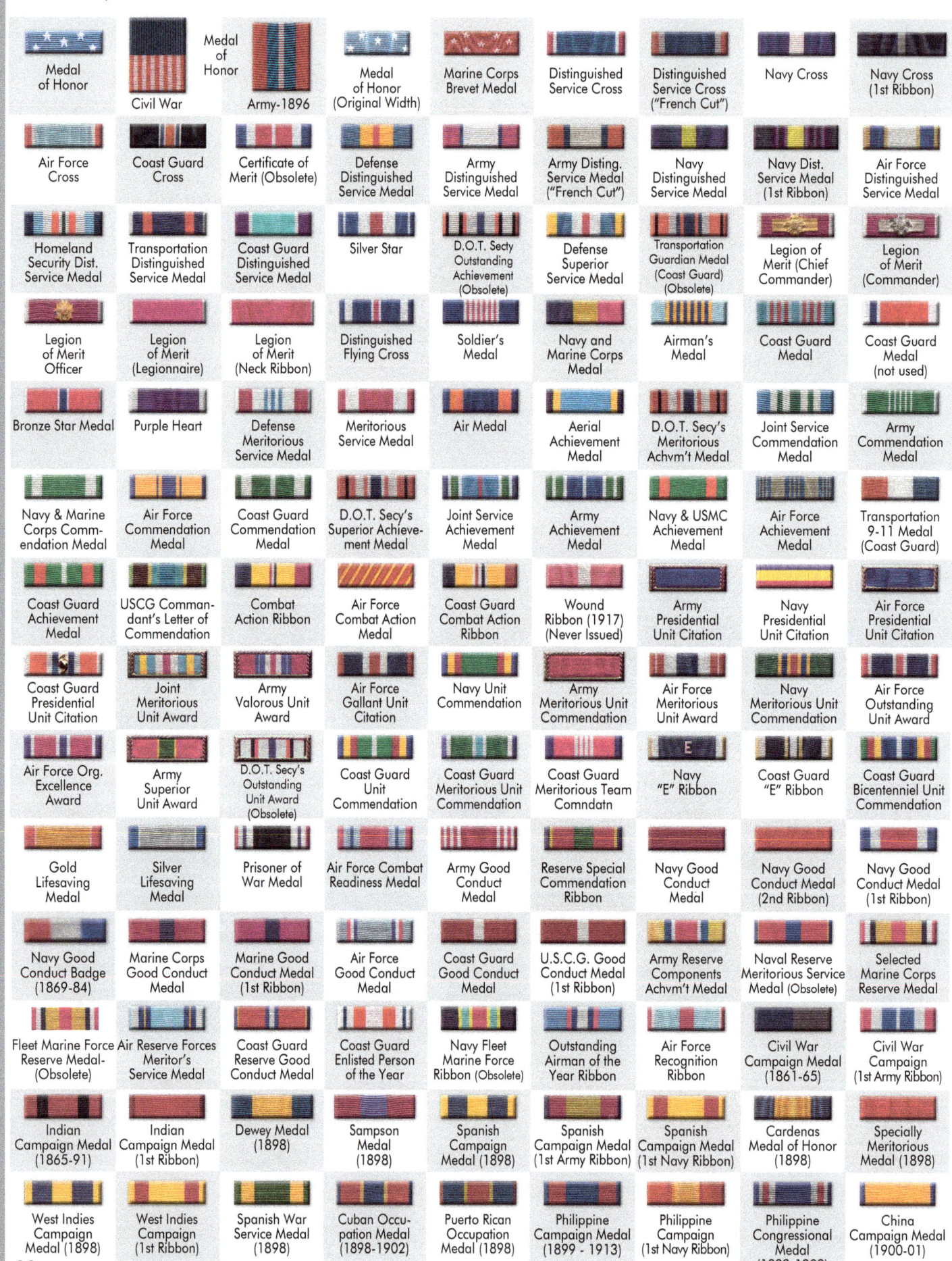

A History of United States Armed Forces Decorations, Unit Awards & Service Ribbons

China Relief Expedition (1st Navy Ribbon)	Cuban Pacification Medal (1906-09)	Peary Polar Expedit'n Medal (1908-09)	Mexican Service Medal (1911-17)	1st Nicaraguan Campaign Medal (1912)	Haitian Campaign Medal (1915)	Dominican Campaign Medal (1916)	Mexican Border Service Medal (1916-17)	World War I Victory Medal (1917-18)
Texas Cavalry Congressional Medal (1918)	Occupation of Germany (1918-23)	N.C.-4 Medal (1919)	Haitian Campaign Medal (1919-20)	2nd Nicaraguan Camp'n Medal (1926-33)	Yangtze Service Medal (1926-32)	1st Byrd Antarctic Expedit'n (1928-30)	Navy Expeditionary Medal	Marine Corps Expeditionary Medal
2nd Byrd Antarctic Expedit'n (1933-35)	China Service Medal (1937, 1945)	Amer. Defense Service Medal (1939-41)	Women's Army Corps Service Medal	American Campaign Medal (1941-46)	Asiatic-Pacific Camp'n Medal (1941-46)	Europe-African-Mid East Cam-p'gn (1941-46)	World War II Victory Medal (1941-46)	U.S. Antarctic Expedit'n Medal (1939-41)
World War II Occupat'n Medal (1945-57)	Medal for Humane Action (1948-49)	Nat'l Defense Service Medal 50,61,90,01,23	Korean Service Medal (1950-54)	Antarctica Service Medal	Coast Guard Arctic Service Medal	Armed Forces Expeditionary Medal	Vietnam Service Medal (1965-73)	Southwest Asia Service Medal (1991-95)
Kosovo Campaign Medal (1999-2013)	Afghanistan Campaign Medal (2001-2021)	Iraq Campaign Medal (2003-2011)	Inherent Resolve Campaign Medal (2014-)	War on Terrorism Expeditionary Medal (2001-)	War on Terrorism Service Medal (2001-2022)	Korea Defense Service Medal (1954-)	Armed Forces Service Medal	Humanitarian Service Medal
Mil. Outstanding Volunteer Service Medal	Army Sea Duty Ribbon	Armed Forces Reserve Medal	Army NCO Prof. Development Ribbon	Army Service Ribbon	Army Overseas Service Ribbon	Army Reserve Comp. Overseas Training Ribbon	Navy Sea Service Deployment Ribbon	Navy Arctic Service Ribbon & Medal
Naval Reserve Sea Service Ribbon	Navy & Marine Corps Overseas Service Ribbon	Navy Recruiting Service Ribbon	Navy Acession Training Service Ribbon	Navy Ceremonial Duty Ribbon	Navy Basic Military Tng Honor Graduate Ribbon	Naval Reserve Medal (Obsolete)	Marine Corps Recruiting Ribbon	Marine Corps Drill Instructor Ribbon
Marine Corps Security Guard Ribbon	Marine Corps Combat Instructor Ribbon	Marine Corps Reserve Ribbon (Obsolete)	Remote Combat Effects Medal	Air & Space Campaign Medal	USAF Nuclear Deterrence Opns Medal	Air Force Overseas Ribbon (Short Tour)	Air Force Overseas Ribbon (Long Tour)	Air Force Expeditionary Service Ribbon
Air Force Longevity Service Award	Air Force Special Duty Ribbon	Air Force Miltry Trnng Instructor Rib'n (Obsolete)	Air Force Recruiter Ribbon (Obsolete)	Air Force NCO Prof. Military Education Grad.	Air Force Basic Military Training Honor Graduate	Air Force Small Arms Expert Marksman	Air Force Training Ribbon	Transprttn 9-11 Ribbon (Coast Guard) (Obsolete)
Coast Guard Special Oper'ns Service Ribbon	Coast Guard Sea Service Ribbon	Coast Guard Restricted Duty Ribbon	Coast Guard Overseas Service Ribbon	Coast Guard Basic Training Honor Graduate Ribbon	Coast Guard Recruiting Service Ribbon	Philippine Presidential Unit Citation	Korean Presidential Unit Citation	Vietnam Presidential Unit Citation
Vietnam Gallantry Cross Unit Citation	Philippine Defense Medal	Philippine Liberation Medal (1944-45)	Philippine Independence Medal (1946)	United Nations Korean Service Medal	UN Palestine Mission (UNTSO)	UN India/Pakistan Mission (UNMOGIP)	UN New Guinea Mission (UNTEA)	UN Iraq/Kuwait Mission (UNIKOM)
UN Western Sahara Mission (MINURSO)	UN Cambodia Mission 1 (UNAMIC)	UN Yugoslavia Mission (UNPROFOR)	UN Somalia Mission (UNOSOM)	UN Haiti Mission (UNMIH)	UN Special Service Medal (UNSSM)	NATO Meritorious Service Medal	NATO Medal for Bosnia	NATO Medal for Kosovo
NATO Medal for Operation Eagle Assist	NATO Medal for Operation Active Endeavor	NATO Medal for Balkan Operations	NATO Medal for Afghanistan, Sudan, Iraq	Multinational Force & Observers Medal	Inter-American Defense Board Medal	Republic of Vietnam Campaign Medal	Kuwait Liberation Medal (Saudi Arabia)	Kuwait Liberation Medal (Kuwait)
Republic of Korea War Service Medal	Navy Distinguished Marksman Badge	Navy Distinguished Pistol Shot Badge	Navy Dist. Marksman & Pistol Shot	Navy Rifle Marksmanship Ribbon	Navy Pistol Marksmanship Ribbon	Coast Guard Dist. Marksman & Pistol Shot	Coast Guard Rifle Marksmanship Ribbon	Coast Guard Pistol Marksmanship Ribbon

Medals of America Press

Types of Medals, Ribbons and Attachments

Decoration - An award conferred on an individual for a specific act of gallantry or for meritorious service.

There are two general categories of "medals" awarded by the United States to its military personnel, namely, decorations and service medals.

The terms "decoration" and "medal" are used almost interchangeably today *(as they are in this book)*, but there are recognizable distinctions between them. Decorations, are awarded for acts of gallantry and meritorious service and usually have distinctive *(and often unique)* shapes such as crosses or stars.

Medals are awarded for good conduct, participation in a particular campaign or expedition, or a noncombatant service and normally come in a round shape. Campaign or service medals are issued to individuals who participate in particular campaigns or periods of service for which a medal is authorized. The fact that some very prestigious awards have the word "medal" in their titles *(e.g.: Medal of Honor)*, can cause some confusion.

Medal-An individual award presented for performance of certain duties or to those who have participated in designated wars, campaigns, expeditions, etc., or who have fulfilled specified service requirements.

Unit Ribbon Only Awards

Unit Award - *An award made to an operating unit for outstanding performance. See the chart to your right.*

Ribbon Only Award - *An award made to an individual for completion of certain training or specific assignment for which there is no medal. See the chart to your right.*

Example - *This example shows three decoration (one from the Army), and other awards you can identify from the chart to your right.*

Attachments and Devices

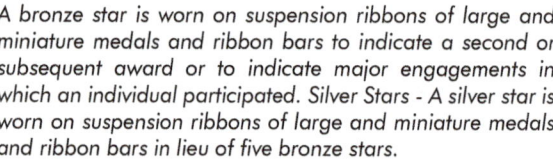

Attachment - *Any device such as a star, clasp, or other appurtenance worn on a suspension ribbon of a medal or on the ribbon bar (also called device). See pages 38 and 39 for all.*

Bronze and Silver Service Stars
A bronze star is worn on suspension ribbons of large and miniature medals and ribbon bars to indicate a second or subsequent award or to indicate major engagements in which an individual participated. Silver Stars - A silver star is worn on suspension ribbons of large and miniature medals and ribbon bars in lieu of five bronze stars.

Letter "V"
A bronze letter "V" is worn on specific combat decorations if the award is approved for valor (heroism). Only one "V" is worn.

Navy Occupation Service Medal Clasp
The bronze Navy of Occupation Medal clasp marked "ASIA" and or "Europe" is worn on suspension ribbons of large and miniature Navy Occupation Medals to denote service in those areas.

Gold and Silver Stars
A Gold starr denotes a second or subsequent award of a personal naval decoration. A silver Silver star is worn in lieu of five Gold Stars

Hour Glass
 A bronze hour glass device denotes ten years service on the Armed Forces Reserve Medal. Upon the completion of the ten year period, reservists are awarded the Armed Forces Reserve Medal with a bronze hourglass device. Silver and gold hourglass devices are awarded at the end of twenty and thirty years of reserve service, respectively.

Letter "M"
 A bronze letter "M" on the Armed Forces Reserve Medal denotes reservists mobilized and called to active duty.

Oak Leaf Cluster
 A bronze Oak Leaf Cluster denotes a second or subsequent award of a personal Dept. of Defense decoration. A silver Oak Leaf Cluster is worn in lieu of five bronze Oak Leaf Clusters.

Bronze Numerals	**Bronze Eagle, Globe and Anchor** Denotes Combat Service with USMC Units.
Denotes total number of awards of the Air Medal and other awards.	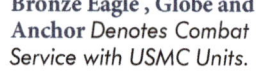 

New Bronze C and R Devices
  The C device indicates the award was issued in a comabat zone while the R indicateds the award was presented for action remote from the combat zone.

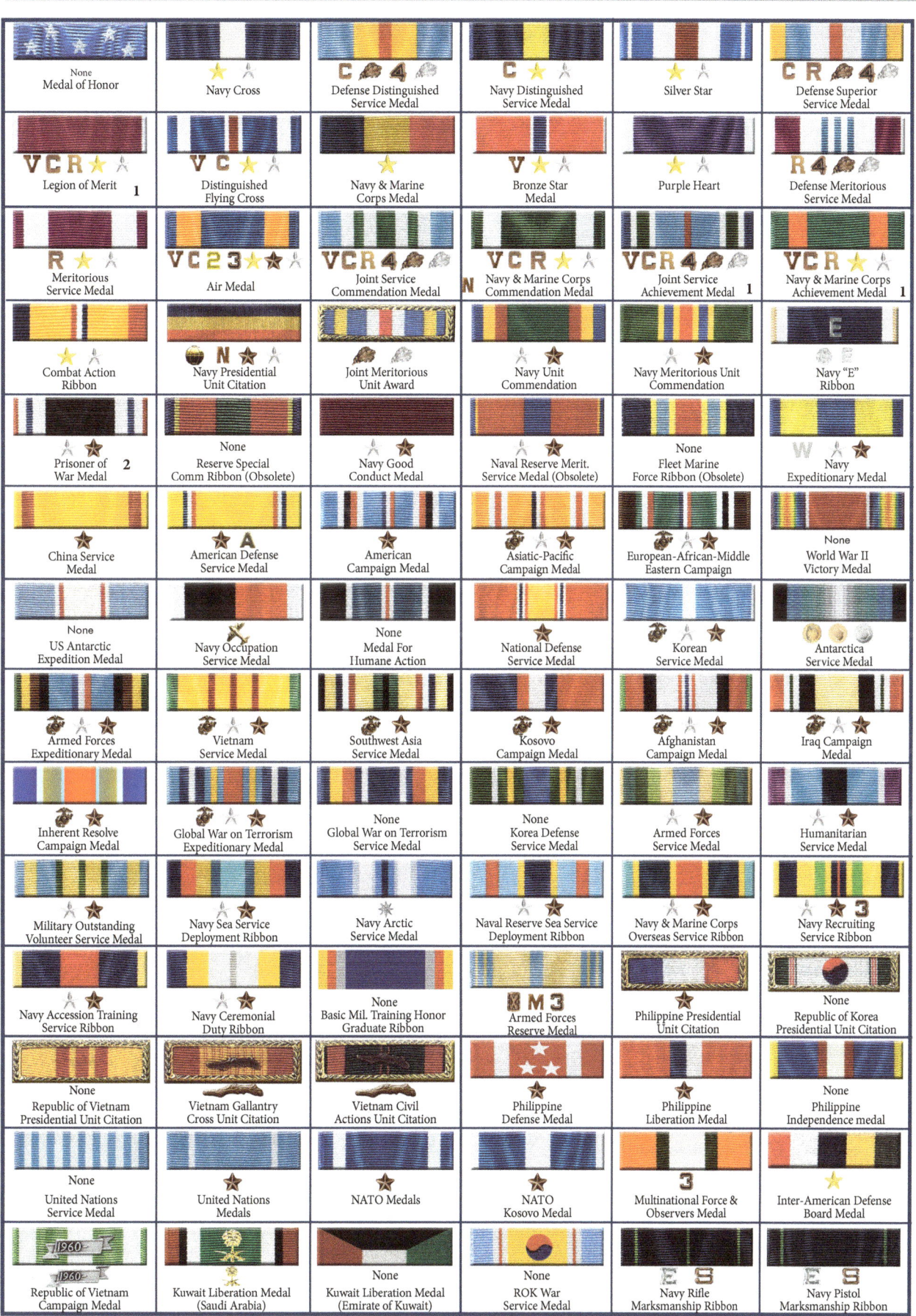

United States Navy Multi Service Decorations, Unit Awards & Service Ribbons Page A

When Sailors are entitled to similar awards from two or more services; for example, good conduct awards, the Navy award will take precedence. After the navy award, similar awards of other services will be worn in the following precedence: Marine Corps, Army, Air Force, and Coast Guard.

Shown below are examples of Multi service awards and a chart laying out the correct order of wear for naval personnel who have been awarded decorations, unit awards or service medals while assigned or while serving in other branches of the Armed Forces.

Prior Air Force Service

Prior Army Service

Prior USCG Service

Prior Marine Service

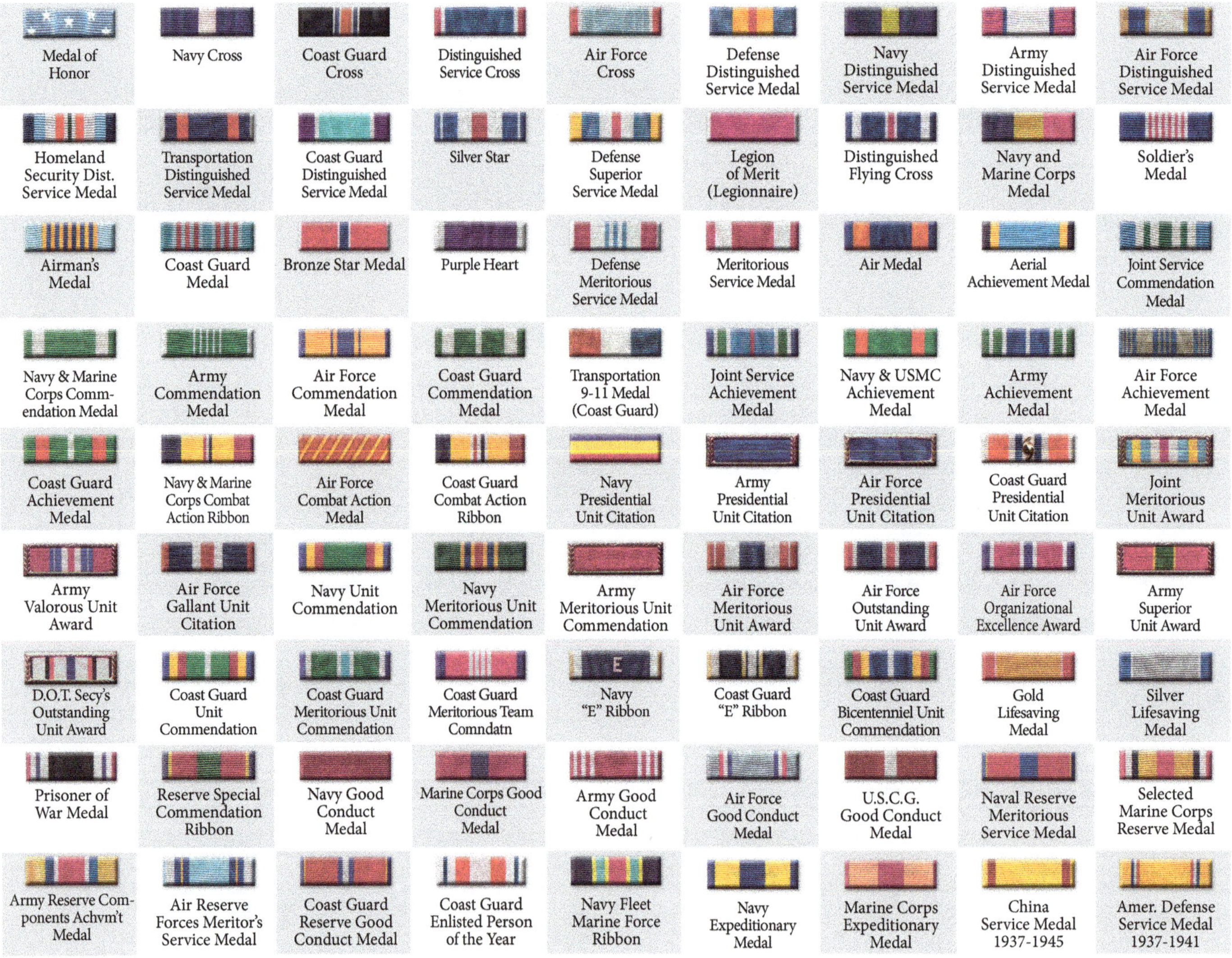

Medal of Honor	Navy Cross	Coast Guard Cross	Distinguished Service Cross	Air Force Cross	Defense Distinguished Service Medal	Navy Distinguished Service Medal	Army Distinguished Service Medal	Air Force Distinguished Service Medal	
Homeland Security Dist. Service Medal	Transportation Distinguished Service Medal	Coast Guard Distinguished Service Medal	Silver Star	Defense Superior Service Medal	Legion of Merit (Legionnaire)	Distinguished Flying Cross	Navy and Marine Corps Medal	Soldier's Medal	
Airman's Medal	Coast Guard Medal	Bronze Star Medal	Purple Heart	Defense Meritorious Service Medal	Meritorious Service Medal	Air Medal	Aerial Achievement Medal	Joint Service Commendation Medal	
Navy & Marine Corps Commendation Medal	Army Commendation Medal	Air Force Commendation Medal	Coast Guard Commendation Medal	Transportation 9-11 Medal (Coast Guard)	Joint Service Achievement Medal	Navy & USMC Achievement Medal	Army Achievement Medal	Air Force Achievement Medal	
Coast Guard Achievement Medal	Navy & Marine Corps Combat Action Ribbon	Air Force Combat Action Medal	Coast Guard Combat Action Ribbon	Navy Presidential Unit Citation	Army Presidential Unit Citation	Air Force Presidential Unit Citation	Coast Guard Presidential Unit Citation	Joint Meritorious Unit Award	
Army Valorous Unit Award	Air Force Gallant Unit Citation	Navy Unit Commendation	Navy Meritorious Unit Commendation	Army Meritorious Unit Commendation	Air Force Meritorious Unit Award	Air Force Outstanding Unit Award	Air Force Organizational Excellence Award	Army Superior Unit Award	
D.O.T. Secy's Outstanding Unit Award	Coast Guard Unit Commendation	Coast Guard Meritorious Unit Commendation	Coast Guard Meritorious Team Comndatn	Navy "E" Ribbon	Coast Guard "E" Ribbon	Coast Guard Bicentenniel Unit Commendation	Gold Lifesaving Medal	Silver Lifesaving Medal	
Prisoner of War Medal	Reserve Special Commendation Ribbon	Navy Good Conduct Medal	Marine Corps Good Conduct Medal	Army Good Conduct Medal	Air Force Good Conduct Medal	U.S.C.G. Good Conduct Medal	Naval Reserve Meritorious Service Medal	Selected Marine Corps Reserve Medal	
Army Reserve Components Achvm't Medal	Air Reserve Forces Meritor's Service Medal	Coast Guard Reserve Good Conduct Medal	Coast Guard Enlisted Person of the Year	Navy Fleet Marine Force Ribbon	Navy Expeditionary Medal	Marine Corps Expeditionary Medal	China Service Medal 1937-1945	Amer. Defense Service Medal 1937-1941	

34 Medals and Ribbons of the U.S. Navy

United States Navy Multi Service Decorations, Unit Awards & Service Ribbons Page B

| Women's Army Corps Service Medal | American Campaign Medal (1941-46) | Europe-African-Mid East Cam-p'gn | Asiatic-Pacific Camp'n Medal (1941-46) | World War II Victory Medal (1941-46) | U.S. Antarctic Expedit'n Medal (1939-41) | World War II Occupat'n Medal (1945-57) | Medal for Humane Action (1948-49) | Nat'l Defense Service Medal (1950,61,90,01) |

| Korean Service Medal (1950-54) | Antarctica Service Medal | Coast Guard Arctic Service Medal | Armed Forces Expeditionary Medal | Vietnam Service Medal (1965-73) | Southwest Asia Service Medal (1991-95) | Kosovo Campaign Medal (1999-) | Afghanistan Campaign Medal (2001-) | Iraq Campaign Medal (2003-11) |

| Inherent Resolve Campaign Medal | War on Terrorism Expeditionary Medal (2001-) | War on Terrorism Service Medal (2001-) | Korea Defense Service Medal (1954-) | Armed Forces Service Medal | Humanitarian Service Medal | Outstanding Volunteer Service Medal | Navy Sea Service Deployment Ribbon | Navy Arctic Service Ribbon |

| Naval Reserve Sea Service Ribbon | Navy & Marine Corps Overseas Service Ribbon | Navy Recruiting Service Ribbon | Marine Corps Recruiting Ribbon | Marine Corps Drill Instructor Ribbon | Marine Corps Security Guard Ribbon | Marine Corps Combat Instructor Ribbon | Navy Accessions Training Service Ribbon | Navy Ceremonial Duty Ribbon |

| Navy BMT Honor Graduate Ribbon | Transportation 9-11 Ribbon (Coast Guard) | Coast Guard Special Oper'ns Service Ribbon | Coast Guard Sea Service Ribbon | Coast Guard Restricted Duty Ribbon | Coast Guard Overseas Service Ribbon | CG Basic Tng Honor Graduate Ribbon | Coast Guard Recruiting Service Ribbon | Air Force Air & Space Campaign Medal |

| USAF Nuclear Deterrence Opns Medal | Air Force Overseas Ribbon (Short Tour) | Air Force Overseas Ribbon (Long Tour) | Air Force Expeditionary Service Ribbon | Air Force Longevity Service Award Ribbon | Air Force Special Duty Ribbon | Air Force Military Training Instructor Rib'n | Air Force Recruiter Ribbon | Army Sea Duty Ribbon |

| Armed Forces Reserve Medal | Naval Reserve Medal (Obsolete) | Marine Corps Reserve Ribbon (Obsolete) | Army NCO Prof. Development Ribbon | Army Service Ribbon | Army Overseas Service Ribbon | Army Reserve Comp. Overseas Training Ribbon | Air Force NCO Prof. Military Education Grad. | Air Force Basic Military Training Honor Graduate |

| Air Force Small Arms Expert Marksman | Air Force Training Ribbon | Philippine Presidential Unit Citation | Korean Presidential Unit Citation | Vietnam Presidential Unit Citation | Vietnam Gallantry Cross Unit Citation | Vietnam Civil Actions Unit Citation | Philippine Defense Medal | Philippine Liberation Medal (1944-45) |

| Philippine Independence Medal (1946) | United Nations Korean Service Medal | UN Palestine Mission (UNTSO) | UN India/Pakistan Mission (UNMOGIP) | UN New Guinea Mission (UNTEA) | UN Iraq/Kuwait Mission (UNIKOM) | UN Western Sahara Mission (MINURSO) | UN Cambodia Mission 1 (UNAMIC) | UN Yugoslavia Mission (UNPROFOR) |

| UN Somalia Mission (UNOSOM) | UN Haiti Mission (UNMIH) | UN Special Service Medal (UNSSM) | NATO Meritorious Service Medal | NATO Medal for Bosnia | NATO Medal for Kosovo | NATO Medal for Operation Eagle Assist | NATO Medal for Operation Active Endeavor | NATO Medal for Balkan Operations |

| NATO Medal for Afghanistan, Sudan, Iraq | Multinational Force & Observers Medal | Inter-American Defense Board Medal | Republic of Vietnam Campaign Medal | Kuwait Liberation Medal (Saudi Arabia) | Kuwait Liberation Medal (Kuwait) | Republic of Korea War Service Medal | Navy Distinguished Marksman Badge | Navy Distinguished Pistol Badge |

| Navy Dist. Marksman & Pistol Shot | Navy Rifle Marksmanship Ribbon | Navy Pistol Marksmanship Ribbon | Coast Guard Dist. Marksman & Pistol Shot | Coast Guard Rifle Marksmanship Ribbon | Coast Guard Pistol Marksmanship Ribbon | | | |

Multi Service Ribbons Not Authorized by the United States Navy
(Basically the Navy does not authorize ribbons for which it does not have an equivalent ribbon.)

Air Force Combat Readiness Medal

USCG Commandant's Letter of Commendation

Outstanding Airman of the Year Ribbon

Air Force Recognition Ribbon

Placement of Recent Campaign Stars on Ribbons

Over the past decade there has been confusion on the number of campaign stars individual sailors have earned for service in Iraq and Afghanistan. Shown below is a summary of the campaigns as of 2019 for both the Iraq and Afghanistan campaign medals. To date there have been six campaign stars authorized in Afghanistan and seven campaign stars authorized for service in Iraq.

Bronze and silver campaign stars designate the number of campaign phases in which a sailor has served. One day's service during any phase earns a bronze campaign star to be worn on the service medal. Service in five different phases of a campaigns is indicated by a silver campaign star. The campaign stars indicate how many phases in which a sailor has participated and do not represent additional awards of the respective campaign medal. One campaign star is worn on a suspension ribbon of the medal or on the ribbon bar for one or more days of service in each designated campaign phase.

The Afghanistan Campaign Medal and the Iraq Campaign Medal will always be awarded with at least one bronze campaign star. The policy is the same for the Southwest Asia Service Medal, the Vietnam Service Medal and the Korean Service Medal. If a sailor's service extends at least one day into a subsequent campaign phase then an additional bronze campaign star is awarded.

Iraq Phase Name	Campaign From	Medal To
Phase 1: Liberation of Iraq	March 19, 2003	May 1, 2003
Phase 2: Transition of Iraq	May 2, 2003	June 28, 2004
Phase 3: Iraqi Governance	June 29, 2004	December 15, 2005
Phase 4: National Resolution	December 16, 2005	January 9, 2007
Phase 5: Iraqi Surge	January 10, 2007	December 31, 2008
Phase 6: Iraqi Sovereignty	January 1, 2009	August 31, 2010
Phase 7: New Dawn	September 1, 2010	December 31, 2011

Afghanistan Phase Name	Campaign From	Medal To
Phase 1: Liberation of Afghanistan	September 11, 2001	November 30, 2001
Phase 2: Consolidation I	December 1, 2001	September 30, 2006
Phase 3: Consolidation II	October 1, 2006	November 30, 2009
Phase 4: Consolidation III	December 1, 2009	June 30, 2011
Phase 5: Transition I	July 1, 2011	December 31, 2014
Phase 6: Transition II	January 1, 2015	August 31, 2021

United Nations Ribbons for Wear on the U.S. Navy Uniform

Only one United Nations Ribbon maybe worn. A second or additional award of a United Nations Service Medal is indicated by a 3/16s Bronze Star Device.

Placement of Devices on Ribbons

No. of Awards	3/16 Bronze and Silver Campaign Stars	Letter V*	Air Medal Individual	Air Medal Strike Flight
1				
2				
3				
4				
5				
6				
7				
8				
9				
10				

Air Medal (1980-1989, 2006-2017)

 Bronze Arabic Numerals

Air Medal (1989-2006)

Gold Numerals

Armed Forces Reserve Medal

After 10 years of reserve service | With 1 mobilization | With 2 mobilizations | After 10 years of reserve service and 3 mobilizations

LEGEND:

	= Bronze Letter "M"		= 5/16" dia. Gold Star		= Bronze Oak Leaf Cluster
	= Hourglass		= 5/16" dia. Silver Star		= 3/16" dia. Bronze Star
	= Bronze Letter "V"		= Bronze Arabic Numerals		= 3/16" dia. Silver Star

U.S. Navy Ribbon Devices

1. Airplane, C-54, Gold

SERVICES: All
WORN ON: World War II Occupation Medals
DENOTES: Service during Berlin Airlift *(1948-49)*

2. Bar, Date, Silver

SERVICES: All
WORN ON: Republic of Vietnam Campaign Medal
DENOTES: Worn upon initial issue; has no significance

3. Letter "C", Serif, Bronze

SERVICES: All
WORN ON: Personal Decorations
DENOTES: Award earned in a combat setting.

4a. Disk, Bronze, Gold, Silver

WORN ON: Antarctica Service Medal
DENOTES: Wintered over 1,2 or 3 times on the Antarctic continent

4b. Globe, Gold

SERVICES: Navy
WORN ON: Navy Presidential Unit Citation
DENOTES: Service with USS Triton during 1st submerged cruise around the world

5a. Hourglass, Bronze

SERVICES: All
WORN ON: Armed Forces Reserve Medal
DENOTES: 10 Years of service in the Reserve Forces

5b. Hourglass, Silver

SERVICES: All
WORN ON: Armed Forces Reserve Medal
DENOTES: 20 Yrs of service in the Reserve Forces

5c. Hourglass, Gold

SERVICES: All
WORN ON: Armed Forces Reserve Medal
DENOTES: 30 Years of service in the Reserve Forces

6. Letter "A", Block, Bronze

SERVICES: Navy, Marine Corps, Coast Guard
WORN ON: American Defense Service Medal
DENOTES: Atlantic Fleet service prior to WW II

7. Letter "E", Block, Silver

SERVICES: Navy, Marine Corps.
WORN ON: Navy "E" Ribbon
DENOTES: Initial and subsequent awards (3 maximum)

8. Letter "S", Serif, Bronze

SERVICES: Navy
WORN ON: Marksmanship Ribbons
DENOTES: "Sharpshooter" weapons qualification

9. Letter "E", Serif, Silver

SERVICES: Navy, Coast Guard
WORN ON: Marksmanship Ribbons
DENOTES: "Expert" weapons qualification

10. Letter "E", Wreathed, Silver

SERVICES: Navy, Marine Corps.
WORN ON: Navy "E" Ribbon
DENOTES: Fourth *(Final)* award

11. Letter "M", Block, Bronze

SERVICES: All
WORN ON: Armed Forces Reserve Medal
DENOTES: Mobilization for active military service

12. Letter "N", Block, Gold

SERVICES: Navy
WORN ON: Navy Presidential Unit Citation
DENOTES: Service aboard USS Nautilus, 1st cruise under the Arctic ice cap

13. Letter "V", Serif, Bronze

SERVICES: All *(Except Marine Corps)*
WORN ON: Personal decorations
DENOTES: Valorous actions in combat

14. Letter "V", Serif, Bronze

SERVICES: All
WORN ON: Joint Service Commendation Medal
DENOTES: Valorous actions in combat

15. Letter "W", Block, Silver

SERVICES: Navy, Marine Corps.
WORN ON: Expeditionary Medals
DENOTES: Participation in defense of Wake Island *(12/1941)*

16. Maltese Cross, Bronze

SERVICES: Navy
WORN ON: World War I Victory Medal
DENOTES: Service by Navy personnel with the AEF

17. Marine Device, Bronze

SERVICES: Navy
WORN ON: Campaign medals since World War II
DENOTES: Service by Naval combat personnel with Marine Corps units

18. Numeral, Block, Bronze

SERVICES: Navy, Marine Corps.
WORN ON: Air Medal
DENOTES: Total number of Strike/Flight awards

19. Numeral, Block, Bronze

SERVICES: All *(Except Coast Guard)*
WORN ON: Humanitarian Service Medal
DENOTES: Number of additional awards *(Obsolete)*

20. Numeral, Block, Bronze

SERVICES: All
WORN ON: Armed Forces Reserve Medal
DENOTES: Number of times mobilized for active duty

21. Numeral, Block, Bronze

SERVICES: Navy
WORN ON: Navy Recruiting Service Ribbon
DENOTES: Total number of "Gold Wreath" awards

22. Numeral, Block, Bronze

SERVICES: All
WORN ON: Multinational Force & Observers Medal
DENOTES: Total number of awards

23. Numeral, Block, Gold

SERVICES: Navy, Marine Corps
WORN ON: Air Medal
DENOTES: Total number of individual awards

24. Numeral, Scroll, Bronze

SERVICES: Navy
WORN ON: World War II Campaign Medals
DENOTES: Number of battle clasps earned *(Obsolete)*

25. Oak Leaf Cluster, Bronze

SERVICES: All
WORN ON: Joint Service Decorations and Joint Meritorious Unit Award
DENOTES: One (1) additional award

26. Palm, Bronze

SERVICES: All *(Except Army)*
WORN ON: Vietnam Gallantry Cross Unit Citation
DENOTES: No significance, worn upon initial issue

27. Palm, Bronze

SERVICES: All
WORN ON: Vietnam Civil Actions Unit Citation
DENOTES: No significance, worn upon initial issue

28. Palm & Swords Device, Gold

SERVICES: All
WORN ON: Kuwait Liberation Medal (Saudi Arabia)
DENOTES: No significance, worn upon initial issue

29. Star 3/16" dia., Blue

SERVICES: Navy, Marine Corps
WORN ON: Navy Presidential Unit Citation
DENOTES: Initial and subsequent awards *(Obsolete)*

30. Star 3/16" dia., Bronze

SERVICES: All
WORN ON: Campaign awards since World War II
DENOTES: Battle participation

31. Star 3/16" dia., Bronze

SERVICES: All
Worn on: Expeditionary Medals
DENOTES: Additional service *(one star per designated expedition)*

32. Star 3/16" dia., Bronze

SERVICES: All
WORN ON: Prisoner of War and Humanitarian Service Medals
DENOTES: One (1) additional award

33. Star 3/16" dia., Bronze

SERVICES: Navy, Marine Corps.
WORN ON: Unit Awards
DENOTES: One (1) star per each additional award

34. Star 3/16" dia., Bronze

SERVICES: All
WORN ON: Service Awards
DENOTES: One (1) star per each additional award

35. Star 3/16" dia., Bronze

SERVICES: Navy
WORN ON: Letter of Commendation Ribbon with Pendant
DENOTES: One additional award *(Obsolete)*

36. Star 3/16" dia., Bronze

SERVICES: Navy and Marine Corps.
WORN ON: Air Medal
DENOTES: First individual award *(Obsolete)*

37. Star 3/16" dia., Bronze

SERVICES: All
WORN ON: World War I Victory Medal
DENOTES: One (1) star for each campaign clasp earned

38. Star 3/16" dia., Bronze

SERVICES: Navy, Marine Corps, Coast Guard
WORN ON: China Service Medal (1937-39)
DENOTES: Additional award for service during (1945-57)

39. Star 3/16" dia., Bronze

SERVICES: All
WORN ON: American Defense Service Medal
DENOTES: Overseas service prior to World War II

40. Star 3/16" dia., Bronze

SERVICES: All
WORN ON: National Defense Service Medal
DENOTES: Additional awards *(one star per designated period)*

41. Star 3/16" dia., Bronze

SERVICES: All
WORN ON: Philippine Defense and Liberation Ribbons
DENOTES: Additional battle honors

42. Star 3/16" dia., Bronze

SERVICES: All *(Except Army)*
WORN ON: Philippine Presidential Unit Citation
DENOTES: Additional award

43. Star 3/16" dia., Bronze

SERVICES: All
WORN ON: United Nations and NATO mission medals
DENOTES: One (1) star for each additional mission

44. Star 3/16" dia., Silver

SERVICES: All
WORN ON: Campaign awards since WW II
DENOTES: Battle participation in five (5) major engagements

45. Star 3/16" dia., Silver

SERVICES: All
WORN ON: Expeditionary Medals
DENOTES: Five (5) additional expeditions

46. Star 3/16" dia., Silver

SERVICES: All
WORN ON: Prisoner of War and Humanitarian Service Medals
DENOTES: Five (5) additional awards

47. Star 3/16" dia., Silver

SERVICES: Navy, Marine Corps
WORN ON: Unit awards
DENOTES: Five (5) additional awards

48. Star 3/16" dia., Silver

SERVICES: All
WORN ON: Service Awards
DENOTES: Five (5) additional Awards

49. Star 3/16" dia., Silver

SERVICES: Navy
WORN ON: World War I Victory Medal
DENOTES: Receipt of Letter of Commendation

50. Star 5/16" dia., Bronze

SERVICES: Navy, Marine Corps.
WORN ON: Navy, USMC Expeditionary Medals
DENOTES: One (1) additional award *(Obsolete)*

51. Star 5/16" dia., Bronze

SERVICES: Navy, Marine Corps.
WORN ON: Haitian Campaign Medal (1915)
DENOTES: Subsequent award of the "1919-1920" Clasp

52. Star 5/16" dia., Gold

SERVICES: Navy, Marine Corps, Coast Guard
WORN ON: Personal Decorations
DENOTES: One (1) additional award

53. Star 5/16" dia., Gold

SERVICES: Navy, Marine Corps
WORN ON: Combat Action Ribbon
DENOTES: One (1) additional award

54. Star 5/16" dia., Gold

SERVICES: All
WORN ON: Inter-American Defense Board Medal
DENOTES: One (1) additional award for 5 years service.

55. Star 5/16" dia., Silver

SERVICES: Navy, Marine Corps, Coast Guard
WORN ON: Personal Decorations
DENOTES: Five (5) additional awards

56. Star 5/16" dia., Silver

SERVICES: Navy
WORN ON: World War II Campaign Medals
DENOTES: Five (5) major campaigns *(Obsolete)*

57. Letter "R", serif, Bronze

SERVICES: All
WORN ON: Personal Decorations
DENOTES: Recognizes remote combat action

Examples of Navy Ribbons and Devices

Placement of the Letter "V" (Valor) and Gold & Silver Stars

No. of Awards	Current Navy V Device	No. of Awards	Gold & silver Stars	Current V Device
1	V	1		
2	★ V	2	★	
3	★ V ★	3	★ ★	
4	★★ V ★	4	★ ★ ★	
5	★★ V ★★	5	★ ★ ★ ★	
6	☆ V	6	☆	
7	☆ V ☆	7	☆ ☆	

Same as ribbons to the left but devices placed vertically in order to display when overlapping medals cover devices.

Legend:
V = Letter V   ☆ = 5/16" Silver Star   ★ = 5/16" Gold Star

Placement of Devices on the Armed Forces Reserve Medal

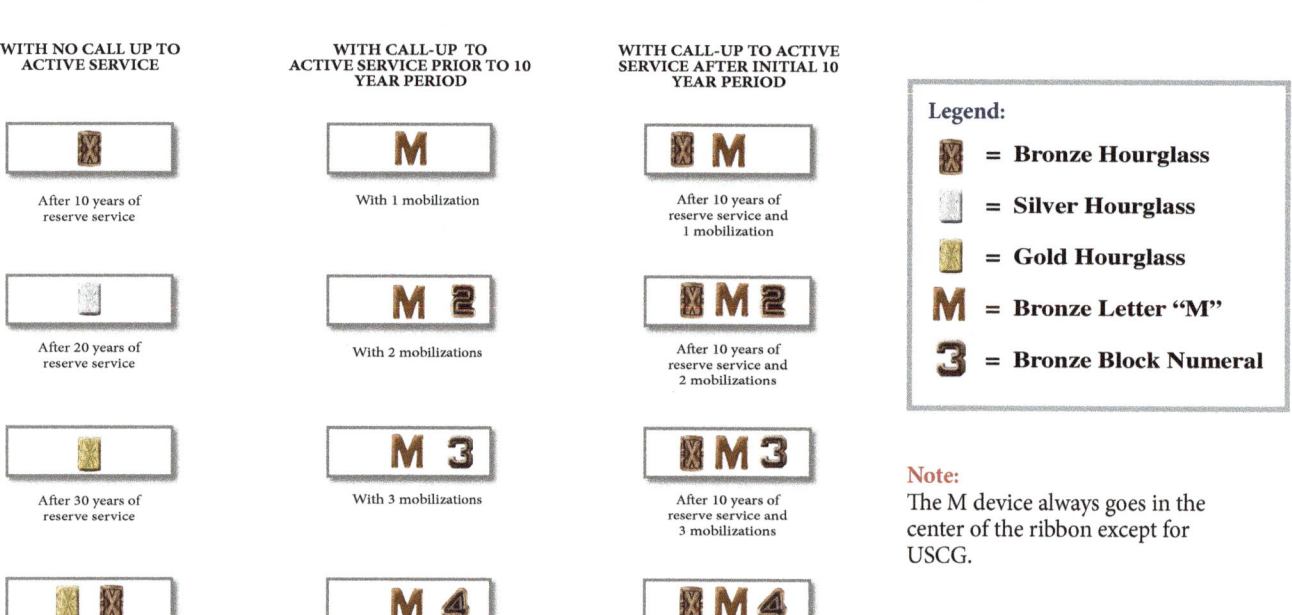

Legend:
- ⌛ = Bronze Hourglass
- ⌛ = Silver Hourglass
- ⌛ = Gold Hourglass
- M = Bronze Letter "M"
- 3 = Bronze Block Numeral

Note: The M device always goes in the center of the ribbon except for USCG.

40 Medals and Ribbons of the U.S. Navy

Placement of Bronze and Silver Campaign Stars

No. of Campaigns	Navy	No. of Campaigns	Navy	Navy
1	★	6	☆ ★	
2	★★	7	★ ☆ ★	
3	★★★	8	★ ☆ ★ ★	
4	★★★★	9	★★ ☆ ★★	
5	☆	10	☆ ☆	

Placement of Oak Leaf Cluster Devices on the Ribbon

No. of Awards	All Services	No. of Awards	
1		6	🍃
2	🍂	7	🍃 🍂
3	🍂🍂	8	🍃 🍂🍂
4	🍂🍂🍂	9	🍃 🍂🍂🍂
5	🍂🍂🍂🍂	10	🍃 🍃

Legend:
🍂 = Bronze Oak Leaf Cluster   🍃 = Silver Oak Leaf Cluster

The following ribbon attachments of a one-piece construction in multiples of two, three, and four are authorized for optional purchase and wear:

(1) 3/16-inch bronze stars ★★★
(2) 5/16-inch gold stars ★★
(3) Bronze oak leaf clusters 🍂🍂

These multiple attachments are worn centered on ribbon bars and are not worn on the same ribbon in combination with single stars or other devices. They are not worn on suspension ribbons of large or miniature medals.

Device Usage on the Navy Air Medal

No. of Awards	Single Mission Gold Numeral	Strike/Flight Bronze Numeral
1	1	1
2	2	2
3	3	3
4	4	4
5	5	5

Navy (Individual Awards)

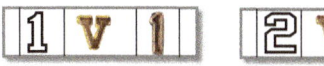

Since April 5, 1974, the Combat "V" may be authorized for awards for heroism or meritorious action in conflict with an armed enemy.

Ribbon devices (1989–2006)

Between November 22, 1989, and September 27, 2006, 3/16 inch bronze stars, 5/16 inch gold stars, and 5/16 inch silver stars denoted the number of "Individual" Air Medals. A bronze star denoted a first award. Gold stars were used for the second through the fifth awards with Silver stars used for five gold stars. For "Individual" Air Medals, the Combat "V" could be authorized.

Air **Medal Device Arrangements**. As of September 27, 2006, gold Numeral devices are used to denote the number of "Individual" Air Medals.

Bronze Strike/Flight numerals denote the total number of Strike/Flight awards. Strikes are combat sorties that encounter enemy opposition. Flights are combat sorties that do not encounter enemy opposition.

Bronze Strike/Flight numerals denoted the number of Strike/Flight awards authorized for operations in hostile or disputed territory and count the total number of Strikes (operations that faced enemy opposition) and Flights (operations that did not encounter enemy opposition) added together.

Combat & R Remote Device Placement on the Ribbon

No. of Awards	Navy	No. of Awards	Navy
1	C	1	R
2	★C	2	★R
3	★C★	3	★R★
4	★★C★	4	★★R★
5	★★C★★	5	★★R★★

When both C and R device are awarded the C goes before the R and the V before both.

CR   VCR   CR🍃   ★CR

Right Breast Displays on U.S. Navy Full Dress Uniforms

The three Naval Services prescribe the wear of *"ribbon only"* awards on the right breast of the full dress uniform when large medals are worn. The Navy and Coast Guard align their ribbons inboard to outboard while the Marines align theirs outboard to inboard.

	Navy Presidential Unit Citation	Combat Action Ribbon
Navy Meritorious Unit Commendation	Navy Unit Commendation	Joint Meritorious Unit Award
Fleet Marine Force Ribbon	Reserve Special Commendation Ribbon	Navy "E" Ribbon
Navy Reserve Sea Service Service Ribbon	Arctic Service Ribbon	Sea Service Deployment Ribbon
Navy Recruit Training Service Ribbon	Navy Recruiting Service Ribbon	Navy & Marine Corps Overseas Service Ribbon
Philippine Presidential Unit Citation	Navy Recruit Honor Graduate Ribbon	Navy Ceremonial Guard Ribbon
Vietnam Gallantry Cross Unit Citation	Vietnam Presidential Unit Citation	Korean Presidential Unit Ribbon
Philippine Liberation Ribbon	Philippine Defense Ribbon	Vietnam Civil Actions Unit Citation
Pistol Marksmanship Ribbon	Rifle Marksmanship Ribbon	Philippine Independence Ribbon

42   Medals and Ribbons of the U.S. Navy

Officer, CPO and E1-E6 Ribbons with Medals

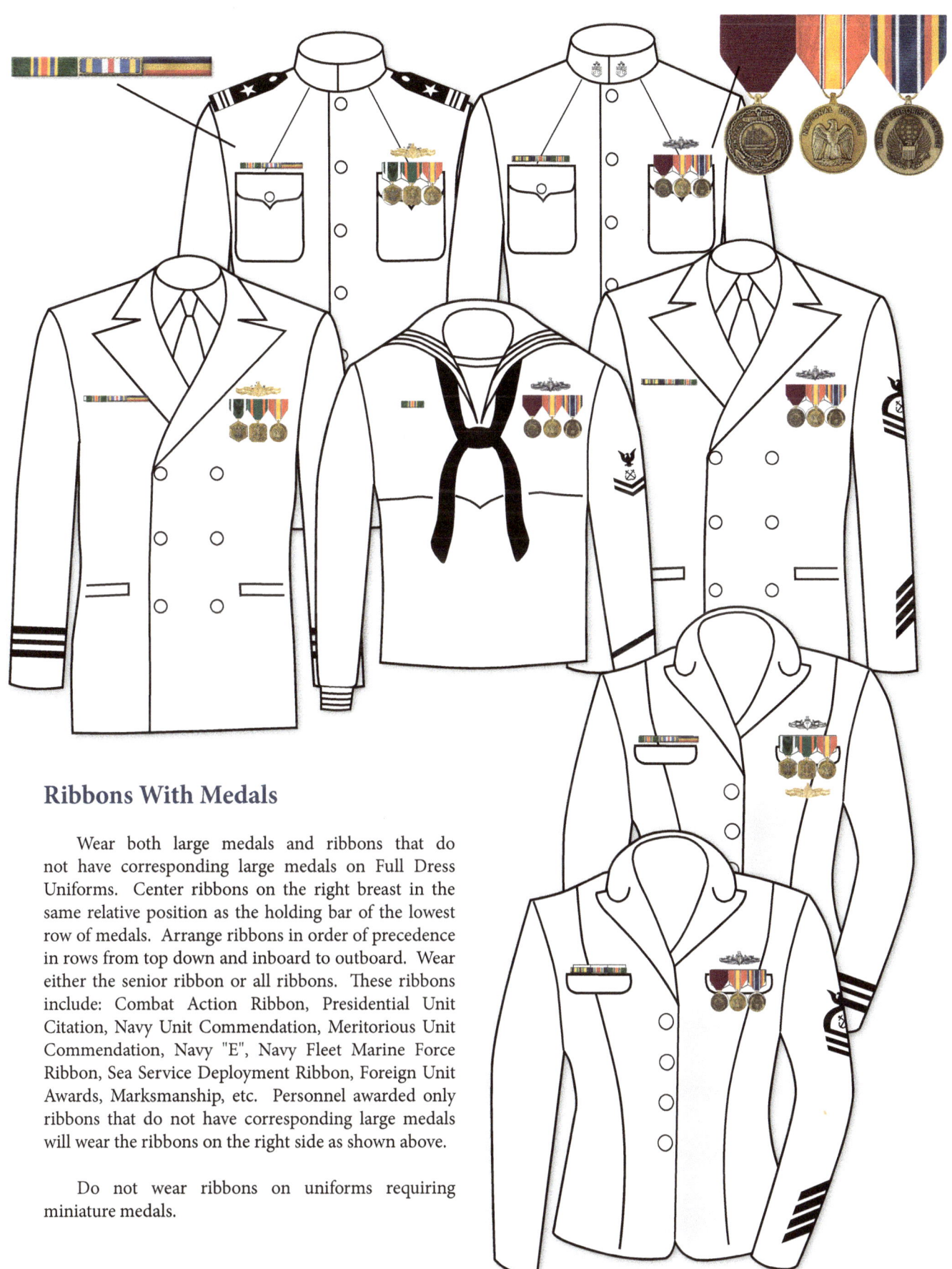

Ribbons With Medals

Wear both large medals and ribbons that do not have corresponding large medals on Full Dress Uniforms. Center ribbons on the right breast in the same relative position as the holding bar of the lowest row of medals. Arrange ribbons in order of precedence in rows from top down and inboard to outboard. Wear either the senior ribbon or all ribbons. These ribbons include: Combat Action Ribbon, Presidential Unit Citation, Navy Unit Commendation, Meritorious Unit Commendation, Navy "E", Navy Fleet Marine Force Ribbon, Sea Service Deployment Ribbon, Foreign Unit Awards, Marksmanship, etc. Personnel awarded only ribbons that do not have corresponding large medals will wear the ribbons on the right side as shown above.

Do not wear ribbons on uniforms requiring miniature medals.

Medals of America Press 43

Male Officer and CPO Ribbon Wear

Ribbons are worn on the service coat or jumper of Service Dress Blue, Dress White, and on the shirt of Service Khaki. Wear up to three ribbons in a single row. When more than three ribbons are authorized, wear them in horizontal rows of three each. If ribbons are not in multiples of three, the top row contains the lesser number, and the center of this row sits over the center of the one below it. Wear ribbons without spaces between ribbons or rows of ribbons. Wear ribbons with the lower edge of the bottom row centered 1/4 inch above the left breast pocket and parallel to the deck. To prevent coat lapels from covering ribbons, ribbons may be aligned so the border to wearer's left is aligned with left side of pocket. Rows of ribbons where more than 50% of the ribbon is covered by the coat lapel may contain two ribbons each and be aligned with left border.

Placement on Ribbon Bar. Ribbons will be arranged on a bar(s) and attached to uniforms. Ribbons will not be impregnated with preservatives which change their appearance, or have any transparent covering.

Arrange ribbons in order of precedence in rows from top down, inboard to outboard. Wear either the three senior ribbons, or all ribbons if you have earned three or more.

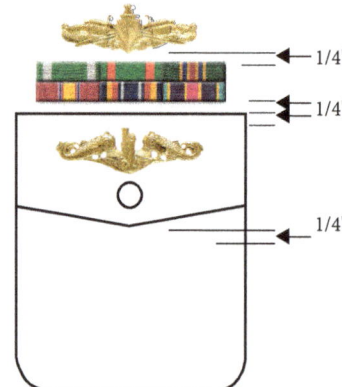

Qualification Insignia - When wearing ribbons, you may wear two qualification badges from any category for which you are qualified. When wearing two badges, put the most current or recently earned uppermost. With ribbons: the most recent badge is centered 1/4" above the ribbons. If a second badge is worn, it is centered 1/4" below the top of the left pocket.

44 Medals and Ribbons of the U.S. Navy

Male Officer, CPO and E6-E1 Medal Wear

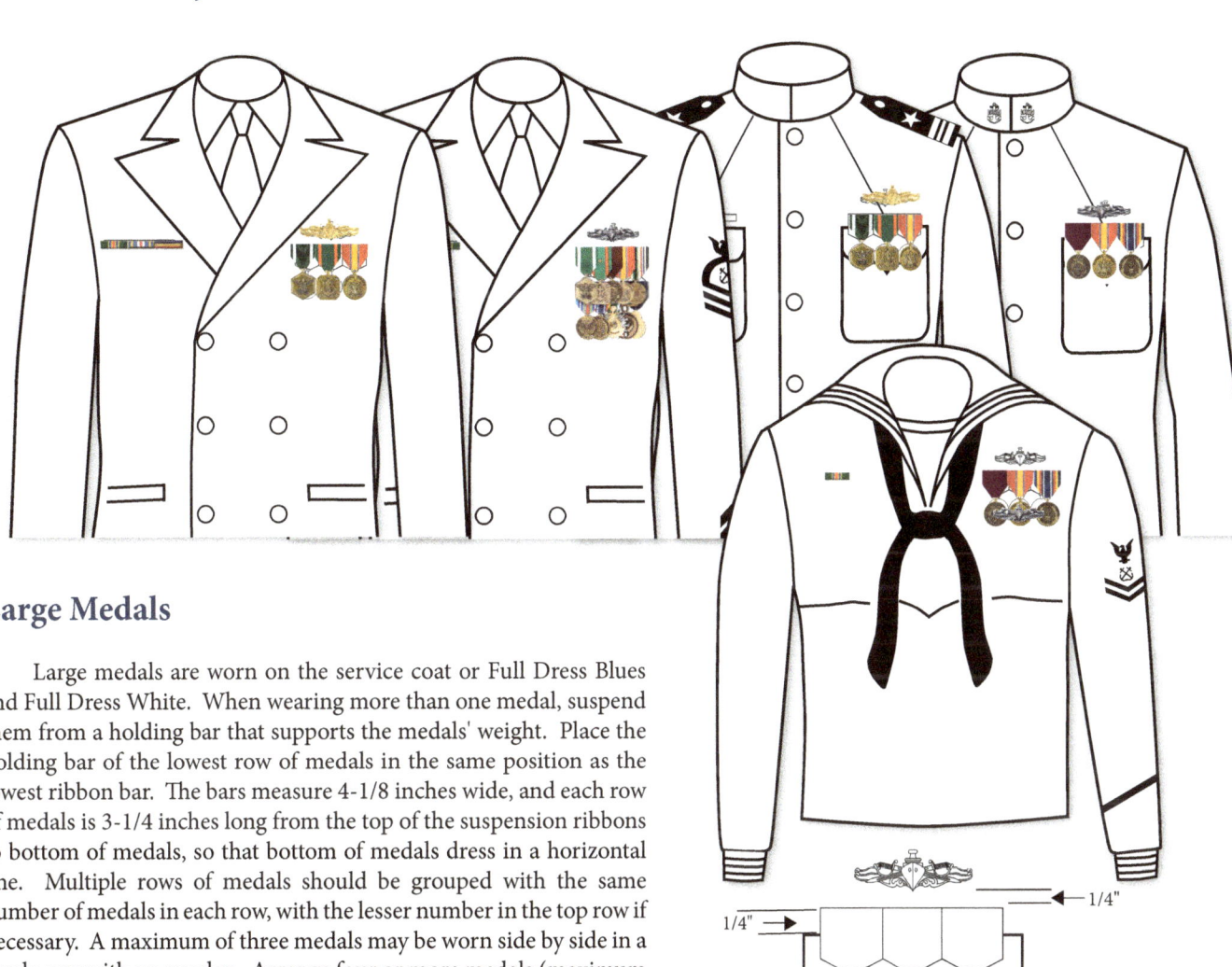

Large Medals

Large medals are worn on the service coat or Full Dress Blues and Full Dress White. When wearing more than one medal, suspend them from a holding bar that supports the medals' weight. Place the holding bar of the lowest row of medals in the same position as the lowest ribbon bar. The bars measure 4-1/8 inches wide, and each row of medals is 3-1/4 inches long from the top of the suspension ribbons to bottom of medals, so that bottom of medals dress in a horizontal line. Multiple rows of medals should be grouped with the same number of medals in each row, with the lesser number in the top row if necessary. A maximum of three medals may be worn side by side in a single row with no overlap. Arrange four or more medals (maximum of five in a single row) following the layout in table. Overlapping will be proportional and the inboard medal will show in full. Mount the medals so they cover the suspension ribbons of the medals below.

Arrangement. Arrange medals in order of precedence in rows from top down, inboard to outboard, within rows. Service members possessing more than five medals may either wear the five senior medals or all of them.

Wearing of Large and Miniature Medals by Navy Male Personnel

Total Number of Medals	Number of Rows	Number of Medals First Row	Number of Medals 2d Row	Number of Medals 3rd Row
1-5	1 row only	1-5	-	-
6	2	3	3	-
7	2	3	4	-
8	2	4	4	-
9	2	4	5	-
10	2	5	5	-
11	3	3	4	4
12	3	4	4	4
13	3	3	5	5
14	3	4	5	5

Medals of America Press

Male Officer, CPO and E6-E1 Miniature Medal Wear

Miniature Medals

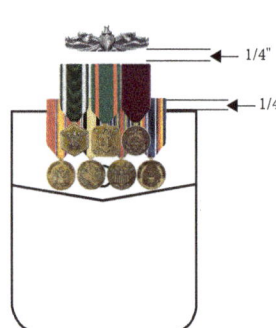

Wear miniature medals with all formal dress uniforms and dinner dress uniforms. Each row of miniatures is 2-1/4 inches long, from top of the suspension ribbons to bottom of medals, so the bottom of medals dress in a horizontal line. Position medals so they cover the suspension ribbons of the medals in the rows below. Male officers and CPOs, and E6 and below: on formal and dinner dress jackets, place the holding bar of the lowest row of miniature medals 3 inches below the notch, centered on the lapel, parallel to the deck. On blue and white service coats, center the holding bar 1/4 inch above the left breast pocket parallel to the deck. Female officers and CPOs, and E6 and below: on formal dress or dinner dress jackets, place the holding bar in the same relative position as on the men's dinner dress jackets, down 1/3 the distance between the shoulder seam and coat hem. On blue and white coats, center the holding bar 1/4 inch above the left pocket flap parallel to the deck. E6 and Below: on jumper uniforms, men and women place the holding bar of the lowest row of miniature medals 1/4 inch above the pocket parallel to the deck.

Arrangement. Wear up to five miniature medals in a row with no overlap. Arrange six or more miniature medals following the layout in the table.

a. Arrange medals in order of precedence in rows from top down, inboard to outboard, within rows. Service members possessing five or more medals may either wear the five senior medals or all of them. On the dinner dress jacket, center up to three miniature medals on the lapel. Position four or more miniatures starting at the inner edge of the lapel extending beyond the lapel on to the body of the jacket.

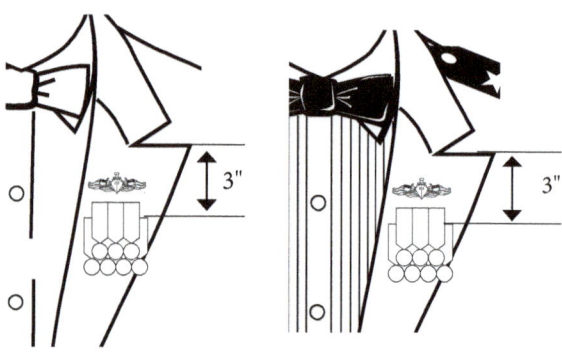

Female Officer and CPO Ribbon Wear

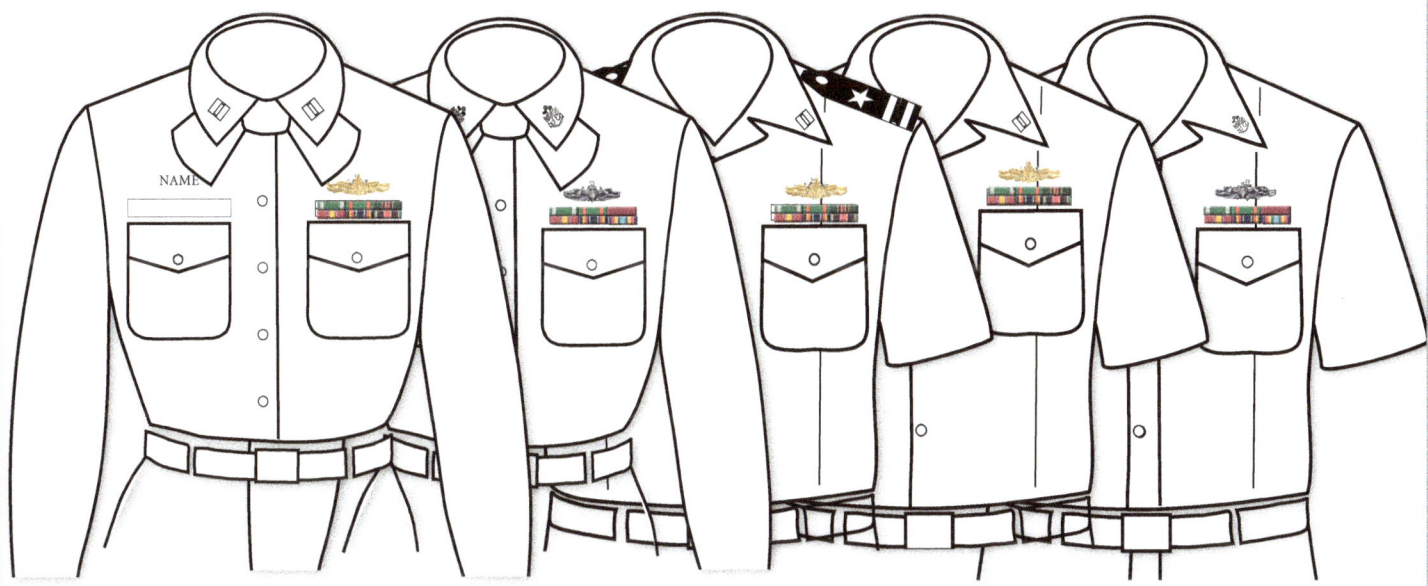

Ribbons are worn on the service coat or jumper of Service Dress Blue, Dress White, and on the shirt of Service Khaki. Wear up to three ribbons in a single row. When more than three ribbons are authorized, wear them in horizontal rows of three each. If ribbons are not in multiples of three, the top row contains the lesser number, and the center of this row sits over the center of the one below it. Wear ribbons without spaces between ribbons or rows of ribbons.

Wear ribbons with the lower edge of the bottom row centered 1/4 inch above the left breast pocket and parallel to the deck. To prevent coat lapels from covering ribbons, ribbons may be aligned so the border to wearer's left is aligned with left side of pocket.

Rows of ribbons where more than 50% of the ribbon is covered by the coat lapel may contain two ribbons each and be aligned with left border.

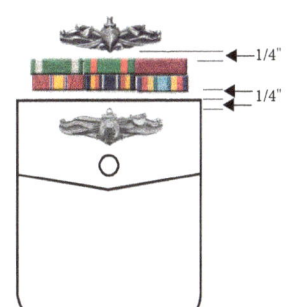

Qualification Insignia - When wearing ribbons, you may wear two qualification badges from any category for which you are qualified. When wearing two badges, put the most current or recently earned uppermost. With ribbons: the most recent badge is centered 1/4" above the ribbons. If a second badge is worn, it is centered 1/4" below the top of the left pocket.

Officer, CPO and E6-E1 Female Full Size Medal Wear

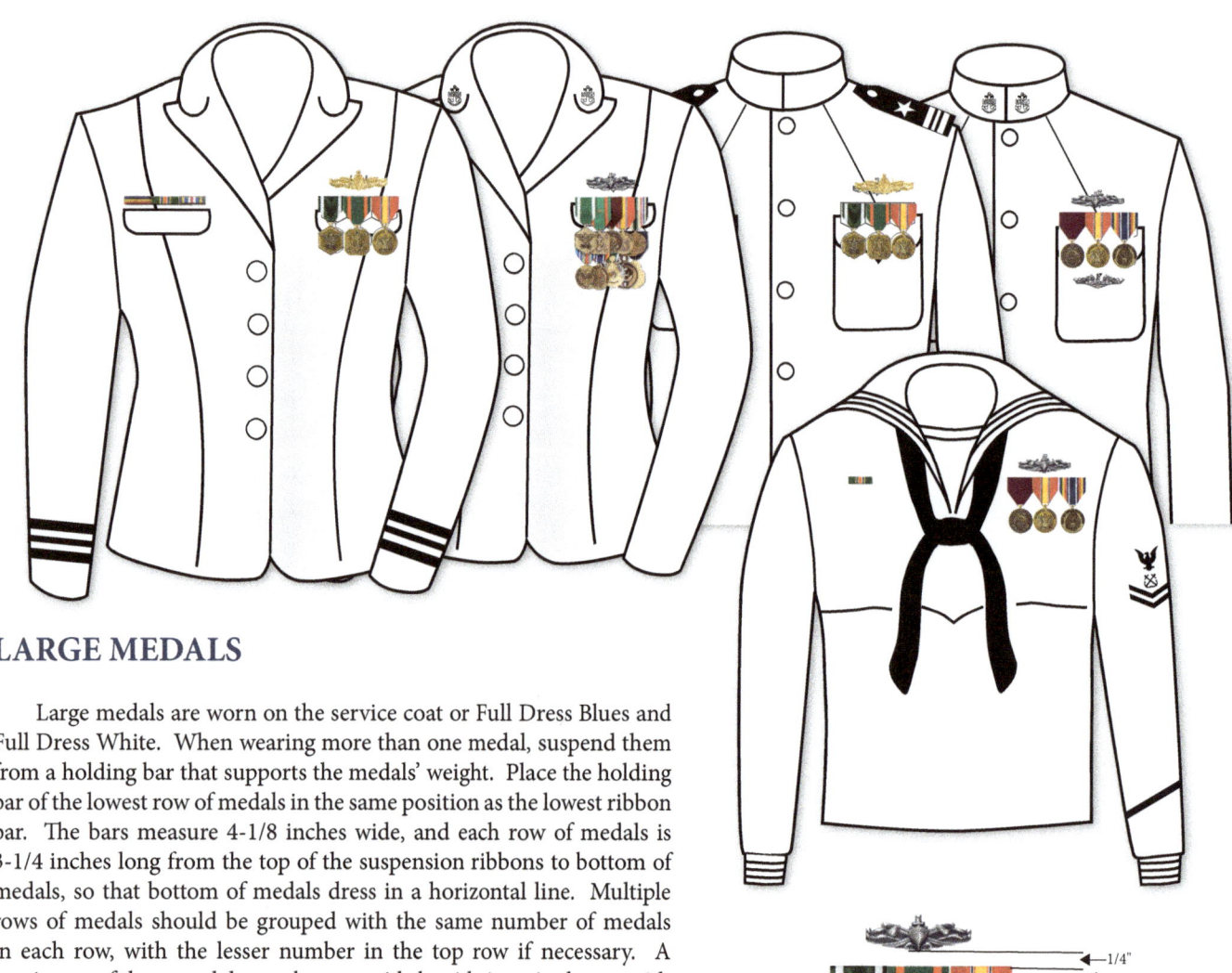

LARGE MEDALS

Large medals are worn on the service coat or Full Dress Blues and Full Dress White. When wearing more than one medal, suspend them from a holding bar that supports the medals' weight. Place the holding bar of the lowest row of medals in the same position as the lowest ribbon bar. The bars measure 4-1/8 inches wide, and each row of medals is 3-1/4 inches long from the top of the suspension ribbons to bottom of medals, so that bottom of medals dress in a horizontal line. Multiple rows of medals should be grouped with the same number of medals in each row, with the lesser number in the top row if necessary. A maximum of three medals may be worn side by side in a single row with no overlap. Arrange four or more medals *(maximum of five in a single row)* following the layout in table. Overlapping will be proportional and the inboard medal will show in full. Mount the medals so they cover the suspension ribbons of the medals below.

Arrangement. Arrange medals in order of precedence in rows from top down, inboard to outboard, within rows. Service members possessing more than five medals may either wear the five senior medals or all of them.

Wearing of Large and Miniature Medals by Navy Female Personnel

Total Number of Medals	Number of Rows	Number of Medals First Row	Number of Medals 2d Row	Number of Medals 3rd Row
1-5	1 row only	1-5	-	-
6	2	3	3	-
7	2	3	4	-
8	2	4	4	-
9	2	4	5	-
10	2	5	5	-
11	3	3	4	4
12	3	4	4	4

Officer, CPO and E6-E1 Female Miniature Size Medal Wear

Miniature Medals

Wear miniature medals with all formal dress uniforms and dinner dress uniforms. Each row of miniatures is 2-1/4 inches long, from top of the suspension ribbons to bottom of medals, so the bottom of medals dress in a horizontal line. Position medals so they cover the suspension ribbons of the medals in the rows below.

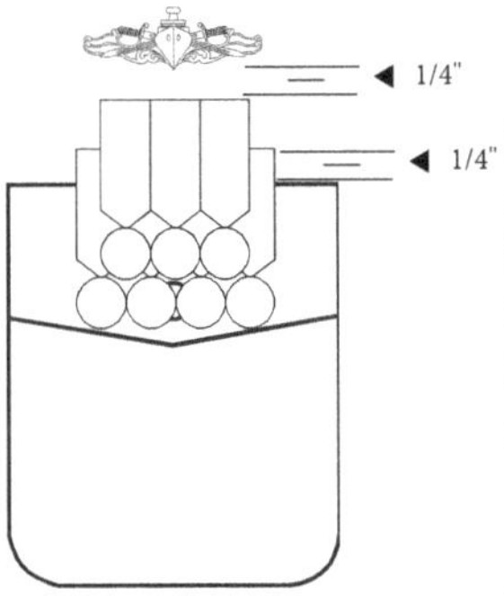

Female officers and CPOs, and E6 and below: on formal dress or dinner dress jackets, place the holding bar in the same relative position as on the men's dinner dress jackets, down 1/3 the distance between the shoulder seam and coat hem.

On blue and white coats, center the holding bar 1/4 inch above the left pocket flap parallel to the deck. E6 and Below: on jumper uniforms, men and women place the holding bar of the lowest row of miniature medals 1/4 inch above the pocket parallel to the deck.

Arrangement. Wear up to five miniature medals in a row with no overlap. Arrange six or more miniature medals following the layout in the table to the left.

Arrange medals in order of precedence in rows from top down, inboard to outboard, within rows. Service members possessing five or more medals may either wear the five senior medals or all of them. On the dinner dress jacket, center up to three miniature medals on the lapel. Position four or more miniatures starting at the inner edge of the lapel extending beyond the lapel on to the body of the jacket.

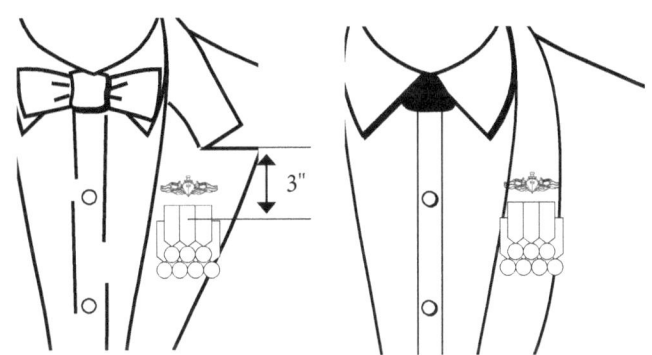

Place the holding bar in the same relative position as on the men's dinner dress jackets, down 1/3 the distance between the shoulder seam and coat hem.

E1-E6 Male & Female Dress Blues and Whites

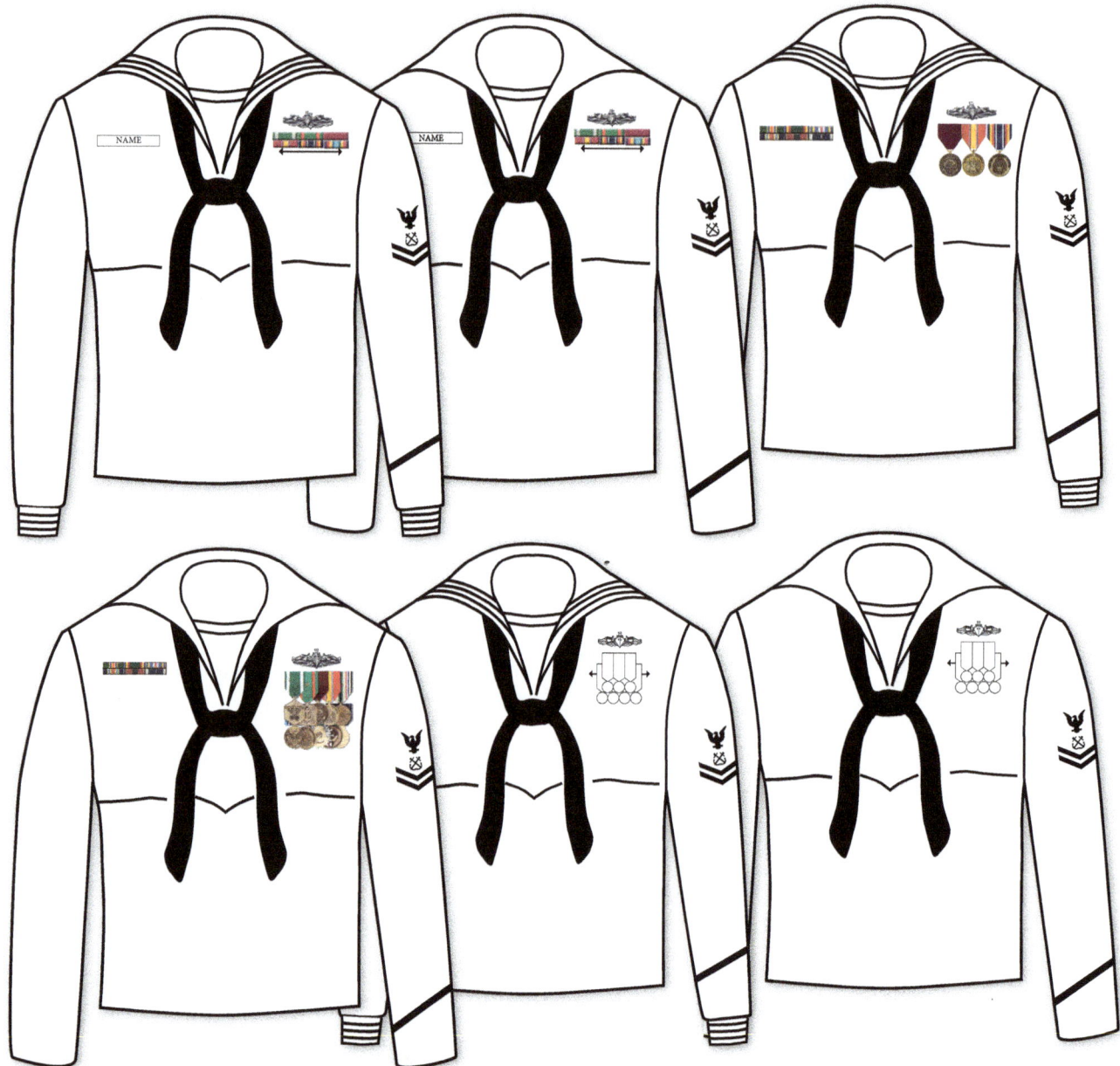

Ribbons are worn on the jumper of Service Dress Blue and Dress White. Wear up to three ribbons in a single row. When more than three ribbons are authorized, wear them in horizontal rows of three each. If ribbons are not in multiples of three, the top row contains the lesser number, and the center of this row sits over the center of the one below it. Wear ribbons without spaces between ribbons or rows of ribbons. Wear ribbons with the lower edge of the bottom row centered 1/4 inch above the left breast pocket and parallel to the deck. Large Medals are worn on Full Dress Blues and Full Dress White. When wearing more than one medal, suspend them from a holding bar that supports the medals' weight. Place the holding bar of the lowest row of medals in the same position as the lowest ribbon bar. The bars measure 4-1/8 inches wide, and each row of medals is 3-1/4 inches long from the top of the suspension ribbons to bottom of medals, so that bottom of medals dress in a horizontal line. Multiple rows of medals should be grouped with the same number of medals in each row, with the lesser number in the top row if necessary. A maximum of three medals may be worn side by side in a single row with no overlap. Arrange four or more medals *(maximum of five in a single row)* following the layout in table. Overlapping will be proportional and the inboard medal will show in full. Mount the medals so they cover the suspension ribbons of the medals below. Arrange medals in order of precedence in rows from top down, inboard to outboard, within rows. Service members possessing more than five medals may either wear the five senior medals or all of them.

Miniature medals for E6 and Below: on jumper uniforms, men and women place the holding bar of the lowest row of miniature medals 1/4 inch above the pocket parallel to the deck. Arrange miniatures the same as for full size medals i.e. in order of precedence in rows from top down, inboard to outboard, within rows.

A Summary of How Navy Medals Are Worn

Military Ribbons

United States Navy

Wear of Service Ribbons — Wear up to 3 in a row; if more than three ribbons, wear in horizontal rows of three each. The top row contains the lesser number, centered above the row below, no spaces between ribbon rows. Rows of ribbons covered by coat lapel may contain two ribbons each and be aligned. Wear ribbons with lower edge of bottom row centered 1/4 inch above left breast pocket and parallel to the deck.

Wear of Full Size Decorations & Service Medals — When wearing large medals on full dress uniforms align the bottom row same as ribbon bars. All rows may contain maximum of 3 medals side by side or up to 5 overlapping. Overlapping is proportional with inboard medal showing in full. Mount a second row of medals so they cover the suspension ribbon of the medals below. When large medals are worn, all unit citations and ribbons with no medal authorized are centered over the right breast pocket the bottom edge 1/8 inch above the top of the pocket.

Wear of Miniature Medals — Wear miniature medals with all formal and dinner dress uniforms. Place holding bar of lowest row of miniatures 3 inches below the lapel notch, centered on the lapel. Center the holding bar immediately above the left breast pocket on the blue and white service coat. You may wear up to five miniature medals in a row with no overlap on the dinner jacket, center up to 3 miniature medals on the lapel. Position 4 or more miniatures at the inner edge of the lapel extending beyond the lapel to the body of the jacket.

Military Miniature Medals

Medals of America Press 51

How to Determine a Navy Veteran's Military Medals

Many veteran sailors and their families are unsure of which military medals they were awarded and often for good reasons. Twenty-five, thirty, even fifty years after military service, it is often difficult to remember or clearly identify the awards a veteran may have earned the right to wear or display. Thousands of veterans have been heard to say *"I don't want any awards I'm not authorized, but I want everything I am authorized."* So the question is, *"What are the medals authorized the veteran for his military service during each conflict?"*

There are a number of reasons besides the passage of time that veterans are not always sure of their military awards. At the end of World War II many campaign medals had not yet been struck and were only issued as ribbons due to the restriction on brass and other metals for the war effort. Many unit awards had not yet been authorized and on the whole, most Soldiers, Sailors, Marines and Airmen were more interested in going home than they were in their military records.

Perhaps the most striking example is the recently-approved Republic of Korea War Service Medal. The Republic of Korea offered the medal to all U.S. Korean War veterans but it was not accepted by our government until 1999. In other cases, veterans came home and stuffed their medals and awards into a cigar box which usually found its way into the hands of children and these magnificent symbols of valor and service from a grateful nation simply disappeared over time.

Today there is a wonderfully renewed interest in wearing and displaying United States military medals, both to honor veterans' patriotic service and to display a family's pride in military service. World War II, Korea, Vietnam, Desert Storm, Iraq, Afghanistan and the Gobal war on Terror veterans now wear their medals at formal social and patriotic events and a display of military medals and insignia is often in the family home place of honor.

As mentioned earlier, military medals are divided into two categories: Decorations awarded for valor or meritorious service and Campaign and Service medals awarded for a particular service or event. Additionally there are Unit Awards which are for unit valor and meritorious service and ribbon-only awards presented for completing special training or recognizing certain service.

Decorations are individual awards which are of such singular significance that most veterans and their family will remember when such awards have been presented. Decorations are noted on a veteran's official discharge papers *(called a DD Form 214)* as well as published in official unit orders. However there are exceptions, such as the Bronze Star Medal issued for meritorious service after World War II and in some cases Purple Heart medals that were never officially presented. Someone who is unsure if they received a decoration can request the National Records Center in St. Louis or other veterans records holding areas to check their records. Home of Heroes at www.homeofheroes.

52   Medals and Ribbons of the U.S. Navy

com list all Medal of Honor, Service Crosses and most Silver Star awardees. Bronze Star, Air Medal, Purple Heart, Commendation and Achievement medals are announced in unit orders which are normally found in the individual's military service record.

Campaign and service medals, unit awards and ribbon-only awards are more clearly identifiable. The Navy has ship and campaign records which provides a clear indication of which campaign medals, unit awards, campaign stars and foreign unit awards are authorized a particular ship or unit during certain periods of time. To aid in identifying the campaign medals authorized veterans of different conflicts and to show how they can be displayed, United States and allied campaign medals authorized since World War II are summarized later in this chapter. Exact criteria for each medal and the campaigns associated with it are shown in detail later in the book.

Basically, there are several ways to identify the military medals a veteran has earned. The early medals such as the Civil War Campaign Medal are easy. If an ancestors served during the Civil War then they earned it *(see the Civil War medal description)*. The other early campaign medals prior to World War I, such as the Spanish-American Campaign Medals were earned by both 250,000 federal and state volunteers and their records are in the National Archives on microfilm. These files can be found by going to www.familysearch.com.

World War I is fairly straight forward, with few exceptions all of the soldiers, sailors, marines and airmen received the World War I Victory Medal. Their campaign bars and any other awards are also available on the government website: www.archives.gov.

World War II and Later

The identification of World War II and later veterans is the information most veterans and families want and that really just comes from two places. The first is the sailor's discharge certificate which has his service history. Early World War II Navy versions were Notice of Seperation from the Naval service which later became the Department of Defense Form 214 *(DD 214)*. While this is the official record, it is often incomplete or missing information which was not available at the time of the veteran's discharge. Which, of course, is the purpose of this book, to bring veterans and their families up to date on their military awards. So let's start with how you obtain a copy of your DD 214 or for the veteran in your family.

All of the federal government's military records for World War II veterans are stored at the National Personnel Records Center (NPRC) in St. Louis, Missouri. The National Personnel Records Center is part of the National Archives and Records Administration.

There are specific rules for requesting a veterans records because of the privacy act. As long as the veteran is still living, he is the only one who may request his complete military records.

However, if the veteran is deceased, then the next of kin is entitled to the complete military file. By the next of kin the NRPC means the unmarried widow or widower, son or daughter, father or mother, brother or sister of a deceased veteran. Grandchildren, nieces or nephews are not generally included as next of kin.

So, if you are not the next of kin of the deceased veteran you really must have one of the next of kin make the request for the records. One exception is the military files will be provided if you are really the only living relative of a deceased veteran. While the NPRC will provide the complete military files for the purpose of identifying the military awards you are really only interested in the DD 214 record of discharge.

Unfortunately, in 1973 there was a huge fire at the NPRC that destroyed nearly 18 million official military personnel records. However, eighty percent of those records destroyed were for Army and Army Air Force personnel that had been discharged between 1912 and 1960. So most Naval records are still there. Even if you're relatively sure that the veterans records may have been burned you should go ahead and send them a request because NPRC has been able to reconstruct some files.

There is a another source for locating a veteran's DD214. Surprisingly, a very high percentage of all veterans recorded a copy of their DD 214 in the local county courthouse. At the time of a Sailors discharge it was recommended that they do this because it was the single most important document for them to have for applying for any veteran's benefits. By having it recorded at the local County Courthouse they could always obtain a copy. If you are researching a veteran's file you might be very pleasantly surprised to find a copy on file at the county courthouse that your veteran came home to.

This Petty Officer Gunner's Mate Vietnam service display is a source of pride and family history that tells the story of his military service through his military meedals, ribbons and insignia.

Medals of America Press 53

Issue of U.S. Medals to Veterans, Retirees and Their Families

How to Request the DD214

Veterans of any United States military service may request medals never issued (the majority of WW II veterans for example) or replacement of medals which have been lost, stolen, destroyed or rendered unfit through no fault of their own. Requests may also be filed for awards that were earned but, for any reason, were never issued to the veteran. A good example is the Korea Defense Service Medal which was recently approved and back dated to cover everyone who served in Korea after 1954. More than 2 million former service personnel are now authorized this medal. The next-of-kin of deceased veterans may also make the same request for the medals of their veteran family member.

The National Personnel Records Center, Military Personnel Records *(NPRC-MPR)* is the repository of millions of military personnel, health, and medical records of discharged and deceased veterans of all services during the 20th century. Information from the records is made available upon written request *(with signature and date)* to the extent allowed by law. Please note that NPRC holds historical Military Personnel Records of nearly 100 million veterans. The vast majority of these records are paper-based and not available on-line.

There are two ways for those seeking information regarding military personnel records stored at NPRC *(MPR)*. If you are a veteran or next-of-kin of a deceased veteran, you may now use **vetrecs.archives.gov** to order a copy of your military records. For all others, your request is best made using a **Standard Form 180**. It includes complete instructions for preparing and submitting requests.

Using the vetrecs.archives.gov Requests for the issuance or replacement of military service medals, decorations, and awards should be directed to the specific branch of the military in which the veteran served. However, for Air Force *(including Army Air Corps)* and Army personnel, the National Personnel Records Center will verify the awards to which a veteran is entitled and forward the request with the verification to the appropriate service department for issuance of the medals.

The Standard Form *(SF 180)*, Request Pertaining to Military Records, is recommended for requesting medals and awards. Provide as much information as possible and send the form to the appropriate address shown on the next page.

1. **How to Obtain Standard Form 180 (SF-180), Request Pertaining to Military Records**

    A. Download and print a copy of the SF-180 in PDF format by going to: ***http://www.archives.gov/facilities/mo/st_louis/military_personnel_records standard_form_180.html#sf.***

    B. Write to The National Personnel Records Center 9700 Page Avenue, St. Louis, Missouri 63132.

The SF 180 may be photocopied as needed. You must submit a separate SF 180 for each individual whose records are being requested.

2. **Write a Letter to Request Records**

If you are not able to obtain SF-180, you may still submit a request for military records by letter. The letter should indicate if the request is for a specific medal(s), or for all medals earned. It is also helpful to include copies of any military service documents that indicate eligibility for medals, such as military orders or the veteran's report of separation (DD Form 214 or its earlier equivalent). Federal law [5 USC 552a(b)] requires that all requests for information from official military personnel files be submitted in writing. Each request must be signed (in cursive) by the veteran or his next-of-kin indicating the relationship to the deceased and dated (within the last year). For this reason, no requests are accepted over the internet.

Requests must contain enough information to identify the record among the more than 70 million on file at NPRC (MPR). Certain basic information is needed to locate military service records. This information includes:

- The veteran's complete name used while in service, Service number or social security number

- Branch of service

    If the request pertains to a record that may have been involved in the 1973 fire, also include:

- Place of discharge

- Last unit of assignment

- Place of entry into the service, if known.

Submit a separate request *(either SF 180 or letter)* for each veteran whose records are being requested. Response times for records requested from the *(NPRC)* vary greatly depending on the nature of the request. For example, the NPRC Military Records Facility can run a backlog of 180,000 requests and receives approximately 5,000 requests per day. The Center may have a difficult time locating records since millions of records were lost in a fire in 1973. Although the requested medals can often be issued on the basis of alternate records, the documents sent in with the request are sometimes the only means of determining proper eligibility.

Finally, you should exercise extreme patience. It may take several months or, in some cases, a year to determine eligibility and dispatch the appropriate medals. The Center asks that you not send a follow-up request for 90 days. Because of these delays, many veterans simply purchase their medals from a supplier such as *www.usmedals.com*.

Generally, there is no charge for medal or award replacements from the government. The length of time to receive a response or your medals and awards varies depending upon the branch of service sending the medals.

Cold War Recognition Certificate

In accordance with section 1084 of the Fiscal Year 1998 National Defense Authorization Act, the Secretary of Defense approved awarding Cold War Recognition Certificates to all members of the armed forces and qualified federal government civilian personnel who faithfully served the United States during the Cold War era, from Sept. 2, 1945 to Dec. 26, 1991. The application for the certificate is best obtained by doing an internet search for Cold War Recognition Certificate since the site location has changed several times.

ARMY

| If the person served in the Army, the request should be sent to: | National Personnel Records Center
1 Archives Drive
St. Louis, MO 63138 | In case of a problem or an appeal write to:
U.S. Army Human Resources Cmd
Awards Division
Attn: AHRC-PDP-A
1600 Spearhead Ave.
Fort Knox, KY 40122-5408 |

AIR FORCE

| The Air Force processes requests for medals through the National Personnel Records Center, which determines eligibility through the information in the veteran's records. Once verified, a notification of entitlement is forwarded to Randolph Air Force Base, Texas, from which the medals are mailed to the requestor. To request medals earned while in the Air Force or its predecessors, the Army Air Corps or Army Air Force veterans or their next-of-kin should write to: | National Personnel Records Center
1 Archives Drive
St. Louis, MO 63138 | In case of a problem or an appeal write to:
Headquarters Air Force Personnel Ctr
AFPC/DPPPR
550 C Street West, Suite 12
Randolph AFB, TX 78150-4714 |

NAVY

| If the person served in the Navy, the request should be sent to: | National Personnel Records Center
1 Archives Drive
St. Louis, MO 63138 | In case of a problem or an appeal write to:
Department of the Navy
Chief of Naval Operations (DNS-35)
2000 Navy Pentagon
Washington, DC 20350-2000 |

MARINE CORPS

| If the person served in the Marine Corps, the request should be sent to: | National Personnel Records Center
1 Archives Drive
St. Louis, MO 63138 | In case of a problem or an appeal write to:
Commandant of the Marine Corps
Military Awards Branch (MMMA)
2008 Elliot Road
Quantico, VA 22134 |

COAST GUARD

| If the person served in the Coast Guard, the request should be sent to: | Coast Guard Personnel Center
4200 Wilson Blvd, Suite 900
(PSC-PSD-MA) STOP 7200
Arlington, VA 20598-7200 | In case of a problem or an appeal write to:
Commandant U.S. Coast Guard
Medals and Awards Branch (PMP-4)
Washington, DC 20593-0001 |

World War II Military Medals Records

Many readers of earlier editions ask for detail information about determining a veterans military awards. As mentioned on the previous pages the veterans DD214 or equallivant is the key. Shown below is a senior officer's World War II DD214 with the individuals name removed. It is also a good example of the need to be able to translate the military abbreviations of that period and figure out what may be missing. In this case can you find the clue that tells you the Sailor's complete list of medals and ribbons authorized.

This senior officer example and an enlisted example will give you a good idea of the hugh amount of information on a discharge certificate..

CHARACTER OF SEPARATION: HONORABLE

REPORT OF SEPARATION FROM THE ARMED FORCES OF THE UNITED STATES

ARTMENT: U.S. NAVY

SEPARATION DATA

1. LAST NAME – FIRST NAME – MIDDLE NAME: veteran's name
2. SERVICE NUMBER: 60331
3. GRADE – RATE – RANK AND DATE OF APPOINTMENT: CAPTAIN 8/3/43
4. COMPONENT AND BRANCH OR CLASS: USN
5. QUALIFICATIONS – SPECIALTY NUMBER OR SYMBOL: 1100; RELATED CIVILIAN OCCUPATION AND D.O.T. NUMBER: SHIPMASTER & ADMINISTRATION
6. EFFECTIVE DATE OF SEPARATION: DAY 30 MONTH JUNE YEAR 1956
7. TYPE OF SEPARATION: RETIREMENT
8. REASON AND AUTHORITY FOR SEPARATION: BUPERS ORDERS 1259 OF 12 JANUARY 1956
9. PLACE OF SEPARATION: U.S. NAVAL RECEIVING STATION, BROOKLYN, NY
10. DATE OF BIRTH: DAY 31 MONTH JULY YEAR 1902
11. PLACE OF BIRTH (City and State): GREENSBURG, PENNSYLVANIA
12. DESCRIPTION: SEX MALE; RACE CAU; COLOR HAIR GRAY; COLOR EYES HAZEL; HEIGHT 5'7"; WEIGHT 145

SELECTIVE SERVICE DATA

13. REGISTERED: YES / NO X; SELECTIVE SERVICE NUMBER: –
14. SELECTIVE SERVICE LOCAL BOARD NUMBER (City, County, State): –
15. INDUCTED: DAY – MONTH – YEAR –
16. ENLISTED IN OR TRANSFERRED TO A RESERVE COMPONENT: YES / NO X; COMPONENT AND BRANCH OR CLASS: –; COGNIZANT DISTRICT OR AREA COMMAND: FOURTH NAVAL DISTRICT, PHILADELPHIA, PA

SERVICE DATA

17. MEANS OF ENTRY OTHER THAN BY INDUCTION: ENLISTED [ ] REENLISTED [ ] COMMISSIONED [X] CALLED FROM INACTIVE DUTY [ ]
18. GRADE – RATE OR RANK AT TIME OF ENTRY INTO ACTIVE SERVICE: ENSIGN
19. DATE AND PLACE OF ENTRY INTO ACTIVE SERVICE: DAY 3 MONTH JUNE YEAR 1926 PLACE (City and State): ANNAPOLIS, MARYLAND
20. HOME ADDRESS AT TIME OF ENTRY INTO ACTIVE SERVICE (St., R.F.D., City, County and State): 1312 PENN AVENUE, WILKINSBURG, PENNSYLVANIA

STATEMENT OF SERVICE FOR PAY PURPOSES	A. YEARS	B. MONTHS	C. DAYS
21. NET (– –) SERVICE COMPLETED FOR PAY PURPOSES EXCLUDING THIS PERIOD	00	00	00
22. NET SERVICE COMPLETED FOR PAY PURPOSES THIS PERIOD	30	00	28
23. OTHER SERVICE (Act of 16 June 1942 as amended) COMPLETED FOR PAY PURPOSES	00	00	00
24. TOTAL NET SERVICE COMPLETED FOR PAY PURPOSES Does not include Naval Academy Time	30	00	28

25. ENLISTMENT ALLOWANCE PAID ON EXTENSION OF ENLISTMENT, IF ANY: DAY – MONTH – YEAR – AMOUNT –
26. FOREIGN AND/OR SEA SERVICE: YEARS – MONTHS 00 DAYS 28
27. DECORATIONS, MEDALS, BADGES, COMMENDATIONS, CITATIONS AND CAMPAIGN RIBBONS AWARDED OR AUTHORIZED: Purple Heart, Navy Cross, Second Nicaraguan Camp., NUC, China ServMed, AmerDefMed, AmerAreaMed, ETC Med, AsiaPacArea PhilLibMed, Nicaraguan Merit Med w/Silver Star, Occup (Asia), WWII VictMed, Peruvian **
28. MOST SIGNIFICANT DUTY ASSIGNMENT: COMDESRON 18 AND ACTING FLOTILLA COMMANDER DD SIXTH FLEET–TWO TOURS WITH THAT FLEET
29. WOUNDS RECEIVED AS A RESULT OF ACTION WITH ENEMY FORCES (Place and date, if known): LEG WOUNDS IN THE BATTLE OF KULA GULF WHILE SERVING ABOARD U.S.S. HELENA CV-50

30. SERVICE SCHOOLS OR COLLEGES, COLLEGE TRAINING COURSES AND/OR POST-GRAD. COURSES SUCCESSFULLY COMPLETED	DATES (From-To)	MAJOR COURSES	31. SERVICE TRAINING COURSES SUCCESSFULLY COMPLETED
TORPEDO SCHOOL	JAN–MAY 1929	TORPEDO OVERHAUL & CONTROL	CORRESPONDENCE COURSE IN STRATEGY AND TACTICS
GUNNERY SCHOOL	1930–1931–1932	FIRE CONTROL	
ASW SCHOOL	MARCH 1952	ANTI-SUBMARINE WARFARE	
SPECIAL WEAPONS	FEB1953	FAMILIARIZATION	

INSURANCE AND PAY DATA

GOVERNMENT INSURANCE INFORMATION: (A) Permanent plan premiums must continue to be paid when due, or within 31 days thereafter, or insurance will lapse. (B) Term insurance not under waiver same as (A) above. (C) Term insurance under waiver – prompt payment must be resumed within 120 days after separation. Forward premiums on NSLI to Veterans Administration District Office having jurisdiction over the area shown in Item 47. Forward premiums on USGLI to Veterans Administration, Washington 25, D. C. (See VA Pamphlet 9-3) When paying premiums give full name, address, Service Number, Policy Number(s), Branch of Service, date of separation. Contact nearest VA office for information concerning Government Life Insurance.

37A. KIND & AMT. OF INSURANCE & MTHLY. PREMIUM: –
37B. ACTIVE SERVICE PRIOR TO 25 APRIL 1951: [X] YES [ ] NO [ ] UNKNOWN
33. MONTH ALLOTMENT DISCONTINUED: –
34. MONTH NEXT PREMIUM DUE: –
35. TOTAL PAYMENT UPON SEPARATION: –
36. TRAVEL OR MILEAGE ALLOWANCE INCLUDED IN TOTAL PAYMENT: –
37. DISBURSING OFFICER'S NAME AND SYMBOL NUMBER: –

AUTHENTICATION

38. REMARKS (Continue on reverse): I HEREBY CERTIFY THAT THE INFORMATION ENTERED IN ITEM 26 IS CORRECT TO THE BEST OF MY KNOWLEDGE AND BELIEF
**Navy Cross, ArmServDefMed
Spanish Cross
39. SIGNATURE OF OFFICER AUTHORIZED TO SIGN: J. B. McAuliffe
NAME, GRADE AND TITLE (Typed): J.B. McAULIFFE, CDR, USN 59983, Executive Officer

40. V.A. BENEFITS PREVIOUSLY APPLIED FOR (Specify type) COMPENSATION, PENSION, INSURANCE BENEFITS, ETC.: –; CLAIM NUMBER: –

PERSONAL DATA

41. DATES OF LAST CIVILIAN EMPLOYMENT: FROM – TO –
42. MAIN CIVILIAN OCCUPATION: –
43. NAME AND ADDRESS OF LAST CIVILIAN EMPLOYER: –
44. UNITED STATES CITIZEN: [X] YES [ ] NO
45. MARITAL STATUS: MARRIED
46. NON-SERVICE EDUCATION (Years successfully completed): GRAMMAR 8; HIGH SCHOOL 4; COLLEGE 6; DEGREE(S) B.S.; MAJOR COURSE OR FIELD: MEC & ELECT ENGINEERING & NAVAL SCIENCE
47. PERMANENT ADDRESS FOR MAILING PURPOSES AFTER SEPARATION (St., R.F.D., City, County and State): 1312 PENN AVENUE, WILKINSBURG, PENNSYLVANIA
48. SIGNATURE OF PERSON BEING SEPARATED

DD FORM 1 JUL 52 214 — EDITION OF 1 JAN 50 IS OBSOLETE — INDIVIDUAL'S COPY (TO BE DELIVERED TO THE INDIVIDUAL BEING SEPARATED) — 1

ALL ENTRIES APPLY TO CURRENT PERIOD OF SERVICE (unless otherwise indicated)

Interpreting the DD 214 for Awards World War II Military Medals

 A Campaign star

Just to the right of the veteran's name shows his final rank in case his retirement after 30 years.

Box 22 shows his total time of naval service.

Box 27 and 38 are the ones that you will always be most interested in as they identify decorations and awards. Box 27 says He was awarded the Navy Cross, the Purple Heart and he served in the 2d Nicaraguan Campaign (between 1926 and 1933), the China Service Medal, American Defense Medal, the American Campaign Medal, American Theater Campaign ribbon, Asiatic Pacific Campaign Medal, European African Middle Eastern, the Occupation Medal with Asia Bar and a Victory Medal. This a good reference because many of the medals had been minted and available for veterans by the 1950s. It also identifies the Phillipine Liberation Medal and three foreign awards from Nicaragia, Peru and Spain. Surprising it does not identify how many campaign stars go on his Asiatic Pacific and ETO medal.

The three letters NUC, what do they stand fo? NUC is a Navy unit award: The Unit Commendation, a ribbon only award.

In box 34, the remarks section, it indicates he is authorize the American Theater Campaign Medal (called America Area Campaign Medal), Asiatic Pacific Campaign Medal with 2 stars, and a Victory Medal. The Bronze Star was a rare decoration for Seaman 3rd class and must have been related to his assignment to UDT Team 12. This discharge has some mystery yet to be researched. during WW II the Navy required 3 years service for a Good Conduct Medal so he did not qualify; however, a little research indicates UDT Team 12 recieved a Navy Presidential Unit Citation for the Battle of Iwo Jima.

What the DD214 does not tell *but does give clues is that this seaman started out as a Seabee and volunteered for Underwater Demotion Duty.* By researching UDT Team 12 you can find out everyman on the team was awarded the Bronze Star for their clearing the beaches for the invasion of Iwo Jima and Okinawa. he would have also been awarded the Honorable Discharge Insignia as shown.

❖ World War II Navy Campaign Medals

The basic service medals of World War II are shown above. The Navy had already established a Good Conduct Medal before WW I.

The American Defense Service Medal was authorized for the period of national emergency prior to 7 December 1941. After America declared war, the conflict was divided into (1) the American theater, (2) the European, African, Middle Eastern theater, and the (3) Asiatic Pacific Theater. Examples of the medals awarded are shown above.

American Defense was awarded for service between 1939 and 7 Dec. 1941.

American Campaign was for service in the American Theater, outside the US for 30 days or in the US for a year. Most veterans qualified for this medal. The Asiatic Pacific and Europe, Africa and Middle East Campaign Medals award requirements are defined in the medal section.

All World War II veterans qualified for the Victory Medal.

World War II veterans who served 30 days in an occupied country qualify for an Occupation Medal.

Philippine Defense and Liberation Medals for service in the Philippines.

NOTICE OF SEPARATION FROM U. S. NAVAL SERVICE

Book 103 Page 310 — No. 10296

Place of Separation: USN Personnel Separation Center, Lido Beach, L.I., N.Y.

Serial or File No.: 806 194

Means of Entry: ☒ Enlisted ☒ Inducted ☐ Commissioned
Date: 12-11-43 / 12-11-43

Date of Entry Into Active Service: 12-18-43
Net Service (for pay purposes): 2-5-9
Place of Entry Into Active Service: Buffalo, N.Y.

Ratings Held: AS, F2c, F1c, WT3c.
Foreign and/or Sea Service World War II: ☒ Yes ☐ No

Qualifications, Certificates Held, Etc.: Those of Rating. See Rating Description Booklet

Service Schools Completed: Recruit Trg., Sampson, N.Y. — 6 weeks

Service (Vessels and Stations Served On):
AFISTA, Rochester, N.Y./ NRS, Buffalo, N.Y.
NTS, Sampson, N.Y./ NTS, NorVa./
USS FRYBARGER/ NTS, NorVa./
USS JOSEPH E. CONNOLY/
PSC Lido Beach, L.I., N.Y.

Kind of Insurance: NTS
Effective Month of Allotment Discontinuance: 5/46
Mo. Next Premium Due: 6 46
Amount of Premium Due Each Month: $6.70
Intention of Veteran to Continue Ins.: Yes
Total Payment Upon Discharge: $36.82
Travel or Mileage Allowance Included In Total Payment: $19.75
Initial Mustering Out Pay: $100.
Name of Disbursing Officer: EP O'ROURKE

Signature: F. R. Ahmuty JM
F. R. AHMUTY, Lieut., USNR
By direction

Remarks:
American Theater Medal
European African Middle Eastern Medal
Asiatic Pacific Medal 1 Star
Victory Medal

This sailor's World War II discharge shows the rating he held in box 21 (WT3/c) Water Tender 3rd Class and the ships he served on. In July 1942 the Navy discontinued the procurement and issuance of Good Conduct Medals for the duration of World War II to conserve metal and offset the increased clerical work. Notations of eligibility were made in service jackets for later issue, however, the Navy required 3 years service for a Good Conduct Medal and his discharge shows 2 years, 5 months and 9 days active service so he did not qualify for a Good Conduct Medal. However, his European African Middle Eastern Theater Campaign Medal should show at least 1 battle/campaign star as you can not earn the medal without being in at least one campaign. He is authorized the 4 medals shown plus 1 star on his European African Middle Eastern Theater Campaign Medal.

Medals of America Press

Korean Campaign Medals 1950-1954

The Armed Forces approved acceptance of the ROK War Service Medal in Oct. 1999 for all Korean War Veterans. The Korea Defense Service Medal for 30 days service in Korea after 27 July 1954 was approved in 2003.

Good Conduct Medals (Current issue) · National Defense Service · US - Korean Service · US - Korea Defense · UN - Korean Service · ROK War Service

Medal Displays are shown with the addition of approiate Commeorative Medals (See page 173)

Vietnam Campaign Medals 1965-1973

Good Conduct Medals (Current issue) — National Defense Service Medal — U.S. Vietnam Service Medal — Vietnam Campaign Medal — RVN Gallantry Cross Unit Citation

This Sailor's Vietnam era discharge is missing the campaign stars for his Vietnam Service Medal and while it shows 2 years and 2 months foreign service, or sea service, it is difficult to tell how many campaign stars he rates on his service medal. If you know the dates of his service in Vietnam you can compute the campaign stars from the table listed on the page describing the Vietnam Service Medal. The Vietnamese Cross of Gallantry listed after the Unit Commendations has to be a unit award and not a personal decoration such as the one shown on the discharge above. The clerk most likely left off the words Unit Citation since he was running out of room. Naval personnel would have recieved the RVN Navy Gallantry Cross as a personnel decoration not an Army verison. The Vietnamese Cross of Gallantry Unit Citation was a blanket wwaward to all Armed Forces personnel who served in Vietnam.

Medals of America Press 61

Cold War 1947-1991

Millions of Americans served in the Armed Forces during the Cold War often in dangerous and difficult places. In many cases the current Good Conduct Medals of the Army, Navy, Marine Corps, Air Force and Coast Guard were all they were authorized. A nice example of a Cold War Navy veteran's case is shown to the right.

Southwest Asia, Bosnia/Kosovo, Afghanistan & Iraq Campaign Medals

- **Southwest Asia Service Medal 1991-1995**
- **Bosnia/Kosovo Campaign Medal 1999-2013**
- **Afghanistan Campaign Medal 2001-2021**
- **Iraq Campaign Medal 2003-2011**
- **Inherent Resolve Campaign Medal 2014-To a date To Be Determined**

After Vietnam, the Armed Forces began a much better job desciribing the decorations and awards of honorably discharged personnel. Current DD214s clearly spell all authorized awards the veteran has earned. Examples of the campaign medals for the period above are shown below.

| Good Conduct Medals (Current issue) | National Defense Service Medal | Southwest Asia Service | Saudi Arabia Liberation of Kuwait | Kuwait Liberation of Kuwait | Kosovo Campaign Medal | NATO Bosnia Medal |

| NATO Kosovo Medal | National Defense Service Medal | Afghanistan Campaign | Iraq Campaign | War on Terrorism Expeditionary | War on Terrorism Service | Inherent Resolve Campaign |

Introduction to Awards Display Cases of the
United States Navy

World War II • Korea • Cold War • Vietnam • Kuwait • Global War on Terror • Afghanistan • Iraq

The most appropriate use of military medals after active service is to mount the medals for permanent display in home or office. This reflects the individual's patriotism and the military service rendered to the United States.

United States decorations are usually awarded in a presentation set which normally consists of a medal, ribbon bar and lapel pin, all contained in a special case. During World War II, the name of the decoration was stamped in gold on the front of the case. However, as budget considerations assumed greater importance, this practice was gradually phased out and replaced by a standard case with "United States of America" emblazoned on the front. At the present time, the more common decorations, (e.g., Achievement and Commendation Medals), come in small plastic cases suitable only for initial presentation and storage of the medal.

The most effective method of protecting awards involves the use of a shadow box or glass front display case with at least 1/2 inch between the medals and the glass. This provides a three dimensional view and protects the medal display in a dust-free environment.

Any physical alteration destroys the integrity of the medal and the use of glue ruins the back of the ribbon and medal. The best way to mount medals is in a display case specially designed for that purpose.

The mounting board is absolutely critical. Acid-free Gator board at least 1/4 inch thick covered with a high quality velour-type material to which Velcro© will adhere will allow the medals to be mounted using Velcro© tape which locks the medal firmly into place without damage. The added advantage is the medals and insignia can be moved without damage.

Medals of America Press 63

A Case in Point on How Not to Display Medals

Admiral R. A. Ofstie, a veteran of World War I and World War II.

The correct display of Admiral R. A. Ofstie's career awards. It would be even better with individual medal name plates.

Here is an example of someone who went to a lot of work to do a poor job of displaying a naval hero's medals. The display in question is of Vice Admiral R. A. Ofstie, a veteran of World War I and World War II whose final assignment was commanding the American Sixth Fleet. Admiral Ofstie was a distinguished naval commander in World War II who was awarded the Navy Cross and Silver Star for valor as well as the Navy Distinguished Service Medal and the Legion of Merit.

This haphazard public display of the Admiral's medals shown above is a perfect example of why this book goes into the detail of the order precedence of the medals and an understanding of the campaign medals that accompany military service during different conflicts. In this case someone went to a great deal of trouble to take a box of some of the admiral's medals and carefully cut out a form for each medal in a piece of styrofoam (unfortunately a very bad material to preserve the medals). The medals are displayed in such a haphazard manner that they certainly confuses Navy veterans, family members or historians who view the display.

The admiral was awarded the Navy Cross, our country's second highest award for valor, but for some reason two of the medals are displayed and inserted haphazardly in the line of other medals. In actuality the admiral was awarded the Navy Cross only once as well as a Distinguished Service Medal, the Silver Star and the Legion of Merit as his prominent decorations. Two World War I Victory Medals are displayed as well as the Spanish Order of Military Merit and the Polish Cross of Military Merit but no campaign medals of World War II.

His naval aviator wings are displayed at the bottom of the case over a group of miniature medals which are mounted in reverse order showing the foreign decorations first. The display leaves out his World War II campaign medals in addition to the World War II Victory Medal and National Defense Service Medal. Based on his World War II service he would've also received the Philippine Liberation Medal.

A correctly assembled display above shows his full military honors. This is the attention to detail we owe every American veteran.

An Easy way to Display Medals

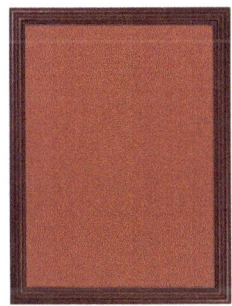

The first six veterans I asked to read the draft of this book all made the suggestion, "Before you show examples of medal displays take a minute to show how simple it is to mount the medals correctly."

Basically, you start with identifying the veteran's medals which can be done for major conflicts in the earlier sections of the book. While it will not identify decorations for valor or merit it gives everyone a great starting point and a veterans discharge *(DD214)*, pictures in uniform or oral family history often fill in the rest.

In this case I prepared a display for an enlisted Marine Korean War veteran *(Naval Infantry?)*. He was a member of the 1st Marine Division and had earned a Good Conduct Medal, National Defense Service Medal, Korean Service Medal, UN Campaign Medal and the later approved Korean War Service Medal. As a combat Marine he was authorized the Combat Action Ribbon and his unit was authorized the Presidential Unit Citation and the Korean Presidential Unit Citation. He had not served in Korea after the conflict so he was not authorized the newer Korean Defense Service Medal

I then selected a red background and 12 by 16 inch display with a red Velcro© friendly fabric. After removing the fabric covered backboard from the frame I laid flat on a table and decided on placement or arrangement of awards.

You then layout your medals, ribbons, badges and patches upside down, side to be taped up, on your colored back. You can then arrange them in the design that you like. Decide if you want to clip pins or tape over them with Velcro©. Prongs can be pushed into the foam core backing.

Cut Velcro© tape into pieces as needed. Peel off protective paper and FIRMLY press onto back of object to be mounted. Place Velcro© tape at strategic points where objects make contact with the fabric backboard. All spots where Velcro© is applied should be clean *(no dust or fingerprints)*. Velcro backs can be reused indefinitely. Velcro© tape can be removed from collectable items. If the sticky tape is removed from the object it is holding for any reason NEW tape should be used.

Once you have the layout you want, press the medal, patch or insignia FIRMLY into place on fabric backboard. Insert the fabric covered gator board into the frame, close it up, attach your hanger and you've done a great job. Spot something wrong or want to add something just open up the case, peel off the medals and badges and rearrange by pressing into a new postion. No glue no mess.

Awards Displays that Honor U.S. Navy Veterans!

The most positive thing a Navy veteran or their family can do to honor and remember their service to our country is to display their military awards for future generations. Many veterans or families are not sure where to start. Sometimes there is an old uniform, a cigar box full of old insignia that children or grandchildren once played with or perhaps some old photographs.

The picture above shows a World War II submarine Sailor's medals and ribbons along with his rating and submarine dolphins His medals are: the World War II Navy Good Conduct Medal, the American Campaign Medal, the Asiatic Pacific Campaign Medal with battle stars, the World War II Victory Medal, the Occupation Medal, the Naval Reserve Meritorious Service Medal. The two foreign awards are the Philippine Liberation Medal and the Philippine Independence Medal. Three Commemorative Medals honor his Combat Service, Sea Service and Navy Service. (There is a section on the use of Commorative Medals at the back of the book.) The Honorable Discharge Pin over his Brass name plate is flanked with his Petty Officer collar insignia and dog tags.

A unique and personal display of naval service that will be admired by generations to come. The following pages present example of Navy veterans' service over the past 75 years.

66 Medals and Ribbons of the U.S. Navy

U.S. Navy World War II Award Displays

World War II Pacific
The display above shows the awards and insignia that tell the unique story of a Navy veteran's service. Medals, badges, insignia, rating, brass plates and ribbons, each tell an event in the history and the life of the veteran it honors.

U.S. Navy in WW II
WW II sailors fought in 3 theaters;
1) Defending America from U-boats.
2) Carrying the war across the Atlantic into Europe and the Mediterranean.
3) Stopping the Japanese fleet in the Pacific, liberating the Philippines and destroying the Imperial Navy.

When the most victorious Navy in the world demobilized, there were no medals to honor these great sailors, only ribbon bars to symbolize their hard earned medals.

Most World War II medals were not struck until after the war and many awards were not officially approved until years after the war.

World War II
This Pharmacist's Mate, 1st Class is a typical USN WW II display. In addition to his Good Conduct and service medals displayed he has the American Defense Medal showing service before WW II.

World War II
This Seaman 1st Class did not recieve a Good Conduct Medal (one liberty too many?). However he did see service in Europe as well as the Pacific and saw occupation duty in Japan for several months after the war.

Medals of America Press

Letters

I joined the USS Mifflin October 1944 and we sailed to Pearl with 1000 4th Marines and then landed them at Iwo Jima. We lost almost 20 crew men before sailing for Saipan. We then carried the 2d Marines to Okinawa and back to Saipan. After a refit in San Francisco, we transported Army replacements to Manila and took on the 33rd Infantry for duty in Japan. The best was " magic carpet ride "duty taking veterans back home until 1946.

Honor the Service... Remember the Sailor

World War II
This Chief Petty Officer served in the American Theater and in addition to his Good Conduct and Victory Medals displays the Occupation of Japan and National Defense Medals..

World War II
This Aerographer's mate, was awarded the DFC as well as the Air Medal. He has 9 campaign stars (1 silver and 4 bronze) on his Pacific Campaign Medal in addition to his Good Conduct and other service medals.

World War II
This Boatswain Mate, 1st Class has added his ribbons over his Medals but left off his campaign stars. In addition to his Good Conduct and service medals he added a Divers badge, and modern Small craft and Surface Warfare badges.

68 Medals and Ribbons of the U.S. Navy

Navy Korean War Displays

Korean War
This Petty Officer 3rd class does not show campaign stars on the Korean Campaign Medal (he would have at least one) but added the Korean Service Medal for his service after the conflict ended. He also has the Navy Combat Action Ribbon and Korean PUC.

U.S. Navy Officer in Korea
This USN Lieutenant with 3 campaign stars added a Korean Service Commemorative and Navy and Korean PUC.

Letters

After high school I enlisted in 1949 and ended up as a crew man on the minesweeper USS Mockingbird (AMS – 27). We were a tight crew with a good captain. The work was cold, wet and dangerous. The mine chasing operations off of Inchon and Wonsan were really scary. I saw the sweeper Magpie go down and the Pirate and the Pledge sink from mines. After we rescued the survivors, they made us the flagship of Mine Division 31. This honor allowed us to be the first into any mine field. I was really happy to finally see our home port Yokosuka for repairs. We earned our battle stars for Korean service.

Korean War
This Radio Man Petty Officer's picture of the USS Missouri adds a very personal touch to a handsome display of war service. He has added numerous commemorative medals to reflect his combat service.

Korean War
This Navy pilot served in all 10 Korean war campaigns and earned the DFC and Air Medal. Today he would also be authorized the Offical Korean War Service medal.

Medals of America Press

Navy Korea and Cold War Award Displays
1947-1991

Korean War with China and Occupation Service
This Chief Petty Officer Radioman's dog tags adds a very personal touch to a handsome display of war service medals.

This Cold War veteran displays his Submarine Badge over his ribbons and medals. He has added two Commemorative Medals for Sea service and Navy Service.

Cold War Navy
This Petty Officer Storekeeper served on the USS Boxer from 1961 to 1965 and in addition to his medals added the ribbons his father earned on an aircraft carrier in WW II and Korea. Dogtags and his old ID card add a personal touch.

Cold War veteran Senior Chief has added the Navy Commemorative medal to reflect his Navy pride. The Bullion crest balances the picture in a display that proudly shows his naval service and is the pride and joy of his daughter.

U.S. Navy Vietnam Award Displays

Vietnam
This brave "Seabee" earned the Combat Seabee badge and a V for valor on his Commendation Medal.

Vietnam
This sailor mounted his ribbons and medals three abreast as for uniform wear.

Vietnam
This Air Crewman Petty Officer added Commemorative medals to represent his ribbon only awards.

Letters

I will never forget the eerie feeling as the USS Coral Sea (CVA-43) aircraft carrier was joined along side by a supply ship. It seemed all to close as they shot the line across and pulled a heavier one until we were sending cargo back and forth. The ships would seem to pitch, and then the load would swing as we steamed straight ahead. It was an ammo supply replenishment and we were taking on 500 pound bombs on the line stretched between two ships. What an awesome experience to be rolling 500 pounders across the hangar bay in a hurried fashion but yet slow enough to control in case the ship would shift in the waves. It's just one of the many exercises that happened and it is all too hard to describe if you have never done it. It's hard to envision; if you have done it, you'll never forget.

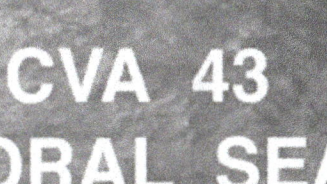

CVA 43
CORAL SEA

U.S. Navy Desert Storm (SWA) Award Displays

Liberation of Kuwait
This Desert Storm veteran added a Combat Action Commemorative medal to represent his Combat Action Ribbon. Commemoratives are used to show service not recognized elsewhere. Challenge coins add another personal touch.

This Navy veteran's display is a source of family pride.

Letters
Our Aegis class cruiser USS San Jacinto fired the first Tomahawk missile on Iraq from our position in the Red Sea. I think over 100 Tomahawk missiles were fired that day from our ships. It was awesome watching missile after missile rise from the other ships. It was something to be part of the greatest Navy in the world.

U.S. Navy Afghanistan, Iraq and War on Terror Displays

This Iraq veteran used his ribbons and medals to show his service in Iraq and at sea. Brass name plates help identify his medals.

U.S. Navy Afghanistan, Iraq and War on Terror Displays

This Hospital Corpsman veteran used his ribbons and medals to show his service in Afghanistan; Iraq and in Korea. The Fleet Marine Force Badge over his ribbons is awarded for service with the Marines. The Brass name plates under the medals help his family recognize the medals.

This Global War on Terror veteran used his ribbons and medals to show his service in Iraq and at sea. Brass name plates under the medals help recognize the medals while the challenge coins are unique personal items.

This Iraq veteran used his ribbons and medals to show his service in Iraq and at sea. Brass name plates help identify his medals and his "dogtag" and challenge coin add a nice personal touch.

This Radioman First Class' display reflects many years of service at sea all over the world. He has been decorated 6 times for meritorious service.

74   Medals and Ribbons of the U.S. Navy

United States Merchant Marine

The Merchant Marine primarily transports cargo and passengers during peacetime but in times of war the Merchant Marine is often an auxiliary to the United States Navy, and is called upon to deliver military personnel and materiel for the armed forces. Merchant Marine officers may also be commissioned as military officers by commissioning unlimited tonnage Merchant Marine officers as Strategic Sealift Officers in the Naval Reserves.

The federal government maintains fleets of merchant ships via organizations such as Military Sealift Command *(part of the US Navy)* and the National Defense Reserve Fleet, which is managed by the United States Maritime Administration.

Although in World War II the Merchant Marine suffered a per capita casualty rate greater than those of the US Armed Forces, merchant mariners who served in World War II were denied such veterans recognition until 1988 when a federal court ordered active military service recognition to American merchant seamen who participated in World War II.

Merchant Marine Officer
This Officer severed 20 years in the Merchant Marine from 1942 to 1962. While his medals are not mounted in correct order of precedence they reflect his 20 years service to include two commemorative medals for Korea and WW II.

United States Merchant Marine Medals

Distinguished Service Medal

Meritorious Service Medal

Mariners Medal

Merchant Achievement Medal

Merchant Marine Defense Medal

Atlantic War Zone Medal

Mediterranean Middle East War Zone Medal

Pacific War Zone Medal

Victory Medal

Korean Service Medal

Vietnam service Medal

Merchant Marine Expeditionary Medal

Prisoner of War Medal

Soviet Commendation Medal

 Gallant Ship Citation ribbon

 Merchant Marine Combat Bar

Medals of America Press

Wear of Medals, Insignia and the Uniform by Veterans, Retirees and Former Service Members

Introduction

One of the first lessons taught to new recruits is proper wear of the uniform and insignia. The same rules apply to wear of military awards by veterans and retirees on their old uniform. There are many occasions when tradition, patriotism, ceremonies and social occasions call for the wear of military awards.

Civilian Dress

The most common manner of wearing a decoration or medal is as a lapel pin in the left lapel of a civilian suit jacket. The small enameled lapel pin represents the ribbon bar of a single decoration or medal an individual has received (usually the highest award or one having special meaning to the wearer).

Many well-known veterans such as former Senator Bob Dole, a World War II Purple Heart recipient, wore a Purple Heart lapel pin. Pins are available for all awards and some ribbons such as the Combat Action Ribbon or Presidential Unit Citation. Small miniature wings, parachute badges and Combat Infantry Badges are also worn in the lapel or as a tie tack. Additionally, retirees are encouraged to wear their retired pin and World War II veterans are encouraged to wear their Honorable Discharge Pin (*affectionately referred to as the "ruptured duck"*).

Honorably discharged and retired Armed Forces members may wear full-size or miniature medals on civilian suits on appropriate occasions such as Memorial Day and Armed Forces Day. Female members may wear full-size or miniature medals on equivalent dress. It is not considered appropriate to wear skill or qualification badges on civilian attire.

Formal Civilian Wear

For more formal occasions, it is correct and encouraged to wear miniature decorations and medals. For a black or white tie occasion, the rule is quite simple: if the lapel is wide enough wear the miniatures on the left lapel or, in the case of a shawl lapel on a tuxedo, the miniature medals are worn over the left breast pocket. The center of the holding bar of the bottom row of medals should be parallel to the ground immediately above the pocket. Do not wear a pocket handkerchief. Miniature medals really do make a handsome statement of patriotic service at weddings and other social events.

Miniature medals can also be worn on a civilian suit at veterans' functions, memorial events, formal occasions of ceremony and social functions of a military nature.

Wear of the Uniform by Retired Personnel

On certain occasions, retired Armed Forces personnel may wear either the uniform prescribed at the date of retirement or any of the current active duty authorized uniforms. Retirees should adhere to the same grooming standards as Armed Forces active duty personnel when wearing the uniform *(for example, a beard is inappropriate while in uniform)*. Whenever the uniform is worn, it must be done in such a manner as to reflect credit upon the individual and the service from which he/she is retired. *(Do not mix uniform items.)*

The occasions for uniform wear by retirees are:

- Military ceremonies.

- Military funerals, weddings, memorial services and inaugurals.

- Patriotic parades on national holidays.

- Military parades in which active or reserve units are participating.

- Educational institutions when engaged in giving military instruction or responsible for military discipline.

- Social or other functions when the invitation has obviously been influenced by the member's earlier active service.

Honorably separated wartime veterans may wear the uniform authorized at the time of their service. The occasions are:

- Military funerals, memorial services, and inaugurals.

- Patriotic parades on national holidays.

- Any occasion authorized by law.

- Military parades in which active or reserve units are participating.

Non-wartime service personnel separated are not authorized to wear the uniform but may wear the medals.

The Early United States Military Medals

The first military medals of the United States clearly showed the country's elected leadership's identification with the private soldier, volunteers, militia and a basic avoidance of awards for the professional officer corps. The first six awards on this page were originally only for private Soldiers, Sailors and Marines. The Marine Corps Brevet Medal came into being reflecting the frustration of Marine Corps officers who were not eligible for the Medal of Honor until 1915. Only when Theodore Roosevelt, a former volunteer officer became President did the Congress begin to truly recognize both volunteers and professional military service.

The Fidelity Medallion is the oldest decoration of the United States military by act of the Continental Congress in 1780. Commonly known as the "André Medal", it was awarded to three soldiers who captured British Major John André after he had contacted Benedict Arnold to organize his defection. André was hung as a spy.

The face of the medallion contains the inscription "FIDELITY" and the reverse "AMOR PATRIÆ VINCIT", which means: "The love of country conquers."

The Fidelity Medallion, was never again awarded and became regarded as a commemorative decoration. The Badge of Military Merit is generally considered the first U.S. military decoration although, created two years later in 1782.

The Badge of Military Merit was announced in General Washington's General Orders to the Continental Army on 7 August 1782. Designed by Washington in the form of a purple heart, it was intended as a military order for soldiers who exhibited: "not only instances of unusual gallantry in battle, but also extraordinary fidelity and essential service in any way." General Washington created three badges, two Honorary Badges of Distinction and a Badge of Military Merit on 7 August 1782. These are the first awards presented to the private soldier as opposed to the European practice of honoring high-ranking officers for victory, rather than private soldiers. However General Washington said, "The road to glory in a patriot army and a free country is open to all".

The Army Certificate of Merit was issued in medal form between the years of 1905 to 1918, Replacing the much older Certificate of Merit issued in 1847 for valor in action during the Mexican-American War. Originally only authorized for Privates in 1854 it was approved for Sergeants but never authorized for officers.

In 1892, the criteria was changed to include distinguished service in action. Although awarded for non-combat heroism, it was generally awarded for gallantry against the enemy.

It could only be awarded once and became obsolete July 9, 1918 with the establishment of the Distinguished Service Cross and Distinguished Service Medal.

The Army Medal of Honor was signed into law on July 12, 1862. To be awarded: "to such noncommissioned officers and privates as shall most distinguish themselves by their gallantry in action, and other soldier-like qualities, during the present insurrection." The original design of the Army Medal of Honor shows the goddess Minerva fending off a symbol of discord. The thirty-four stars surrounding the figures represent the number of states in the Union. Later in the war it was approved for award to Army Officers.

The Navy Medal of Valor was signed into law by President Lincoln on December 21, 1861. Soon renamed the Medal of Honor, it was "to be bestowed upon such Petty Officers, Seamen, Landsmen and Marines as shall most distinguish themselves by their gallantry and other seaman like qualities during the present war." It was not approved for Officers until 1915.

The Secretary of the Navy authorized a Good Conduct Badge on April 26, 1869 to help re-enlistments. The badge, a Maltese cross, had the words "FIDELITY - ZEAL - OBEDIENCE" in a circle with "U.S.N." in the center of the disc. The reverse was for the engraved recipients name. A one-half inch wide red, white and blue ribbon was supplied without a suspension pin. Initially, the badge was awarded to "... any man holding a Continuous Service Certificate who: "has distinguished himself for obedience, sobriety, and cleanliness, and is proficient in seamanship and gunnery..." Sailors were presented a separate badge for each discharge and promoted to Petty Officer upon receipt of their third award. It was replaced in 1884 by the now-familiar Navy Good Conduct Medal.

The Marine Corps Brevet Medal was authorized in 1921 for Marine officers who had received brevet commissions between April 15, 1861 and March 3, 1915. As the Medal of Honor was not available to Marine officers until 1915, the brevet promotion was the only means to reward these individuals for outstanding service or gallantry in action. Although originally intended for all Marine officers who qualified, it was ultimately limited to 20 surviving active duty and retired officers. Since the last action for which brevet promotions had been bestowed was the Boxer Rebellion (1900-01), the Brevet Medal became obsolete on the day it was issued. After many years of indecision, the Brevet Medal was elevated to its final precedence immediately after the Medal of Honor in 1937 and declared obsolete in 1940.

With malice toward none with charity for all.

Civil War Campaign Medal (Army)

Service: Army **Instituted:** 1905
Dates: 1861-1866
Criteria: Active Federal service between April 1861 and April 1865 or service in Texas between April 1861 and August 1866.
Devices:

Civil War Service Medal (Navy)

Service: Navy, Marine Corps.
Instituted: 1908 **Dates:** 1861-1865
Criteria: Active service in the Union Navy or Marine Corps afloat or ashore between April 1861 and April 1865.

The Civil War Campaign Medal is chronologically the first campaign service medal and was authorized in 1905 on the fortieth anniversary of the Civil War. The blue and gray ribbon reflects the uniform colors of both U.S. and Confederate soldiers. The Army Civil War Campaign Medal required that a soldier had to serve between 1861 and 1866 when President Johnson signed a Proclamation officially ending the war. The Navy and Marine Civil War Medal was established June 27, 1908.

The front of the Army Civil War Campaign Medal displayed a bust of Abraham Lincoln while the Navy and Marine Corps versions depicted the USS Monitor and CSS Virginia's battle in Hampton Roads. The reverse of the Army medal displays "The Civil War 1861-1865" encircled by a wreath.

The medal was first established as a badge due to costs. In 1956, some 90 years after the Civil War, Congress provided the government provide the medal to all Civil War qualified veterans (whether they were Union or Confederate).

In the center of the bronze Armymedal is the head of Lincoln encircled by inscription, WITH MALICE TOWARD NONE WITH CHARITY FOR ALL.

The back of the medal is inscribed THE CIVIL WAR over a bar, under which appear the dates 1861-1865; surrounded by a wreath composed of a branch of oak on the left and a branch of laurel on the right, joined at the base by a bow. The oak representing the strength of the United States and the laurel representing its victory.

The Navy and Marine Corps versions have different backs as shown above. The medal was designed by Francis D. Millet, a noted sculptor who perished on the RMS Titanic in 1912. The Civil War Campaign Medal was the first campaign medal authorized for Marine Corps veterans and only about 200 medals were minted and numbered on the rims for Marine Corps Civil War veterans. Less than two dozen original issued numbered medals are known to exist making them the rarest of all Marine Corps Campaign Medals.

Confederate Soldiers, Sailors, and Marines who fought in the Civil War, were made U.S. Veterans by an act of Congress in 1957. U.S. Public Law 85-425 May 23, 1958 *(H.R. 358) (attached & link below)*

This made the Confederate Army, Navy, and Marine Veterans equal to U.S. Veterans. Additionally, under U.S. Public Law 810 *(link below),* approved by the 17th Congress on 26 Feb 1929, The War Department was directed to erect headstones and recognize Confederate grave sites as U.S. War grave sites.

US. Public Law 85-425 May 23, 1958 *(H.R. 358)*

"(e) For the purpose of this section, and section 433, the term 'veteran' includes a person who served in the military or naval forces of the Confederate States of America during the Civil War, and the term 'active, military or naval service' includes active service in such forces. The Act of Congress can be founded at:

http://uscode.house.gov/statutes/pl/85/425.pdf
http://uscode.house.gov/statutes/pl/85/810.pdf

Spanish Campaign Medal (Navy)

Service: Navy, Marine Corps
Instituted: 1908 **Dates:** 1898
Criteria: Service by all Navy & Marine Corps personnel in the naval activities of the Spanish-American War.

West Indies Campaign Medal (Navy)

Service: Navy, Marine Corps.
Instituted: 1908 **Dates:** 1898
Criteria: Originally awarded to Naval veterans of the West Indies Campaign. Later replaced by the Spanish Campaign Medal.

Notes: First ribbon version.

Manila Bay ("Dewey") Medal (Navy)

Service: Navy
Instituted: 1898
Dates: 1898
Criteria: Awarded to all officers and men under Commodore George Dewey's command during the defeat of the Spanish Navy at Manila Bay.

West Indies Naval Campaign ("Sampson") Medal (Navy)

Service: Navy, Marine Corps.
Instituted: 1901
Dates: 1868
Criteria: Participation in the naval engagements in the West Indies and on the shores of Cuba.

Specially Meritorious Medal (Navy)

Service: Navy, Marine Corps.
Instituted: 1901
Dates: 1898
Criteria: Performance of specially meritorious service other than battle during the Spanish-American War.

Philippine Campaign Medal (Navy)

Service: Navy, Marine Corps.
Instituted: 1908 **Dates:** 1899-1906
Criteria: Awarded to Navy & Marine Corps personnel who served on ships in Philippine waters and four shore stations.

China Relief Expedition Medal (Navy)

Service: Navy, Marine Corps.
Instituted: 1908 **Dates:** 1900-1901
Criteria: Service ashore in China or as crew members on specific vessels during the period of the Boxer Rebellion.

Cuban Pacification Medal (Navy)

Service: Navy & Marine Corps.
Instituted: 1909 **Dates:** 1898-1902
Criteria: Service by personnel who served on land and aboard ship in Cuban waters during the specified time period.

Nicaraguan Campaign (Navy)

Service: Navy & Marine Corps.
Instituted: 1913 **Dates:** 1912
Criteria: Awarded to personnel who served ashore and specific ships in Nicaraguan waters between Sept 1906 and April 1909.

Mexican Service Medal (Navy)

Service: Navy, Marine Corps.
Instituted: 1918
Dates: 1914-1917
Criteria: Awarded to Navy & Marine Corps personnel who served ashore or on ships in Mexican waters during the above period.

Haitian Campaign Medal (Navy)

Service: Navy & Marine Corps.
Instituted: 1917 **Dates:** 1915
Criteria: Awarded to personnel who served ashore in Haiti or on ships in Haitian waters during the period of July 9 to Dec. 1915. **Devices:**

Dominican Campaign (Navy)

Service: Navy & Marine Corps.
Instituted: 1921 **Dates:** 1916
Criteria: Service ashore in Santo Domingo or on specific ships operating in Dominican waters between May and Dec., 1916.

World War I Victory Medal

Service	All Services
Instituted	1919
Criteria	Awarded to all military personnel who served in the Continental United States or overseas between April, 1917 and April, 1920.
Devices	Bronze Star, Silver Star, Bronze Cross

The Navy only allowed one clasp to be worn on the ribbon. Marine or Medical Corps who served in France but were not eligible for a battle clasp would receive a bronze Maltese cross on their ribbons.

Known until 1947 simply as the "Victory Medal", the World War I Victory Medal was awarded to any member of the U.S. military who had served in the armed forces between the following dates in the following locations: 6 April 1917 to 11 November 1918 for any military service. 12 November 1918 to 5 August 1919 for service in European Russia and 23 November 1918 to 1 April 1920 for service with the American Expeditionary Force Siberia.

The 14 Allied Nations decided on a single ribbon, but pendant design was left up to each Nation. Mr. James E. Fraser was the designer of the U.S. Victory Medal. The bronze medal front shows a Winged Victory holding a shield and sword. The back of the medal reads "The Great War For Civilization" curved along the top of the medal. On the bottom of the back of the medal are six stars, three on either side of the center column of seven Roman staffs wrapped in a cord. The top of the staff has a round ball on top and is winged on the side. The staff overlays a shield saying "U" on the left side of the staff and "S" on the right side. Left of the staff are listed World War I Allied countries: France, Italy, Serbia, Japan, Montenegro, Russia, and Greece. On the right side of the staff are: Great Britain, Belgium, Brazil, Portugal, Rumania (now spelled Romania), and China.

A 3/16 inch Silver Citation Star was authorized to be worn on the ribbon of the Victory Medal by any member of the U.S. Army who had been cited for gallantry in action between 1917 and 1920. In 1932, the Silver Citation Star was redesigned as the Silver Star and, upon application, any holder of the Silver Citation Star could have it converted to a Silver Star decoration. Only one bronze star was authorized for wear on the ribbon regardless of the number of campaign bars earned. The Navy Commendation Star to the World War I Victory Medal was authorized to any person who had been commended by the Secretary of the Navy for performance of duty during the First World War. A 3/16 inch silver star was worn on the World War I Victory Medal, identical in appearance to the Army's Citation Star. Unlike the Army's version, however, the Navy Commendation Star could not be upgraded to the Silver Star medal. Marines and Navy Medical Corps personnel attached to the Army in France earned, and were authorized to wear any Army clasps authorized by their parent command.

For sea-related war duty, the Navy issued operational clasps, which were worn on the World War I Victory Medal and inscribed with the name of the duty type which had been performed:

1. **Armed Guard**: Merchant personnel *(freighters, tankers, and troop ship)*, 2. **Asiatic**: Service on any vessel that visited a Siberian port, 3. **Asiatic**; Port visit Atlantic Fleet: Service in the Atlantic Fleet; 4. **Aviation**: Service involving flying over the Atlantic Ocean, 5. **Destroyer**: Service on destroyers on the Atlantic Ocean, 6. **Escort**: Personnel regularly attached to escort vessels on the North Atlantic, 7. **Grand Fleet**: Personnel assigned to any ship of the "United States Grand Fleet", 8. **Mine Laying**: Service in mine laying sea duty, 9. **Mine Sweeping**: Service in mine sweeping sea duty, 10. **Mobile Base**: Service on tenders and repair vessels, 11. **Naval Battery**: Service as a member of a naval battery detachment, 12. **Overseas**: Service on shore in allied or enemy countries of Europe, 13. **Patrol**: War patrol service on the Atlantic Ocean, 14. **Salvage**: Salvage duty performed on the seas, 15. **Submarine**: Submarine duty performed on the Atlantic Ocean, 16. **Submarine Chaser**, 17. **Anti-submarine**: duty performed on the Atlantic Ocean, 18. **Transport**: Personnel regularly attached to a transport or cargo vessel, 19. **White Sea**: Service on any vessel which visited a Russian port or war patrols in the White Sea.

NC-4 Medal (Navy)

Service: Navy, Coast Guard
Instituted: 1929
Dates: 1919
Criteria: Awarded to personnel who participated in the first Trans-Atlantic flight by Curtiss Army seaplanes from May 8 to May 31, 1919.

2nd Haitian Campaign Medal (Navy)

Service: Navy, Marine Corps
Instituted: 1921   **Dates:** 1919-1920
Criteria: Awarded to personnel who reinforced the Marine garrison in Haiti to assist in the restoration of order to the country.

2nd Nicaraguan Campaign Medal (Navy)

Service: Navy and Marine Corps.
Instituted: 1929   **Dates:** 1926-1933
Criteria: Awarded to personnel who served ashore in Nicaragua between Aug 1926 and Jan 1933 to put an end to local violence.

Yangtze Service Medal (Navy)

Service: Navy & Marine Corps.
Instituted: 1930   **Dates:** 1926-1932
Criteria: Service in the Yangzte River Valley or in surrounding Chinese waters between Sept, 1926 and Dec 1932.

THE PYRAMID OF HONOR

The awards system of the United States has evolved into a structured program often referred to as the "Pyramid of Honor." It is an awards program designed to reward services ranging from heroism of individuals and units on the battlefield to superior meritorious performance of noncombat duties.

The Armed Services, for the most part, embraced Napoleon's concept of liberally awarding medals and ribbons to enhance morale and esprit de corps. This expanded and specifically tailored awards program is generally very popular in all-volunteer armed forces and has played a significant part in improving morale, job performance, recruitment and reenlistment among all military personnel.

The decorations and awards, which represent the rich United States military heritage of all the Armed Forces from 1939 onward, are presented in the chart to the right; displaying the United States Armed Forces' "Pyramid of Honor" and includes commonly awarded foreign medals. Most of the medals pertain to all branches of the service but many are branch specific.

Decorations, medals, ribbons and unit awards as well as commonly awarded foreign medals are shown in the senior service (U.S. Army) order of precedence for wear. These awards paint a wonderful portrait of the Armed Forces dedication to the ideals of freedom, honor and sacrifice required of each member to support those ideals.

Army
Medal of Honor

Navy, Marine Corps and
Coast Guard Medal of Honor

Air Force
Medal of Honor

Britt K. Slabinski, a former senior chief petty officer of the Navy's elite SEAL Team 6, received the Medal of Honor for his leadership during a firefight in Afghanistan in 2002.

Introduction to U.S. Navy Medals
World War II to Present

Beginning with the Navy, Marine Corps and Coast Guard Medals of Honor, the decorations, medals and ribbon and unit awards of the U.S. Navy are presented in Army order of precedence from World War II to present. Consult the various services' ribbon charts for their order of wear precedence.

THE MEDAL OF HONOR

In a country whose government is based upon a totally democratic society, it is fitting that the first medal to reward heroic acts on the field of battle should be for private soldiers, marines, and seamen (although later extended to officers).

The Congressional Medal of Honor (referred to universally as the Medal of Honor in all statutes, awards manuals and uniform regulations) was born in conflict and steeped in controversy during its early years, finally emerging, along with Great Britain's Victoria Cross, as one of the World's premier awards for bravery.

The Medal of Honor comes in three forms (Army, Navy and Air Force); all three medals represent our county's highest reward for bravery. Today there is only one set of directives governing the award of this, the highest of all U.S. decorations.

The medal was created during the Civil War as a reward for "gallantry in action and other soldier-like qualities." However, the reference to "other qualities" led to many awards for actions which would seem less than heroic, including the bestowal of 864 awards upon the entire membership of the 27th Maine Volunteer Infantry for merely reenlisting.

The inconsistencies in this and other dubious cases were apparently resolved in the early 20th Century when 910 names were removed from the lists (including the 864 awarded to the 27th Maine). At the same time, the statutes which intrepidity govern the award of the medal were revised to reflect the present-day criteria of "gallantry and at the risk of one's own life above and beyond the call of duty."

Many Americans today are confused by the term: "Congressional Medal of Honor" when, in fact, the proper term is "Medal of Honor". Part of this confusion stems from a law that was passed on July 1918 authorizing the President to present the medal" ... in the name of Congress". The fact that all Medals of Honor recipients belong to the Congressional Medal of Honor Society, an official organization chartered by Congress, does not help the situation. However, suffice it to state that the medal is referred to universally as the "Medal of Honor" in all statues, awards manuals, uniform regulations and official documents.

Medals of America Press 87

Medal of Honor

The **Medal of Honor** is the highest military award for bravery that can be given to an individual in the United States of America. Conceived in the early 1860's and first presented in 1863, the medal has a colorful and inspiring history which has culminated in the standards applied today for awarding this respected honor.

To judge whether a man is entitled to the Medal of Honor, all of the Armed Services apply regulations which permit no margin of doubt or error: (1) The deed of the person must be proved by incontestable evidence of at least two eyewitnesses (2) It must be so outstanding that it clearly distinguishes gallantry beyond the call of duty from lesser forms of bravery and (3) It must involve the risk of life. However, until passage of Public Law 88-77, the Navy awarded Medals of Honor for bravery in saving lives, and deeds of valor performed in submarine rescues, boiler explosions, turret fires and other types of disasters unique to the naval profession.

A recommendation for the Army or Air Force Medal must be made within 2 years from the date of the deed upon which it depends. Award of the medal must be made within 3 years after the date of the deed. The recommendation for a Navy Medal of Honor must be made within 3 years and awarded within 5 years.

The Medal of Honor was the result of group thought and action and evolved in response to a need of the times. In the winter of 1861-62, following the beginning of hostilities in the Civil War, there was much thought in Washington concerning the necessity for recognizing the deeds of the American soldiers, sailors and marines who were distinguishing themselves in the fighting. The United States, which had given little thought to its Armed Forces during times of peace, now found them to be the focal point of attention. The serviceman was not just fighting, but was fighting gallantly, sometimes displaying a sheer heroism which a grateful Nation now sought to reward in a meaningful and dignified manner.

It was in this spirit that a bill was introduced in the Senate to create a Navy Medal of Honor. It was passed and approved by President Abraham Lincoln on December 21, 1861. It established the Medal of Honor for enlisted men of the Navy and Marine Corps - The first decoration formally authorized by the American Government to be worn as a badge of honor. Action on the Army medal was started two months later, when, on February 17, 1862, a Senate resolution was introduced providing for presentation of "medals of honor" to enlisted men of the Army and Voluntary Forces who *"shall most distinguish themselves by their gallantry in action and other soldier like qualities."* President Lincoln's approval made the resolution law on July 12, 1862. The law was extended later to include Army officers as well as enlisted men and made retroactive to the beginning of the Civil War. Awards to Navy and Marine Corps officers were not authorized until 1915.

There were some sincere men who believed that the idea of a Medal of Honor would not prove popular with Americans. But, after the Civil War and in succeeding years, the medal turned out to be too popular and the honors conferred upon its recipients had the effect of inspiring the human emotion of envy. A flood of imitators, including a number by prestigious veteran and patriotic organizations, sprang up following the Civil War and had the effect of causing Congress, eventually, to take steps to protect the dignity of the original medal. This took the form of major changes to the medal and ribbon and over the years, resulted, depending on the source, in seventeen Medal of Honor variations *(six Army, ten Navy and one Air Force)*. Illustrations of the most notable Navy variants are presented on the following pages.

On April 27, 1916, Congress approved an act which created a *"Medal of Honor Roll"* upon which the names of honorably discharged recipients who had earned the Medal of Honor in combat were to be recorded. The purpose of the act was to provide a special pension of $10 per month for life and to give medal recipients the same recognition shown to holders of similar British and French decoration for valor. Unfortunately, the act had some unforeseen consequences since not all of the awards seemed to be for combat actions. Given these doubts, the Secretary of War appointed a board of five retired general officers for the purpose of *"investigating and reporting upon past awards of the medal of honor by the War Department with a view to ascertaining what medals of honor, if any, had been awarded or issued for any cause other than distinguished conduct involving actual conflict with an enemy."*

By October 16, 1916, the Board had met, gathered all records on the 2,625 Medals of Honor which had been awarded up to that time, prepared statistics, organized evidence and began its deliberations. On February 15, 1917, all of the pertinent documentation had been examined and considered by the Board and 910 names were stricken from the list.

Of these 910 names, 864 were involved in one group, the 27th Maine Volunteer Infantry. The regiment's enlistment was to have expired in June of 1863 but, to keep the regiment on active duty during a critical period *(the Battle of Gettysburg)*, President Lincoln authorized Medals of Honor for any members who volunteered for another tour of duty. It was felt that the 309 men who volunteered for extended duty in the face of possible death, were certainly demonstrating "soldier like" qualities and as such were entitled to the Medal under the original law. But their act in no way measured up to the 1916 standards and a clerical error compounded the abuse. Not only did the 309 volunteers receive the medal, but the balance of the regiment, which had gone home in spite of the President's offer, also received the award.

In that case, as well as in the remaining 46 scattered instances, the Board felt that the medal had not been properly awarded for distinguished services by the definition of the act of June 3, 1916. Among the 46 others who lost their medals were William F. ("Buffalo Bill") Cody, Dr. Mary Walker, the only female medal recipient and the 29 members of the special Honor Guard that had accompanied the body of Abraham Lincoln from Washington, DC to its final resting place in Springfield, Illinois. There have been no instances of cancellation of Medal of Honor awards within the Naval services due to failure to meet the 1916 award criteria.

MEDAL OF HONOR
(Navy-Marine Corps-Coast Guard Design)

Navy Medal of Honor (Current)

THE NAVY MEDAL OF HONOR

The 1861 Navy Medal of Honor, was redesigned by Tiffany and Company in 1917, but returned to the basic 1861 design in 1942 and a neck ribbon added. The medal is a five pointed star with a standing figure of the Goddess Minerva surrounded by a circle of stars representing the number of States in the Union at the outbreak of the Civil War. Minerva, the Goddess of Strength and Wisdom, holds a shield taken from the Great Seal of the United States, and in her left hand she holds a fasces, which represents the lawful authority of the state; she is warding off a crouching figure representing Discord. The design is a five pointed bronze star, with a central circular plaque depicting Minerva repulsing Discord. The reverse is is engraved, *"Personal Valor,"* with room for the recipient's name, rank, ship or unit and date. The medal hangs from the flukes of an anchor, which is attached to the neck ribbon. The ribbon is light blue and has an eight-sided central pad with thirteen white stars.

Navy
Medal of Honor Type 1, with first style ribbon and fouled anchor (1861-1882)

Navy
Medal of Honor Type 2, with first style ribbon and unfouled anchor (1882-1913)

Navy
Medal of Honor Type 3, used Army type ribbon (1896-1913)

Navy
Medal of Honor Type 4, the Type 5 was suspended from a neck ribbon of the same design (1904-1917)

Navy Medal of Honor "Tiffany Cross" (1917-1942)

The Navy version of the Medal of Honor was established in 1861 and named the *"Medal of Valor"* while the Army version established in 1862 was named the *"Medal of Honor."* Both medals were to recognize men who distinguished themselves *"conspicuously by gallantry and intrepidity"* in combat with an enemy of the United States. Because the medal is presented *"in the name of Congress,"* it is often referred to as the *"Congressional Medal of Honor"*. However, the official name is the *"Medal of Honor"* and less frequently referred to as *"Congressional Medal of Honor"*.

In 1919 the so called *"Tiffany Cross"* Medal of Honor version came into use and remained until 1942, when the current Navy Medal of Honor was instituted. This version was often referred to as the *"Tiffany Cross,"* since Tiffany was involved with its design. The medal was a gold cross patee on a wreath of oak and laurel leaves. In the center of the cross was an octagon with the inscription "UNITED STATES NAVY 1917-1919". Inside the octagon was an eagle design of the United States Seal and an anchor appeared on each arm of the cross. The reverse of the medal had the raised inscription "AWARDED TO" and space for the recipient's name. The medal was suspended by a light blue ribbon with thirteen white stars. The ribbon was suspended from a rectangular gold pin bar inscribed with the words "VALOUR".

Captain Joel T. Boone was awarded the Tiffany Cross Medal of Honor while serving with the marines in World War I.

❖ Navy, Marine Corps and Coast Guard Medals of Honor

For conspicuous gallantry and intrepidity at the risk of one's own life, above and beyond the call of duty, in action involving actual conflict with an opposing armed force.

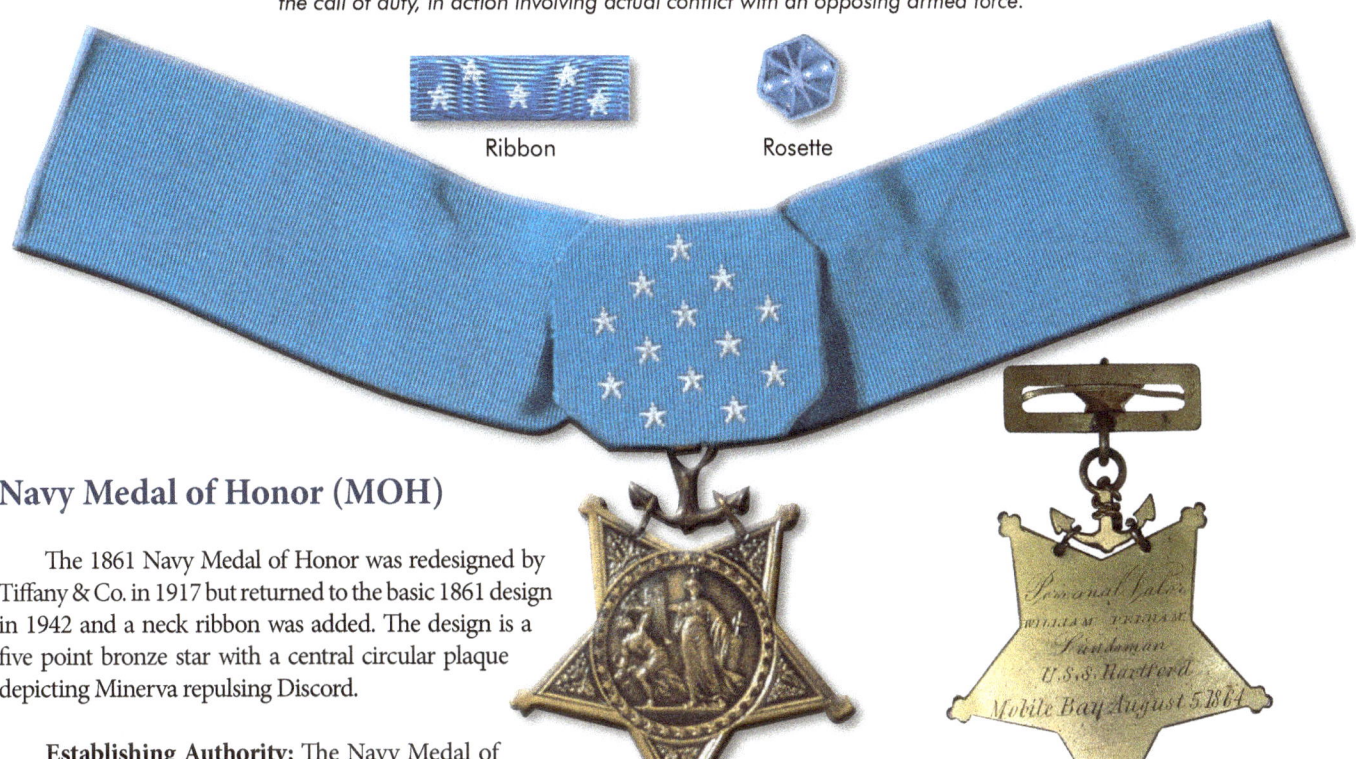

Ribbon   Rosette

Navy Medal of Honor (MOH)

The 1861 Navy Medal of Honor was redesigned by Tiffany & Co. in 1917 but returned to the basic 1861 design in 1942 and a neck ribbon was added. The design is a five point bronze star with a central circular plaque depicting Minerva repulsing Discord.

Establishing Authority: The Navy Medal of Honor signed into law by President Lincoln on December 21, 1861 authorizing the preparation of "200 medals of honor" to promote the efficiency of the Navy. It was followed by a Joint Resolution of Congress on July 12, 1862 (as amended) which actually approved the design and further defined the eligibility and required deeds of potential recipients.

Criteria: For conspicuous gallantry and intrepidity at the risk of one's own life, above and beyond the call of duty, in action involving actual conflict with an opposing armed force. The Navy Medal of Honor is a five pointed star with a standing figure of the goddess Minerva surrounded by a circle of stars representing the number of States in the Union at the outbreak of the Civil War. Minerva, the Roman goddess of Strength and Wisdom, holds a shield taken from the Great Seal of the United States, and in her left hand she holds a fasces, representing the lawful authority of the state with which she is warding off a crouching figure representing Discord. The medal is suspended from an anchor and the reverse is plain for engraving the recipient's name. The ribbon is light blue and has a light blue eight-sided central pad with thirteen white stars.

Navy Medal of Honor
(August 7, 1942 to Present)

In August 1942, Congress readopted the original, Civil War-style five-pointed star, adding a neckband of light blue and eight-sided pad charged with 13 white stars. Although some minor modifications have been made to the neck ribbon/pad in the interim, the award as adopted in 1942 is basically identical to the Medal of Honor design used by the Navy and Marine Corps today.

Ensign Michael Thornton was awarded the Medal of Honor for risking his life in a daring operation against enemy forces in Vietnam.

Navy Cross

Service	Navy, Marine Corps and Coast Guard
Instituted	1919
Criteria	Extraordinary heroism in action against an enemy of the U.S. while engaged in military operations involving conflict with an opposing foreign force or while serving with friendly foreign forces.
Devices	Gold, Silver Star
Notes	Originally issued with a 1-1/2" wide ribbon.

Bronze

Anodized

Miniature Medals

Medal Reverse

Regulation Ribbon Bar

Enamel Lapel Pin

For extraordinary heroism in connection with military operations against an opposing armed force. The Navy Cross (NX) is worn after the Medal of Honor and before all other decorations.

The Navy Cross was established by an Act of Congress and approved on 4 February 1919. Initially the Navy Cross was awarded for extraordinary heroism or distinguished service in either combat or peacetime. The criteria was upgraded in August 1942 to limit the award to those individuals demonstrating extraordinary heroism in connection with military operations against an armed enemy.

The Navy Cross Medal is a cross patee with the ends of the cross rounded. It has four laurel leaves with berries in each re-entrant angle, which symbolizes victory. In the center of the cross is a sailing ship on waves. The ship is a caravel, symbolic of ships of the fourteenth century. On the reverse are crossed anchors with cables attached with the letters USN amid the anchors. The ribbon is navy blue with a white center stripe. Additional awards of the Navy Cross are denoted by gold stars five-sixteenths of an inch in diameter.

HN Luis E. Fonseca, Jr., was a hospital corpsman who was awarded the Navy Cross for his heroic actions during the Battle of Nasiriyah, on March 23, 2003. This was one of the first major battles in the opening stages of the Iraq War.

Hospital Corpsman Chief Petty Officer Justin Wilson salutes after he was awarded the Navy Cross on Nov. 25, 2014, at Camp Pendleton. Wilson earned the medal for his actions in Helmand province, Afghanistan, on Sept. 28, 2011. Wilson is the first sailor in the eight-year history of Marine Special Operations Command to receive a Navy Cross.

Defense Distinguished Service Medal

Service	All Military Services
Instituted	1970
Criteria	Exceptionally meritorious service to the United States while assigned to a Joint Activity in a position of unique and great responsibility.
Devices	Bronze & Silver Oak Leaf Cluster, C Device, Bronze Numeral.

Bronze
Anodized
Miniature Medals
Medal Reverse

Regulation Ribbon Bar
Enamel Lapel Pin

For award by the Secretary of Defense for exceptionally meritorious service in a duty of great responsibility. The Defense Distinguished Service Medal (DDSM) is worn after the Navy Cross and before the Navy Distinguished Service Medal.

The Defense Distinguished Service Medal was established by an Executive Order, which was signed by President Nixon on 9 July 1970. The medal was instituted for senior officers who held positions of authority over elements of other service branches. This eliminated the need to award multiple Distinguished Service Medals from the service branches involved. The medal is the highest award for meritorious service within the Department of Defense.

The Defense Distinguished Service Medal was designed by the Army's Institute of Heraldry and is gold in color featuring a blue enameled pentagon superimposed by a gold eagle with outspread wings. On the eagle's breast is the seal of the United States and in its talons are three arrows. The eagle and pentagon are surrounded by a gold circle consisting of thirteen stars and laurel and olive branches. At the top of the circle are five gold rays extending above the stars, which form the medal suspension.

On the reverse of the pentagon is the raised inscription "FROM THE SECRETARY OF DEFENSE TO," with a space for inscribing the recipient's name. On the reverse of the gold circle is the raised inscription "FOR DISTINGUISHED SERVICE". The ribbon has a narrow red center stripe flanked on either side by stripes of gold and blue. Additional awards of the Defense Distinguished Service Medal are denoted by oak leaf clusters.

Army Gen. Martin E. Dempsey, Chairman of the Joint Chiefs of Staff, pins a Defense Distinguished Service Medal on Navy Adm. James A. Winnefeld Jr., Vice Chairman of the Joint Chiefs of Staff, during Winnefeld's retirement ceremony on Joint Base Myer-Henderson Hall, Va., July 31, 2015.

Navy Distinguished Service Medal

Service	Navy and Marine Corps
Instituted	1919
Criteria	Exceptionally meritorious service to the U.S. Government in a duty of great responsibility.
Devices	Gold, Silver Star, C Device
Notes	107 copies of earlier medal design issued but later withdrawn. First ribbon design was 1 1/2" wide.

For exceptionally meritorious service to the Government in a duty of great responsibility. The Navy Distinguished Service Medal (DSM) is worn after the Defense Distinguished Service Medal and before the Silver Star.

The Navy Distinguished Service Medal was established by an Act of Congress and approved on 4 February 1919 and, like the Navy Cross, was made retroactive to 6 April 1917. During this period there was confusion about what criteria constituted the award of the Navy's Distinguished Service Medal and what criteria constituted the award of the Navy Cross. At the outbreak of World War II laws governing the award of naval decorations were changed with Public Law 702, which placed the Navy Cross above the Navy's Distinguished Service Medal and clearly limited the Navy's Distinguished Service Medal for exceptionally meritorious service and not for acts of heroism. The very first Navy Distinguished Service Medal was awarded, posthumously, to Brigadier General Charles M. Doyen, USMC.

The Navy's Distinguished Service Medal is a gold medallion with an American bald eagle with displayed wings in the center. The eagle is surrounded by a blue enameled ring which contains the words, "UNITED STATES OF AMERICA" with "NAVY" at the bottom. Outside the blue ring is a gold border of waves. The medal is suspended from its ribbon by a five pointed white enameled star with an anchor in the center. Behind the star are gold rays emanating from the re-entrant angles of the star. The reverse of the medal contains a trident surrounded by a wreath of laurel.

The wreath is surrounded by a blue enamel ring with the inscription FOR DISTINGUISHED SERVICE. The blue enamel ring is surrounded by a gold border of waves the same as on the front of the medal. The ribbon is navy blue with a gold stripe in the center. Additional awards of the Navy's Distinguished Service Medal are denoted by gold stars and Silver five sixteenths of an inch in diameter.

Navy Admiral Scott H. Swift wearing the Distinguished Service Medal. (John Gibbins / San Diego Union-Tribune)

Silver Star

Service	All Services *(Originally Army only)*
Instituted	1932
Criteria	Gallantry in action against an armed enemy of the United States or while serving with friendly foreign forces.
Devices	Navy/ Marine Corps/ Coast Guard: Gold, Silver Star.
Notes	Derived from the 3/16" silver "Citation Star" previously worn on Army campaign medals.

Bronze

Anodized or Gold-Plated

Miniature Medals

Medal Reverse

Regulation Ribbon Bar

Enamel Lapel Pin

Mini Ribbon (unofficial)

Enamel Hat Pin (unofficial)

Notes: *Derived from the 3/16 silver "Citation Star" previously worn on Army campaign medals.*

For gallantry in action (1) against an enemy of the United States; (2) while engaged in military operations involving conflict with an opposing foreign force; or, (3) while serving with friendly foreign forces engaged in armed conflict with an opposing foreign force in which the United States is not a belligerent party. The required gallantry, while of a lesser degree than required for the award of the Navy Cross, must nevertheless have been performed with marked distinction. The Silver Star (SS) is worn after the Navy Distinguished Service Medal and before the Defense Superior Service Medal.

The Silver Star was originally established by President Woodrow Wilson on 9 July 1918 as a three-sixteenth inch silver citation star to be worn on the World War I Victory Medal to denote receipt of a special letter of commendation. Although the citation star was widely used during World War I, it was not a popular award. Arguments centered around the fact that the award was "insignificant in size and constitutes very little tangible evidence of gallantry, is not an article which can be handed down to posterity and, therefore, serve as evidence of a grateful nation and people with attendant stimulation to patriotism." Because of these arguments, the Army decided to redesign the citation star by placing it on a medal. The Silver Star as it is today was created in 1932 for the Army and extended to the Navy and Marine Corps on 8 August 1942 retroactive to 7 Dec. 1941.

The medal was designed by Bailey, Banks and Biddle, an retail jeweler. The medal is a five pointed gilt-bronze star with a small silver star centered in the middle, which is actually a representation of the original citation star. The small silver star is surrounded by a laurel wreath with rays radiating outward from the star. The reverse of the medal has the raised inscription "FOR GALLANTRY IN ACTION" and room for inscribing the recipient's name. The ribbon, employing the colors of the American Flag, has a wide red center stripe flanked on either side by a wide white stripe, a wide dark blue stripe, a thin white stripe and a thin dark blue stripe at the edges. Additional awards are denoted by five-sixteenth inch diameter gold stars.

Hospital Corpsman 2nd Class Juan M. Rubio, FMF, of San Angelo, Texas, was awarded the Silver Star Medal for conspicuous gallantry against the enemy on Jan. 1, 2005, while serving as a Marine platoon corpsman in support of Operation Iraqi Freedom (OIF). Rear Adm. Thomas R. Cullison, left, made the presentation in front of the Naval Hospital on board Naval Air Station Corpus Christi. U.S. Navy photo by Mr. Bill W. Love

Defense Superior Service Medal

Bronze

Anodized

Miniature Medals

Medal Reverse

Service	All Services (by Secretary of Defense)
Instituted	6 February 1976
Criteria	Superior meritorious service to the United States while assigned to a Joint Activity in a position of significant responsibility.
Devices	C and R Devices, Bronze Numeral, Bronze & Silver Oak Leaf Cluster.

Regulation Ribbon Bar

Enamel Lapel Pin

Mini Ribbon (unofficial)

Enamel Hat Pin (unofficial)

For award by the Secretary of Defense for superior meritorious service while in a position of significant responsibility while assigned to a joint activity. The Defense Superior Service Medal (DSSM) is worn after the Silver Star and before the Legion of Merit.

The Defense Superior Service Medal was established by an Executive Order, which was signed by President Ford on 6 February 1976. The medal was instituted to recognize duty performed with distinction and significance that would justify an award comparable to the Legion of Merit for members of the Armed Forces assigned to the Office of the Secretary of Defense and other activities in the Department of Defense.

The Defense Superior Service Medal was designed by the Army's Institute of Heraldry and is of the same design as the Defense Distinguished Service Medal. The medal is silver in color featuring a blue enameled pentagon superimposed by a gold eagle with outspread wings. On the eagle's breast is the seal of the United States and in its talons are three arrows. The eagle and pentagon are surrounded by a silver circle consisting of thirteen stars and laurel and olive branches. At the top of the circle are five silver rays extending above the stars, which form the medal suspension. On the reverse of the pentagon is the raised inscription "FROM THE SECRETARY OF DEFENSE TO" with space to inscribe the recipient's name. On the back is the inscription "FOR SUPERIOR SERVICE". The ribbon consists of a central stripe of red flanked on either side by stripes of white, blue and yellow. Additional awards of the Defense Superior Service Medal are denoted by oak leaf clusters and numerals.

Did You Know? At the time of its creation it was decided that this medal would be obtained at the lowest possible cost and "with as little involvement as possible." For these reasons and because it would rank just below the Defense Distinguished Service Medal for similar service, it was decided to use the same design as the Defense Distinguished Service Medal, except that it would be finished in silver rather than gold and the inscription on the reverse would be modified.

Legion of Merit

Service	All Services
Instituted	1942 (retroactive to 8 Sept 1939)
Criteria	Exceptionally meritorious conduct in the performance of outstanding services to the United States.
Devices	C and R Devices and Gold and Silver Stars; Letter "V" (not authorized after 2016).
Notes	Issued in four degrees (Legionnaire, Officer, Commander & Chief Commander) to foreign nationals. V no longer authorized as of 2016.

For exceptionally meritorious conduct in the performance of outstanding service. The Legion of Merit (LOM) is worn after the Defense Superior Service Medal and before the Distinguished Flying Cross.

The Legion of Merit was established by an Act of Congress, which was approved 20 July 1942 and signed by President Franklin D. Roosevelt on 29 October 1942. The medal was instituted to fill the gap below the Distinguished Service Medal and provide an award that could be given for meritorious service in positions of considerable responsibility but below the positions of responsibility greater than called for by the criteria of the Distinguished Service Medal.

The Legion of Merit was designed by Colonel Townsend Heard and followed the basic design of the French Legion of Honor. The medal is a white enameled five-armed cross with ten gold tipped points. The cross is bordered in red enamel. In the center of the cross there is a blue enameled circle with thirteen stars surrounded by a border of gold clouds. Behind the cross is a gold circle bordered by a laurel wreath that is tied in a bow between the two lower arms of the cross.

Gold crossed arrows appear between each of the arms of the cross. The same cross appears on the reverse of the medal except there is no enamel. In the center of the reverse is a rope circle for engraving the recipient's name. Contained in a second rope circle is the raised inscription "ANNUIT COEPTIS MDCCLXXXII". The words "ANNUIT COEPTIS" are Latin meaning "God has favored our undertaking" and comes from the Great Seal of the United States. The "MDCCLXXXII" *(1782)* refers to the date George Washington founded the Badge of Military Merit, from which the Legion of Merit evolved. There is an outer ribbon circle with the raised inscription "UNITED STATES OF AMERICA". The ribbon is ruby (pinkish-red) edged in white. Additional awards are denoted by five-sixteenth inch gold stars. A Combat Distinguishing Device may be authorized prior to 2016.

Rear Adm. Brian Brakke, commander, Navy Expeditionary Combat Command, awards Capt. Joseph Rehak the Legion of Merit during a change of command of Expeditionary Combat Readiness Center (ECRC).

Legion of Merit for Foreign Military Personnel

The Legion of Merit is awarded to members of armed forces of foreign nations in four degrees according to the level of responsibility, rank and position of the receiver of the award.

Chief Commander
Legion of Merit

Commander
Legion of Merit

Officer
Legion of Merit

Legionnaire
Legion of Merit

The degrees of Chief Commander, Commander, Officer, and Legionnaire are awarded only to members of armed forces of foreign nations under the criteria outlined in Army Regulation 672-7 and is based on the relative rank or position of the recipient as follows:

Chief Commander: *Head of state or government. However ,this degree was awarded by President Roosevelt to some Allied World War II theater commanders usually for joint amphibious landings or invasions. (The President had this power under Executive Order 9260 of October 29, 1942 paragraph 3b.[6])*

Commander: *Equivalent of a U.S. military chief of staff or higher position, but not to a head of state.*

Officer: *General or flag officer below the equivalent of a U.S. military chief of staff; colonel or equivalent rank for service in assignments equivalent to those normally held by a general or flag officer in U.S. military service; or military attachés.*

Legionnaire: *All recipients not included above.*

When the Legion of Merit is awarded to members of the uniformed services of the United States it is awarded without reference to degree.

The degrees and the design of the decoration were clearly influenced by the French Legion of Honor *(Légion d'honneur)* The Chief Commander Degree of the Legion of Merit Medal overall width is 2 15⁄16 inches *(75 mm)*. The words "UNITED STATES OF AMERICA" are engraved in the center of the reverse. A miniature of the decoration in gold on a horizontal gold bar is worn on the service ribbon.

The Commander Degree of the Legion of Merit Medal overall width is 2 1⁄4 inches *(57 mm)*. A gold laurel wreath in the v-shaped angle at the top connects an oval suspension ring to the neck ribbon that is 1 15⁄16 inches (49 mm) in width. The reverse of the five-pointed star is enameled in white, and the border is crimson. In the center, a disk for engraving the name of the recipient surrounded by the words "ANNUIT COEPTIS MDCCLXXXII." An outer scroll contains the words "UNITED STATES OF AMERICA." A miniature of the decoration in silver on a horizontal silver bar is worn on the service ribbon.

The Officer Degree of the Legion of Merit Medal is similar to the degree of Commander except the overall width is 1 7⁄8 inches *(48 mm)* and the pendant has a suspension ring instead of the wreath for attaching the ribbon. A gold replica of the medal, 3⁄4 inch (19 mm) wide, is centered on the suspension ribbon.

The Legionnaire Degree of the Legion of Merit Medal and the Legion of Merit Medal issued to U.S. personnel are basically the same as the degree of Officer, except the suspension ribbon does not have the medal replica. The date "MDCCLXXXII" *(1782)*, which is the date of America's first decoration, the Badge of Military Merit, now known as the Purple Heart. The ribbon design also follows the pattern of the Purple Heart ribbon.

Vice Adm. Lisa M. Franchetti, commander, U.S. 6th Fleet (C6F), presents French Vice Adm. Charles-Henri du Ché with the Legion of Merit.

98 Medals and Ribbons of the U.S. Navy

Distinguished Flying Cross

Service	All Services
Instituted	1926
Criteria	Heroism or extraordinary achievement while participating in aerial fight
Devices	Bronze letter "V" (for valor), gold, silver star, C device,

Bronze

Anodized or Gold-Plated

Miniature Medals

Medal Reverse

Regulation Ribbon Bar

Enamel Lapel Pin

Mini Ribbon (unofficial)

Enamel Hat Pin (unofficial)

For heroism or extraordinary achievement while participating in aerial flight. The Distinguished Flying Cross (DFC) is worn after the Legion of Merit and before the Navy and Marine Corps Medal.

The Distinguished Flying Cross was established by an Act of Congress and approved in July 1926. The Act of Congress was implemented in January 1927 by President Coolidge. If the medal is awarded for an act of heroism, the act must involve voluntary action in the face of danger and be above the actions of others in a similar operation. If awarded for extraordinary achievement, it must have resulted in an accomplishment so outstanding or exceptional that the act clearly sets the individual apart from his or her comrades. This is specifically an aviation award.

The Distinguished Flying Cross was designed by the Army's Institute of Heraldry and is a bronze four bladed propeller surmounted on a bronze cross pattee. Behind the cross are bronze rays forming a square. The medal is suspended from a plain bronze suspender. The back of the medal is blank to allow for engraving the recipient's name. The ribbon is blue with a red center stripe bordered in white. The ribbon is outlined with a white stripe on each side. Additional awards are denoted by five-sixteenth inch diameter gold stars. The Combat Distinguishing Device (Combat "V") could be be authorized between 4 April 1974 and Jan. 2016. V for valor and C for Combat can be awarded as of 2016.

Lt. Cmdr. Michael "Mob" Tremel was presented the Distinguished Flying Cross by the Navy's Air Boss Vice Adm. DeWolfe Miller, commander, Naval Air Forces, for his actions in Syria. The Distinguished Flying Cross is given for heroism or extraordinary achievement during aerial flights and was awarded to Tremel during the 2018 Tailhook Association Reunion, in Reno, Nev.

"While monitoring a Russian SU-35 Flanker operating above him, Lt. Cmdr. Tremel identified a Syrian SU-22 Fitter closing quickly on the coalition ground force. He executed three warning passes with flares, but the Fitter disregarded the warnings and delivered ordnance on the coalition ground force," the award citation states. "Tremel immediately fired two air-to-air missiles that destroyed the Fitter and protected the coalition force from further threat."

Navy and Marine Corps Medal

Service	Navy And Marine Corps
Instituted	1942
Criteria	Heroism not involving actual conflict with an armed enemy of the United States
Devices	Gold and Silver Stars
Notes	For acts of life-saving, action must be at great risk to one's own life

Bronze

Anodized or Gold-Plated

Miniature Medals

Medal Reverse

Regulation Ribbon Bar

Mini Ribbons (unofficial)

For heroism that involves the voluntary risk of life under conditions other than those of conflict with an opposing armed force. The Navy and Marine Corps Medal (NM) is worn after the Distinguished Flying Cross and before the Bronze Star Medal.

Navy and Marine Corps Medal awarded to President John F. Kennedy (then Lieutenant (jg) USN) for rescuing crewmembers when PT 109 was sunk by the Japanese August 1942

The Navy and Marine Corps Medal was established by an Act of Congress and approved on 7 August 1942. The medal was established to recognize non-combat heroism. For acts of lifesaving, or attempted lifesaving, it is required that the action be performed at the risk of one's own life. The Navy and Marine Corps Medal is prized above many combat decorations by personnel who have received it.

The Navy and Marine Corps Medal was designed by Lt. Commander McClelland Barclay, USNR. The medal is a bronze octagon with an eagle perched upon a fouled anchor. Beneath the anchor is a globe and below that the inscription "HEROISM" in raised letters. The back of the medal is blank to allow for engraving the recipient's name. The ribbon consists of three equal strips of Navy blue, gold and scarlet. Additional awards are denoted by five-sixteenth inch gold stars.

Lieutenant John F. Kennedy receives one of the Navy's highest honor for his heroic actions as a gunboat pilot during World War II on June 12, 1944. The future president also received a Purple Heart for wounds received during battle. Lieutenant Kennedy received the Navy and Marine Corps Medal for "courage, endurance and excellent leadership which contributed to the saving of several lives and was in keeping with the highest traditions of the United States Naval Service."

100 Medals and Ribbons of the U.S. Navy

Bronze Star Medal

Service	All Services
Instituted	1944 (retroactive to 7 Dec. 1941)
Criteria	The Bronze Star Medal is awarded to individuals who, while serving in the United States Armed Forces in a combat theater, distinguish themselves by heroism, outstanding achievement or by meritorious service not involving aerial flight.
Devices	Letter "V" (for Valor) Device, Gold and Silver Star

Bronze

Anodized or Gold-Plated

Miniature Medals

Medal Reverse

Regulation Ribbon Bar

Enamel Lapel Pin

Enamel Hat Pin (unofficial)

Authorized in 1944, retroactive to December 7, 1941. It is awarded to individuals who, while serving in the United States Armed Forces in a combat theater, distinguish themselves by heroism, outstanding achievement or by meritorious service not involving aerial flight. The Bronze Star Medal (BSM) is worn after the Navy and Marine Corps Medal and before the Purple Heart.

The Bronze Star was originally conceived by the U.S. Navy as a junior decoration comparable to the Air Medal for heroic or meritorious actions by ground and surface personnel. The level of required service would not be sufficient to warrant the Silver Star if awarded for heroism or the Legion of Merit if awarded for meritorious achievement. In a strange twist of fate, the Bronze Star Medal did not reach fruition until championed by General George C. Marshall, the Army Chief of Staff during World War II. Marshall was seeking a decoration that would reward front line troops, particularly infantrymen, whose ranks suffered the heaviest casualties and were forced to endure the greatest danger and hardships during the conflict. Once established, the Bronze Star Medal virtually became the sole province of the Army in terms of the number of medals awarded.

Like the Silver Star, the Bronze Star Medal was designed by the retail jeweler, Bailey, Banks and Biddle. Its design reflects the intent that it be a companion to the Silver Star. The medal is a bronze five pointed star with a smaller raised and centered bronze star three-sixteenth inches in diameter. The reverse of the medal has the raised inscription HEROIC OR MERITORIOUS ACHIEVEMENT forming a circle in the center. The ribbon is red with a narrow blue center stripe. A thin white stripe borders the ribbon and the blue center stripe. Additional awards are denoted by five-sixteenth inch diameter gold stars. The combat distinguishing device (Combat "V") may be authorized prior to 2016. Sailors who had participated in the defense of the Philippine Islands between December 7, 1941 and May 10, 1942 were awarded the Bronze Star Medal if their service was on the island of Luzon, the Bataan Peninsula or the harbor defenses on Corregidor Island.

The "V" Device

The Bronze Star was established as an award for lessor acts of heroism than the Silver Star but also for meritorious service. This created the immediate problem that there was intially no way to tell if the Bronze Star was awarded for bravery or merit.

In late 1945 after World War II had ended a bronze block letter "V," was designated to denote an award for valor. The Navy announced in early 1946 that, "All personnel who have been awarded the Legion of Merit or the Bronze Star Medal for services or acts performed in actual combat with the enemy were authorized to wear a Combat Distinguishing Device upon both the service ribbon and the suspension ribbon of the medal." This changed in 1947 to read "for acts or services involving direct participation in combat operations." Typically the typed Bronze Star Citation from the 1947 period had the line "The Combat Distinguishing Device is Authorized" typed at the bottom of the Official Citation page.

The Navy and Marines Combat Distinguishing Device may be worn on the Bronze Star Medal only if it is specifically authorized in the citation. Award is only based on acts or services of Naval personnel who are exposed to direct hostile actions and not on the location in which the acts or services were performed. The one exception is the Navy authorized blanket awards to Sailors that participated in the defense of the Philippines before it fell to the Japanese. The Combat Distinguishing Device is no longer awarded as of 2016 and is replaced by the V device awarded only for *"Valor"*.

Purple Heart

Service	All Services (Originally Army Only)
Instituted	1932; The Purple Heart is retroactive to 5 April 1917; however, awards for qualifying prior to that date have been made.
Criteria	Awarded to any member of the Armed Forces of the United States or civilian national of the United States who serving under competent authority in the U.S. Armed Forces (since 5 April 1917) has been wounded, killed, or who has died or may die of wounds received from an opposing enemy force while in armed combat or as a result of an act of international terrorism or being a Prisoner of War.
Devices	Gold and Silver stars. 

Bronze

Anodized or Gold-Plated

Miniature Medals

Early Purple Hearts were numbered on the edge of the medal.

Regulation Ribbon Bar

Enamel Lapel Pin

Enamel Hat Pin (unofficial)

Medal Reverse

For wounds or death as a result of an act of any opposing armed force, as a result of an international terrorist attack or as a result of military operations while serving as a part of a peacekeeping force. The Purple Heart (PH) is worn after the Bronze Star Medal and before the Defense Meritorious Service Medal. The Purple Heart was originally last in precedence of all other personal decorations but was elevated in 1985 by an act of Congress to a position just behind the Bronze Star.

The Purple Heart stems from the Badge of Military Merit established by George Washington in 1782, which is the oldest American military decoration. Washington's Badge of Military Merit was referred to as the *"Purple Heart"* and was awarded for military merit. It is believed that the name comes from a wood called "purple heart", which is a smooth-grained plum-colored wood used with firearms and artillery. The wood was considered the best in the world for making gun carriages and mortar beds, because it could withstand extreme stress. The original medal was a heart-shaped purple cloth embroidered in silver with a wreath surrounding the word MERIT. It was designed by Pierre Charles L'Enfant in accordance with Washington's personal instructions. The Badge of Military Merit or "Purple Heart" though intended to be permanent, fell into disuse shortly after the Revolution and was all but forgotten as a military decoration.

The current Purple Heart Medal was revived by the War Department on 22 February 1932 at the urging of Army Chief of Staff, General Douglas MacArthur, who was also the first recipient. The medal was authorized for the Navy and Marine Corps by the Department of the Navy on 21 January 1943. Although the Purple Heart was awarded for meritorious service between 1932 and 1943, the primary purpose was to recognize those who received wounds while in the service of the United States Military. With the development of awards such as the Legion of Merit, the use of the Purple Heart came to be strictly limited to injuries sustained in combat. The current criteria states that it is to be awarded for wounds received while serving in any capacity with one of the U.S. Armed Forces after 5 April, 1917. The wounds may have been received in combat against an enemy, while a member of a peacekeeping force, while a Prisoner of War, as a result of a terrorist attack, or as a result of a friendly fire incident in hostile territory. The 1996 Defense Authorization Act extended eligibility for the Purple Heart to prisoners of war before 25 April 1962; 1962 legislation had only authorized the medal to POWs after 25 April 1962. Wounds that qualify must have required treatment by a medical officer or must be a matter of official record.

Capt. Mark Brouker pins the Purple Heart medal on Hospital Corpsman 3rd Class (FMF) Derek Richey while Rear Adm. C. Forrest Faison III, and Capt. Gordon Smith look on. Richey was presented the medal for being wounded in action while serving in Afghanistan.

The Purple Heart was designed by the Army's Institute of Heraldry from a design originally submitted by General Douglas MacArthur and modeled by John Sinnock, Chief Engraver at the Philadelphia Mint. The medal is a purple heart with a bronze gilt border and a bronze profile of George Washington in the center. Above the heart is a shield from George Washington's Coat of Arms between two sprays of green enameled leaves. On the back of the medal, below the Coat of Arms and leaves, there is a raised bronze heart with the raised inscription FOR MILITARY MERIT and room to inscribe the name of the recipient. Initially the medals were numbered, but this practice was discontinued in July 1943 as a cost-cutting measure. The ribbon is purple edged in white. Additional awards are denoted by five-sixteenth inch diameter gold stars.

The Purple Heart medal has always been highly respected by military personnel since it was earned by giving one's life or being wounded while in military service of our country. During World War II contracts were issued for over a million and a half Purple Heart medals with the largest number being produced in anticipation of the invasion of Japan.

The Japanese Armed Forces determination to fight to the death during the Pacific campaign led everyone, especially the Navy and Marines to anticipate heavy casualties. The government requested so many Purple Hearts be manufactured that it was not until almost 1947 that all the contracts were completed. Meanwhile the Air Force bombing campaign and the use of the first atomic bombs lead to the capitulation of Japan and ended the requirement for the huge order of Purple Heart medals.

Approximately a half million Purple Hearts went into the military inventories after World War II. Even with many of these medals presented during the Korean and Vietnam eras there were over 100,000 World War II Purple Heart medals still in the military supply chain during the Liberation of Kuwait. Refurbished, many of these Purple Hearts continued to be awarded to veterans. The World War II Purple Hearts are generally identified by the high quality of workmanship and a single white stitch under the left and right edge of the ribbon bar of the medal drape. It is not improbable for an Iraq or an Afghanistan veteran to receive the Purple Heart Medal that was originally manufactured for his grandfather's generation.

Shown below is a World War II Purple Heart presentation box and certificate. The presentation came with the medal, a ribbon and a lapel pin.

Defense Meritorious Service Medal

Service	All Services (by Secretary of Defense)
Instituted	3 November 1977
Criteria	Noncombat meritorious achievement or service while assigned to a Joint Activity.
Devices	Bronze, Silver Oak Leaf Cluster, Bronze Letter "R" or Numeral.

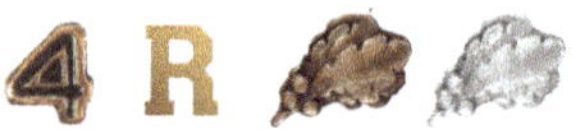

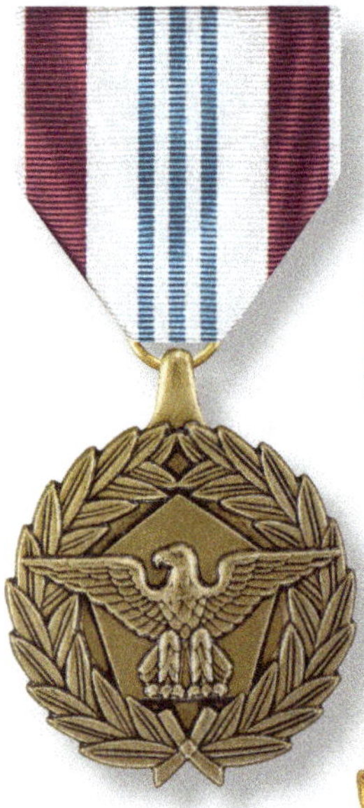

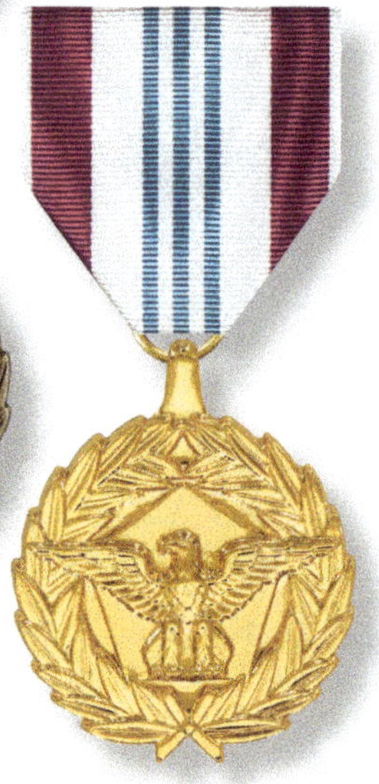

Authorized on November 3, 1977. The Defense Meritorious Service Medal is awarded to any active member of the U.S. Armed Forces who distinguishes him/herself by noncombat meritorious achievement or service while serving in a Joint Activity after November 3, 1977. Examples of Joint assignments that may allow qualification for this medal are: Office of the Secretary of Defense, Office of the Joint Chiefs of Staff, Unified or Specified Commands, Joint billets in NATO or NORAD, Defense Agencies, National Defense University, National War College, Industrial College of the Armed Forces, Armed Forces Staff College and the Joint Strategic Target Planning Staff. Personnel serving with jointly manned staffs within Allied Command Europe, Allied Command Atlantic, the NATO Military Committee, and military agencies associated with functions of the military or other joint activities are also included. In 2014, the President extended eligibility of the DMSM to include any member of the armed forces of a friendly foreign nation, thus authorizing recognition of those NATO, Allied and Coalition officers and senior enlisted personnel assigned to/embedded in the Joint Staff, the Unified Combatant Commands and associated Joint Task Forces.

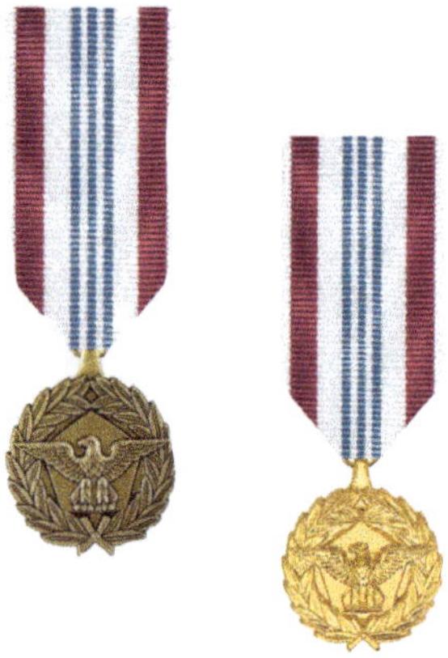

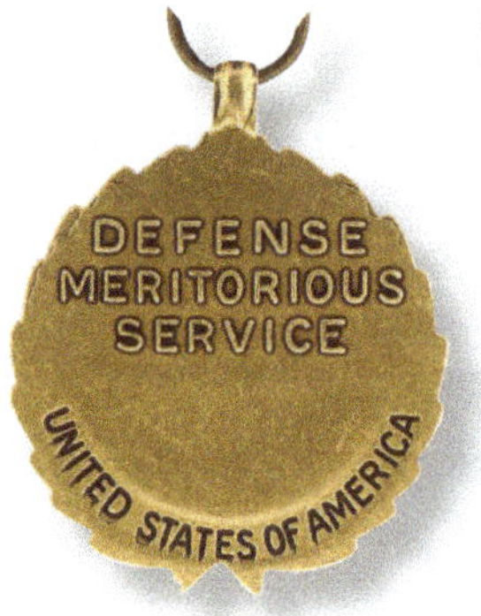

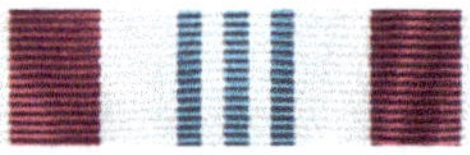

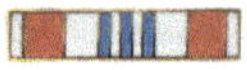

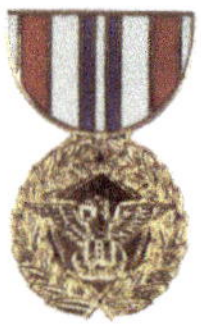

The bronze medal has an eagle with spread wings in the center superimposed on a pentagon in the center of a laurel wreath. The reverse is inscribed with the words, "DEFENSE MERITORIOUS SERVICE" and "UNITED STATES OF AMERICA". The ribbon has a wide white center stripe with three light blue stripes in the middle. The white stripe is flanked by ruby red and white. The ruby red and white are copied from the ribbon of the Meritorious Service Medal with the blue stripes representing the Department of Defense. Subsequent awards are denoted by bronze and silver oak leaf clusters or the R device or bronze numeral as appropriate. The Defense Meritorious Service Medal was designed by Lewis J. King, Jr. of the Institute of Heraldry.

Lt. Denise Romeo, Staff Judge Advocate Office, Combined Joint Interagency Task Force 435 (CJIATF 435), receives a Defense Meritorious Service Medal from U.S. Army Lt. Gen. Keith M. Huber, Commanding General of CJIATF 435 and U.S. Forces-Afghanistan Deputy Commander, Detainee Operations. The award was presented onboard Camp Phoenix, Kabul, Afghanistan.

Meritorious Service Medal

Service All Services
Instituted 16 January 1969
Criteria Outstanding noncombat meritorious achievement or service to the United States.
Devices Gold and Silver stars, Bronze Letter "R".

Bronze

Anodized or Gold-Plated

Miniature Medals

Regulation Ribbon Bar

Medal Reverse

Enamel Lapel Pin

Mini Ribbon (unofficial)

Enamel Hat Pin (unofficial)

Authorized on January 16, 1969 and awarded to members of the Armed Forces for noncombat meritorious achievement or meritorious service after that date. The Meritorious Service Medal (MSM) evolved from an initial recommendation in 1918 by General John J. Pershing, the Commander of the American Expeditionary Forces during World War I. He suggested that an award for meritorious service be created to provide special recognition to deserving individuals by the U.S. government. Although the request by General Pershing was disapproved, it was revisited several more times during World War II and afterwards. During the Vietnam War the proposal to create the medal received significant attention and was eventually approved when President Lyndon B. Johnson signed the executive order on January 16, 1969. The Meritorious Service Medal cannot be awarded for service in a combat theater. It has often been the decoration of choice for both end of tour and retirement recognition for field grade officers and senior enlisted personnel.

The MSM is a bronze medal with six rays rising from the top of a five-pointed star with beveled edges with two smaller stars outlined within. On the lower part of the medal in front of the star there is an eagle with its wings spread. It is standing on two curving laurel branches tied between the eagle's talons. The eagle, symbol of the nation, holds laurel branches representing achievement. The star represents military service with the rays symbolizing individual efforts to achieve excellence. The reverse of the medal has the inscription, "UNITED STATES OF AMERICA" at the top and "MERITORIOUS SERVICE" at the bottom; the space inside the circle formed by the text is to be used for engraving the recipient's name. The ribbon is ruby red with two white stripes and is a variation of the Legion of Merit ribbon. Jay Morris and Lewis J. King of the Institute of Heraldry designed and sculpted the Meritorious Service Medal. Additional awards are indicated by gold and silver stars and as of 2017 by variations of the R device or oak leaf clusters.

Standing left, Capt. Tim Brewer, presents the Meritorious Service Award to Cmdr. Steingold, Commanding Officer, Scientific Development Squadron ONE (VXS-1), at an award ceremony, May 3, 2012.
(Photo: Jamie Hartman)

Did You Know? The Meritorious Service Medal was designed to provide appropriate recognition for non-combat achievement or service comparable to the Bronze Star for combat achievement or service. Normally, the acts or services rendered must be comparable to that required for the Legion of Merit but in a duty of lesser, though considerable, responsibility.

Air Medal

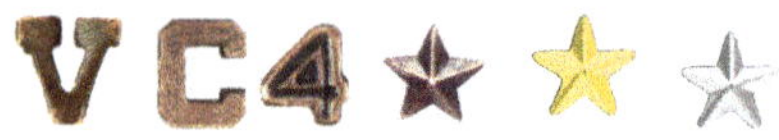

Service	All Services
Instituted	1942 (Retroactive to 8 September 1939)
Criteria	Heroic actions or meritorious service while participating in aerial flight, but not of a degree that would justify an award of the Distinguished Flying Cross
Devices	Navy/Marine Corps: Letter "V" (for valor), Bronze Numeral, Bronze Star, Gold, Silver Star, Gold Numeral;
Notes	The Air Medal devices currently in effect are Gold Arabic Numerals for Single Mission/Individual Awards.

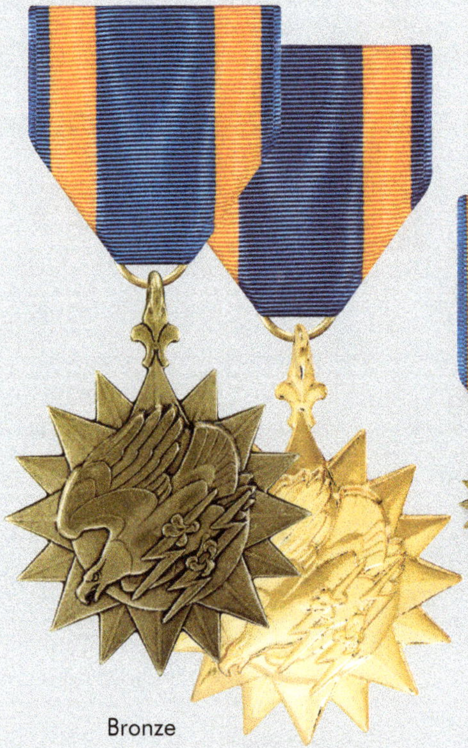

For meritorious achievement while participating in aerial flight. The Air Medal may be awarded to individuals who, while serving in any capacity with the Armed Forces, distinguish themselves by heroism, outstanding achievement, or by meritorious service while participating in aerial flight, but to a lesser degree than which justifies the award of the Distinguished Flying Cross. The Air Medal is worn after the Meritorious Service Medal and before the Joint Service Commendation Medal. The Air Medal is considered by many to be the air version of the Bronze Star Medal.

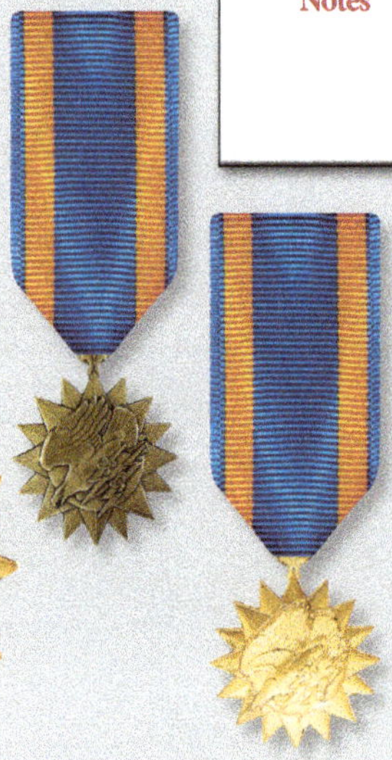

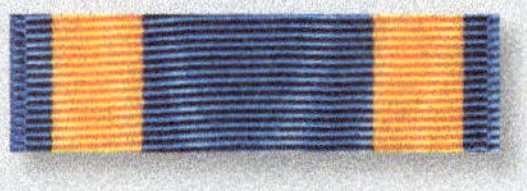

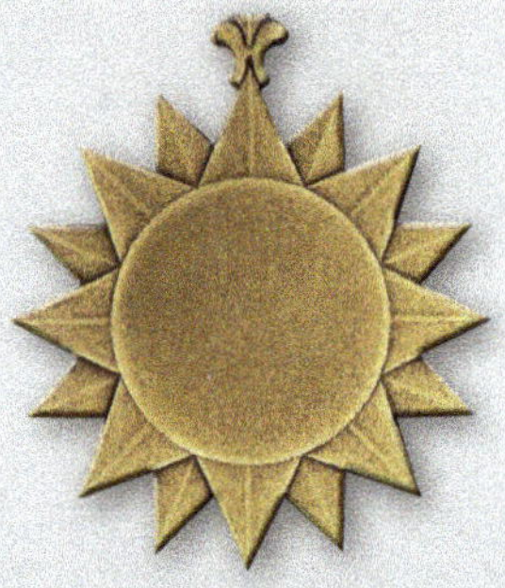

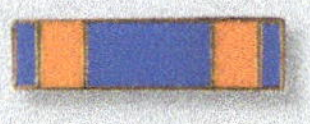

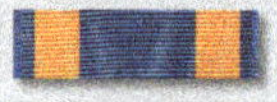

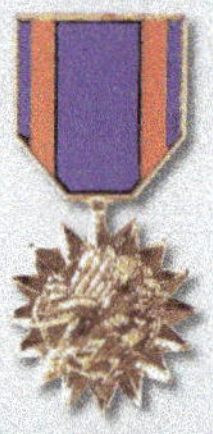

The Air Medal was established by Executive Order, which was signed by President Franklin D. Roosevelt on 11 May 1942. The medal was intended to protect the prestige of the Distinguished Flying Cross and as a morale booster to recognize the same kind of acts that were recognized by the Distinguished Flying Cross, but to a lesser degree

Although the Naval Services were authorized to award the Air Medal during World War II, the numbers never approached those received by the Army Air Force amidst the European bombing campaigns. Subsequent to World War II, however, with the increased role of the Navy in joint operations, the use of the Air Medal was subtly redefined. The Air Medal was still awarded for single acts of outstanding achievement which involve superior airmanship but of a lesser degree than would justify an award of a Distinguished Flying Cross. However, during the Korean, Vietnam and Gulf conflicts, awards for meritorious service were made for sustained distinction in the performance of duties involving regular and frequent participation in aerial flight operations. These operations include "strikes" (sorties which deliver ordnance against the enemy; those which land or evacuate personnel in an assault; or, those which involve search and rescue operations which encounter enemy opposition), "flights" (sorties which involve the same kinds of operations as strikes but which do not encounter enemy opposition) or "direct combat support" (sorties which include such activities as reconnaissance, combat air patrol, electronic countermeasures support, psychological warfare, coastal surveillance, etc.). In addition, the Air Medal was awarded for noncombat aerial achievement, such as, to air weather crews who gather major storm data by flying into hurricanes. The Air Force ceased all noncombat awards of the Air Medal with the

institution of the Aerial Achievement Medal in 1988 but without a comparable peacetime medal, the other Services still award the Air Medal under circumstances not involving actual combat.

The Navy and Marine Corps also use a system for awarding the medal for meritorious achievement while participating in sustained aerial flight operations based on the number of strikes or flights. Strikes are defined as sorties which encounter enemy opposition and flights are sorties without enemy opposition. The requirement calls for 10 strikes, or 20 flights, or 50 missions, or 250 hours in direct combat support or any combination. The combination requires the accumulation of 20 points on the formula of a strike being valued at 2 points, a flight at 1 point, and a mission at .4 points. The Navy and Marine Corps distinguish between the award of the medal on a Strike/Flight basis and those awarded for Single Mission/Individual basis. This is done by placing a bronze arabic numeral (indicating the number of awards) on the ribbon bar on the wearer's left if the award is for Strike/Flight. If the award is for individual heroism or achievement a three-sixteenth inch bronze star is placed in the center of the ribbon for the first award, while five-sixteenth inch gold stars are used to denote additional individual awards (a silver star is used in lieu of five gold stars).

The use of stars to denote the number of Air Medals for Single Mission/Individual awards was discontinued 2006 and a practice of using gold arabic numerals (indicating the number of awards) on the ribbon bar on the wearer's right was substituted. The practice (from 22 November 1989 to 2006) of denoting the number of Air Medals for Single Mission/Individual awards was with the use of five-sixteenth inch gold stars (a silver star is used in lieu of five gold stars).

The Air Medal was designed and sculpted by Walker Hancock and is a bronze sixteen point compass rose suspended by a fleur-de-lis. In the center there is an diving eagle carrying a lighting bolt in each talon. The compass rose represents the global capacity of American air power. The lightning bolts show the United States' ability to wage war from the air and the Fleur-de-lis, the French symbol of nobility, represents the high ideals of American airmen. The reverse of the compass rose is plain with an area for engraving the recipient's name. The ribbon is ultramarine blue with two golden orange stripes representing the original colors of the Army Air Force. A Combat Distinguishing Device "V" was authorized for use with the Air Medal effective 5 April 1974 it was replaced with a V for valor in 2017.

Air Medal w/Attachments
(Current)

Single Mission/Individual Awards
(Gold Arabic Numerals)

Gold Letter "V"
Strike / Flight Awards
(Bronze Arabic Numerals)

Air Medal w/Attachments
(1989- 2006)

Single Mission/Individual Awards
(Gold / Silver / Bronze Stars)

Bronze Letter "V"
Strike / Flight Awards
(Bronze Arabic Numerals)

Medals of America Press 107

Joint Service Commendation Medal

Bronze

Anodized or Gold-Plated

Miniature Medals

Regulation Ribbon Bar

Medal Reverse

Mini Ribbons (unofficial)

Enamel Lapel Pin

Enamel Hat Pin (unofficial)

Service	All Services (by DOD)
Instituted	June 25, 1963
Criteria	Meritorious service or achievement while assigned to a Joint Activity.
Devices	Letter "V" (for valor), Bronze, Silver Oak Leaf, Letter "V, C, R & Numeral.

Established on June 25, 1963, this was the first medal specifically authorized for members of a Joint Service organization. Awarded to members of the Armed Forces for meritorious achievement or service while serving in a Joint Activity after January 1, 1963. The "V" for valor is authorized for award in combat operations.

The medal consists of four conjoined green enameled hexagons edged in gold which represent the unity of the Armed Forces. The top hexagon has thirteen gold five-pointed stars (representing the thirteen original states) and the lower hexagon has a gold stylized heraldic device (for land, air and sea). An eagle with spread wings and a shield on its breast is in the center of the hexagons. The eagle is grasping three arrows in its talons. The hexagons are encircled by a laurel wreath bound with gold bands (representing achievement). On the reverse there is a plaque for engraving the recipient's name. Above the plaque are the raised words, "FOR MILITARY" and below, "MERIT" with a laurel spray below. The words and laurel spray are derived from the Army and Navy Commendation Medals. The ribbon is a center stripe of green flanked by white, green, white and light blue stripes. The green and white are from the Army and Navy Commendation ribbons and the light blue represents the Department of Defense.

The Joint Service Commendation Medal (JSCM) was designed by the Institute of Heraldry's Stafford F. Potter. Oak leaf Clusters and Bronze Numerals denote additional awards.

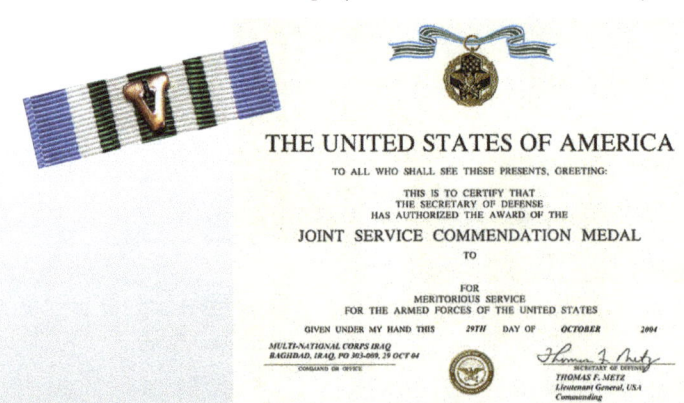

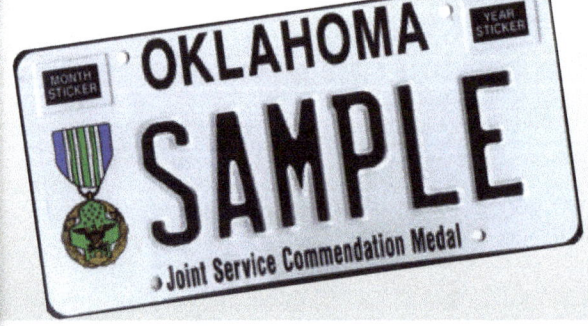

108 Medals and Ribbons of the U.S. Navy

Navy and Marine Corps Commendation Medal

Service	Navy/Marine Corps
Instituted	1944/1950
Criteria	Meritorious service or achievement in a combat or noncombat situation based on sustained performance of a superlative nature.
Devices	Letter "V" (for valor), Letter " C and R", Gold, Silver Star
Notes	Originally a ribbon only award: Changed to present name in 1994.

Bronze

Anodized or Gold-Plated

Miniature Medals

Regulation Ribbon Bar

Enamel Lapel Pin

Mini Ribbon (unofficial)

Medal Reverse

Enamel Hat Pin (unofficial)

The reverse of the medal has a plaque for inscribing the recipient's name and the raised words, "FOR MILITARY" *(above the plaque)* and "MERIT" *(below the plaque)*. The ribbon is dark green with a narrow stripe of white near each edge. Additional awards of the Navy and Marine Corps Commendation Medal are denoted by five-sixteenth inch gold stars. A Combat Distinguishing Device *(Bronze letter "V")* could be authorized until 2016. A V for valor now authorized.

For heroic and meritorious achievement or service. The Navy and Marine Corps Commendation Medal (NC) is worn after the Joint Service Commendation Medal and before the Joint Service Achievement Medal.

The Navy and Marine Corps Commendation Medal was originally established as a ribbon-only award on January 11, 1944. The current medal was authorized by the Secretary of the Navy on March 22, 1950. The medal is awarded for both heroism and meritorious achievement. To be awarded for heroism, the act must be worthy of recognition, but to a lesser degree than required for the Bronze Star Medal in combat or the Navy and Marine Corps Medal in a noncombat situation. To be awarded for meritorious achievement, the act must be outstanding and worthy of special recognition, but to a lesser degree than required for the Bronze Star Medal in combat or the Meritorious Service Medal or Air Medal when in a noncombat situation.

The Navy and Marine Corps Commendation Medal was designed by the Institute of Heraldry. The medal is a bronze hexagon with the eagle from the Seal of the Department of Defense in the center.

A display of a Petty Officer's service in Vietnam. Mounting ribbons over the medals allows diaplay of the unit awards. Commemorative Medals represent the Unit awards.

Medals of America Press 109

Joint Service Achievement Medal

Service	All Services
Instituted	1983
Criteria	Meritorious service or achievement while serving with a Joint Activity.
Devices	Bronze, Silver Oak Leaf Cluster, Bronze Letter "C, R", Brz Numeral.

Bronze

Anodized or Gold-Plated

Miniature Medals

Regulation Ribbon Bar

Medal Reverse

Enamel Lapel Pin

Mini Ribbon (unofficial)

Enamel Hat Pin (unofficial)

The Joint Service Achievement Medal (USAM) was established in 1983 specifically to complete the Department of Defense awards hierarchy and thereby provide a system of decorations for meritorious achievement comparable to those of the separate services. In so doing, the integrity of the more senior Joint Service medals was protected and the opportunity to earn recognition while assigned to a Joint Activity was provided.

It is awarded for meritorious service or achievement while serving in a Joint Activity after August 3, 1983 to military personnel below the rank of colonel. Oak Leaf Clusters and Numerals denote additional awards. No V device is authorized after January 2016.

The medal features an American eagle with the United States coat of arms on its breast holding three arrows in the center of the bronze medal which consists of a star of twelve points chosen to make it distinctive. The eagle was taken from the Seal designed for the National Military Establishment in 1947 by the President and the arrows were adapted from the seal of the Department of Defense. This is the same design seen on the Army and Navy Commendation Medals.

The reverse of the medal contains the inscriptions, "JOINT SERVICE" and "ACHIEVEMENT AWARD" in a circle. There is space in the center for inscribing the recipient's name. The ribbon consists of a center stripe of red flanked on either side by stripes of light blue, white, green, white and blue.

The Joint Service Achievement Medal was designed by Jay Morris and sculpted by Donald Borja, both of the Institute of Heraldry.

> **Did You Know?** ... The JSAM may not be awarded for any act or period of service for which a Military Department medal was awarded, and it should not be awarded for retirement. Bronze oak-leaf clusters are used to denote the 2nd through 5th award. No more than four bronze oak-leaf clusters can be worn. Bronze oak-leaf clusters may be worn with one or more silver oak-leaf clusters to denote 7 or more awards.

Navy and Marine Corps Achievement Medal

Bronze

Anodized or Gold-Plated

Service	Navy / Marine Corps
Instituted	1961
Criteria	Meritorious service or achievement in a combat or noncombat situation based on sustained performance of a superlative nature.
Devices	Bronze Letter "C" and "R", Gold, Silver Star
Notes	Originally a ribbon only award: "Secretary of the Navy Commendation for Achievement Award with Ribbon". Changed to present form in 1967. Changed to present name in 1994. No longer authorized a "V".

Regulation Ribbon Bar

Enamel Lapel Pin

Mini Ribbon (unofficial)

Enamel Hat Pin (unofficial)

Miniature Medals

Medal Reverse

For junior officers and enlisted personnel whose professional and/or leadership achievements on or after May 1, 1961 are clearly of a superlative nature. The Navy and Marine Corps Achievement Medal (NAM) is worn after the Joint Service Achievement Medal and before the Combat Action Ribbon.

The Navy and Marine Corps Achievement Medal was originally established as a ribbon-only award on May 1, 1961. The current medal was authorized by the Secretary of the Navy on July 17, 1967. The medal is awarded for both professional and leadership achievement. To be awarded for professional achievement, the act must clearly exceed that which is normally required or expected and must be an important contribution to benefit the United States Naval Service. To be recognized for leadership achievement, the act must be noteworthy and contribute to the individual's unit mission.

The Navy and Marine Corps Achievement Medal was designed by the Institute of Heraldry. The medal is a bronze square *(having clipped corners)* with a fouled anchor in the center. There is a star in each of the four corners. The reverse of the medal is blank to allow for engraving the recipient's name. The ribbon is myrtle green with stripes of orange near each edge. Additional awards of the Navy and Marine Corps Achievement Medal are denoted by five-sixteenth inch gold stars. A Combat Distinguishing Device *(Combat "V")* could be awarded prior to 2017 but is no longer authorized for any achievement medal.

This Master Chief has 2 awards of the Navy and Marine Corps Achievement Medal with multiply awards of the Good Conduct Medal.

Medals of America Press

Combat Action Ribbon

For active participation in ground or surface combat subsequent to 6 December 1941, while in the grade of Colonel or below. The Combat Action Ribbon (CAR) is worn after the Navy and Marine Corps Achievement Medal and before the Navy's Presidential Unit Citation in a ribbon display. It is worn as the senior ribbon on the right breast when full-sized medals are worn on the left breast.

The Combat Action Ribbon was authorized by the Secretary of the Navy on 17 February 1969 and made retroactive to 1 March 1961. Currently, Public Law 106-65 now also allows the Secretary of the Navy to award the CAR to veterans retroactively for World War II and the Korean War. The two blocks of time indicated by Public Law 106-65, which have been designated are World War II, 7 December 1941 - 14 April 1946 and Korea, 27 June 1950 - July 1954. The principal requirement

Service	Navy/Marine Corps
Instituted	1969 - Retroactive to 7 Dec 1941
Criteria	Active participation in ground or air combat during specifically listed military operations.
Devices	Gold, Silver Star
Notes	This is the only Navy personal decoration which has no associated medal (a "ribbon-only" award).

is that the individual was engaged in combat during which time he/she was under enemy fire and that his/her performance was satisfactory.

The Combat Action Ribbon is a ribbon only award. The ribbon is gold with thin center stripes of red, white and blue and border stripes of dark blue on the left and red on the right. Additional awards are authorized for each separate conflict/war and are represented by five-sixteenth inch gold stars.

Presidential Unit Citation (Navy)

Awarded in the name of the President for service in a unit with outstanding performance in action. The Navy Presidential Unit Citation (PUC) is worn after the Combat Action Ribbon and before the Joint Meritorious Unit Award.

The Navy Presidential Unit Citation (PUC) was established by Executive Order on 6 February 1942 and amended on 28 June 1943. It is awarded by the Secretary of the Navy in the name of the President. The citation is conferred on units for displaying extraordinary heroism subsequent to 16 October 1941. The degree of heroism required is the same as that which is required for the award of the Navy Cross to an individual. An individual assigned to the unit when the

Service	Navy/Marine Corps
Instituted	1942
Criteria	Awarded to Navy/Marine Corps units for extraordinary heroism in action against an armed enemy.
Devices	Bronze, Silver Star, Golden Globe, Gold N.

award was granted may wear the ribbon as a permanent part of the uniform.

The Navy Presidential Unit Citation is a ribbon only award. The ribbon consists of three equal horizontal stripes of navy blue *(top)*, gold *(middle)* and red *(bottom)*. Additional awards of the Navy Presidential Unit Citation are denoted by three-sixteenth inch stars. USS Triton "Golden Globe", USS Nautilus "N".

Joint Meritorious Unit Award

Recognizes joint units or activities for meritorious achievement or service superior to that which is normally expected. The Joint Meritorious Unit Award (JUMA) is worn after the Navy Presidential Unit Citation and before the Navy Unit Commendation.

The Joint Meritorious Unit Award was authorized by the Secretary of Defense on 10 June 1981 and was originally called the Department of Defense Meritorious Unit Award. It is awarded in the name of the Secretary of Defense for meritorious service, superior to that which would normally be expected during combat, or declared national emergency, or under extraordinary circumstances that involve national interest. The service performed by the unit would be similar to that performed by an individual awarded the Defense Superior Service Medal.

Service	All Services
Instituted	1981
Criteria	Awarded to Joint Service units for meritorious achievement, or service in combat or extreme circumstances.
Devices	Bronze, Silver Oak Leaf Cluster

The award is retroactive to 23 January 1979.

The Joint Meritorious Unit Award is a ribbon only award. The ribbon is similar to the Defense Superior Service Medal ribbon with a gold metal frame with laurel leaves. Like the Defense Superior Service Medal, the ribbon consists of a central stripe of red flanked on either side by stripes of white, blue and yellow with blue edges. Additional awards are denoted by oak leaf clusters.

Navy Unit Commendation

For outstanding heroism in action or extremely meritorious service not involving combat, but in support of military operations. The Navy Unit Commendation (NUC) is worn after the Joint Meritorious Unit Award and before the Navy's Meritorious Unit Commendation.

The Navy Unit Commendation was established by the Secretary of the Navy on 18 December 1944. The Commendation is awarded by the Secretary of the Navy with the approval of the President. The Commendation is made to units, which, subsequent to 6 December 1941, distinguish themselves by outstanding heroism in action against an enemy, but to a lesser degree than required for the Presidential Unit Citation. The

Service	Navy/Marine Corps
Instituted	1944
Criteria	Awarded to units Navy/Marine Corps for outstanding heroism in action or extremely meritorious service.
Devices	Bronze, Silver Star

Navy Unit Commendation may also be awarded for extremely meritorious service not involving combat, but in support of military operations, which is outstanding when compared to other units performing similar service.

The Navy Unit Commendation is a ribbon only award. The ribbon is dark green with narrow border stripes of red, gold and blue. Additional awards are denoted by three-sixteenth inch bronze and silver stars.

Meritorious Unit Commendation

For any unit which distinguishes itself by valorous or meritorious achievement or service or outstanding service. The Meritorious Unit Commendation (MUC) is worn after the Navy's Unit Commendation and before the Navy "E" Ribbon.

The Navy's Meritorious Unit Commendation was established by the Secretary of the Navy on 17 July 1967. The Commendation is awarded by the Secretary of the Navy to units which distinguish themselves by either valorous or meritorious achievement considered outstanding, but to a lesser degree than required for the Navy Unit Commendation. The Meritorious Unit Commendation may be awarded for services in combat or non-combat situations.

Service	Navy/Marine Corps
Instituted	1967
Criteria	Awarded to Navy/Marine Corps units for valorous actions or meritorious achievement (combat or noncombat).
Devices	Bronze, Silver Star

The Navy's Meritorious Unit Commendation is a ribbon only award. The ribbon is dark green with a narrow red center stripe flanked on either side by stripes of gold, navy blue and gold. Additional awards are denoted by three-sixteenth inch bronze and silver stars.

Navy "E" Ribbon

To recognize individuals who were permanently assigned to ships or squadrons that won the battle efficiency competitions subsequent to 1 July 1974. The Navy "E" (NE) Ribbon is worn after the Meritorious Unit Commendation and before the Prisoner of War Medal on a ribbon display and on the right breast before the Sea Service Deployment Ribbon if wearing full-sized medals.

The Navy "E" Ribbon was established in June 1976 and is authorized to be worn by all personnel who served as permanent members of ship's company or squadrons winning the Battle Efficiency Award.

The Navy "E" Ribbon is a ribbon only award. The ribbon is navy blue with borders of white and gold with a silver "E" in the center. Additional awards are denoted by additional "E"s. The fourth *(and final)* awards is denoted by an "E" surrounded by a silver wreath.

Service	Navy/Marine Corps
Instituted	1978
Criteria	Awarded to ships or squadrons which have won battle efficiency competitions.
Devices	Silver letter "E", wreathed silver letter "E"
Notes	A "ribbon-only" award.

Medals of America Press 113

Prisoner of War Medal

Service	All Services
Instituted	1985
Criteria	Awarded to any member of the U.S. Armed Forces taken prisoner during any armed conflict dating from World War I.
Devices	Bronze Star.

Bronze

Anodized or Gold-Plated

Miniature Medals

Regulation Ribbon Bar

Medal Reverse

Enamel Lapel Pin

Mini Ribbon (unofficial)

Enamel Hat Pin (unofficial)

The Prisoner of War Medal (POWM) is awarded to any person who was taken prisoner of war and held captive after April 5, 1917. It was authorized by Public Law Number 99-145 in 1985 and may be awarded to any person who was taken prisoner or held captive while engaged in an action against an enemy of the United States, while engaged in military operations involving conflict with an opposing armed force or while serving with friendly forces engaged in armed conflict against an opposing armed force in which the United States is not a belligerent party. The recipient's conduct while a prisoner must have been honorable.

The Prisoner of War Medal is worn after all unit awards (after personal decorations in the case of the Army) and before the various Armed Service Good Conduct Medals (before the Combat Readiness Medal in the case of the Air Force).

The Prisoner of War Medal was designed by the Institute of Heraldry. The medal is a circular bronze disc with an American eagle centered and completely surrounded by a ring of barbed wire and bayonet points. The reverse of the medal has a raised inscription, "AWARDED TO" with a space for the recipient's name and, "FOR HONORABLE SERVICE WHILE A PRISONER OF WAR" set in three lines. Below this is the shield of the United States and the words, "UNITED STATES OF AMERICA." The ribbon is black with thin border stripes of white, blue, white and red. Additional awards are denoted by three-sixteenth inch bronze stars.

Due to a provision in the FY1996 National Defense Authorization Act, service secretaries are required to award the Purple Heart to any POW Medal recipients wounded in captivity. The law specified that a person is considered to be a former prisoner of war for purposes of this section if the person is eligible for the Prisoner-of-War Medal under section 1128 of title 10, United States Code." The corresponding DoD regulation specifies that any "Service member who is killed or dies while in captivity" after April 5, 1917 can receive the Purple Heart medal, "unless compelling evidence shows that the member's death was not the result of enemy action."

The idea of a medal to recognize prisoners of war was first proposed in 1944. However, the military services opposed the idea and only in 1985 did Congress pass legislation creating the POW Medal over the Pentagon's objections.

114 Medals and Ribbons of the U.S. Navy

Good Conduct Medal Type I, Maltese cross, nickel, of the type issued between 1870 and 1884.

WW II Navy Good Conduct Medal

Verisons of the Earlier Navy Good Conduct Medal are shown above and described below.

Early Navy Good Conduct Medals

The older versions of the "U.S. Navy" Good Conduct Medal

The Navy Good Conduct Medal was established on 20 July 1896. The Good Conduct Medal with an all-red ribbon replaced the former red, white, and blue style. The reverse of the medal continued to bear the name of the recipient, but additional information such as the Sailor's continuous service number, discharge date, and ship name, now was to be included. The practice of issuing a new medal for each honorable discharge was also discontinued. Instead, a pin-bar, engraved with the name of the Sailor's last ship or duty station, was provided. The reverse of the bar was also engraved with the Sailor's continuous service number and date of discharge in order to prevent the "borrowing" or theft of medals or bars when re-enlistment time rolled around. The use of award bars to recognize repeat awards continued unchanged from 1884 until the 1930s when the name of the ship or duty station was replaced with the engraved year in which the enlistment ended. The year bars stayed in use until World War II when die struck bars for "SECOND AWARD," "THIRD AWARD," etc. were authorized. The use of all bars was discontinued in approximately 1950, being replaced with the 3/16" bronze and silver stars in use today. Each bronze star represents one additional good conduct enlistment. A silver star is worn in lieu of five bronze stars

Medals of America Press

Navy Good Conduct Medal

Service	Navy
Instituted	1896
Criteria	Outstanding performance and conduct during three years of continuous active enlisted service in the U.S. Navy.
Devices	Bronze, Silver Star
Notes	Earlier ribbon was 1¼" wide

The Navy Good Conduct Medal (NGCM) was authorized on November 21, 1884. The medal is awarded to enlisted personnel of the United States Navy and Naval Reserve (active duty) for creditable, above average professional performance, military behavior, leadership, military appearance and adaptability based on good conduct and faithful service for three-year periods of continuous active service.

Those receiving the award must have had no convictions by court martial and no nonjudicial punishment during the three year period (there was a time from November 1963 to January 1996 when the period was four years). For the first award the medal may be awarded to the next-of-kin in those cases where the individual is missing in action or dies of wounds received in combat. Naval personnel may also receive the medal if separated from the service as a result of wounds incurred in combat.

The Navy Good Conduct Medal is a circular bronze disc with a raised anchor and anchor chain circling a depiction of the *U.S.S. Constitution* and the words, "CONSTITUTION and UNITED STATES NAVY." The reverse side of the medal has the raised inscription, "FIDELITY - ZEAL - OBEDIENCE" around the border with space provided in the center to stamp the recipient's name. The medal is suspended from a plain bronze suspender and is worn after the Prisoner of War Medal and before the Naval Reserve Meritorious Service Medal. The ribbon of the Navy Good Conduct Medal is maroon. Additional awards are denoted by three-sixteenth inch diameter bronze and silver stars.

The forerunner of the Navy Good Conduct Medal was the Navy Good Conduct Badge which was established in 1868 by the Secretary of the Navy, making it our country's second oldest award. The badge, in use from 1868 to 1884, was awarded to men holding a Continuous Service Certificate received upon the successful completion of a term of enlistment. In those early days, any seaman who qualified for three awards was promoted to petty officer.

The Good Conduct Badge was a Maltese cross with a circular medallion in the center. The medallion was bordered with a border inscribed around the edge with the words, "FIDELITY - ZEAL - OBEDIENCE and U.S.A." in the center. The cross was suspended from a 1/2 inch wide red, white and blue ribbon.

In 1880, the Navy redesigned the Good Conduct Badge. The new medallion was proposed by Commodore Winfield Scott Schley from the design used on the letterhead of the Navy Department's Bureau of Equipment and Recruiting. This new medallion was suspended from a 1-5/8 inch wide red ribbon with thin border stripes of white and blue.

In 1884, the medal was redesigned and in 1896, the award period was changed to three years of continuous active service. This new medal maintained the 1880 design but was suspended from a maroon ribbon by a straight bar clasp. Subsequent awards were recognized by the addition of clasps placed on the suspension ribbon between the top of the ribbon and the medallion. These clasps were bordered with rope and were engraved with the recipient's ship or duty station. During World War I, medals were impressed with rim numbers but many were issued without engraving. In the 1930's, the ship or duty station name on the clasps was replaced by the recipient's enlistment discharge date. In 1942, all engraved clasps were replaced with generic clasps having, "SECOND AWARD", "THIRD AWARD", etc. in raised letters. Finally, subsequent to World War II, the Navy discontinued the clasps, began stamping the recipient's information on the medal's reverse and authorized the use of three-sixteenth bronze stars to denote additional awards.

Examples of Navy Good Medals

WW II Navy Good Conduct Medal. The US Navy changed the design of the WW II Good Conduct Medal in 1961. This change involved adopting a ring suspension for the ribbon and medal, which differentiated it from the Marine Corps version and aligned it with other service medals.

Medals of America Press 117

Naval Reserve Meritorious Service Medal (Obsolete)

Service	Navy
Instituted	1964 to January 1, 2014.
Criteria	Outstanding performance and conduct during 3 years of enlisted service in the Naval Reserve.
Devices	Bronze, Silver Star
Notes	Originally a ribbon-only award.

The Naval Reserve Meritorious Service Medal (NRMSM) was an obsolete award for Navy Reservists who fulfilled their obligations with distinction during inactive duty. It was intended as the reserve component equivalent of the Navy Good Conduct Medal. The NRMSM was discontinued on January 1, 2014, when Navy Reserve members became eligible for the Navy Good Conduct Medal.

The Naval Reserve Meritorious Service Medal was authorized on September 12, 1959 originally as a ribbon-only award. The medal was authorized on June 22, 1962 with eligibility backdated to July 1, 1958. The award is made on a selected basis to U.S. Navy Reservists who fulfill, with distinction, the obligations of an inactive Reservists at a higher level than normally expected. The obligations pertain to attendance and performance.

The Naval Reserve Meritorious Service Medal is a circular bronze disc showing an fouled anchor covered with a scroll with the raised words, "MERITORIOUS SERVICE." The words, "UNITED STATES NAVAL RESERVE" encircle the anchor. The reverse of the medal is blank. The ribbon is red with a blue center stripe and thin border stripes of gold and blue. Additional awards are denoted by three-sixteenth bronze stars.

Fleet Marine Force Ribbon (Obsolete)

Service	Navy/
Instituted	1984-Oct. 2006
Criteria	Awarded to Navy personnel serving with the Marine Corps.
Devices	None

The Navy Fleet Marine Force Ribbon (FMF Ribbon) was a military award established by the United States Navy in 1984 to recognize Navy personnel serving with the Marine Corps. It signified the acquisition of specific skills and knowledge beyond what was typically required for Navy personnel in those roles. The ribbon was discontinued on October 1, 2006, as the FMF badges for officers and enlisted were created. However, individuals who earned the FMF Ribbon before its discontinuation are still authorized to wear it

The FMF Ribbon recognizes Navy personnel who have served with Marine Corps units and have achieved a level of expertise and experience above what is typically required for their Navy role within the FMF.

Recipient must have served a minimum of 12 months with Marine Corps operating forces, and have a specific combination of qualifications or service experience.

The FMF Ribbon was not a combat award. It was a service award recognizing the service member's specialized experience and qualifications within the Marine Corps environment.

A recipient could only qualify for the FMF Ribbon once.

Navy Expeditionary Medal

Service	Navy
Instituted	1936
Criteria	Landings on foreign territory and operations against armed opposition for which no specific campaign medal has been authorized.
Devices	Silver Letter "W", Bronze, Silver Star
Notes	Originally a "ribbon only" award.
Bars	"Wake Island"

Bronze

Anodized or Gold-Plated

Miniature Medals

Medal Reverse

Regulation Ribbon Bar

The Navy Expeditionary Medal (NEM) was authorized on August 5, 1936. The medal is awarded to members of the Navy who have engaged in operations against armed opposition in foreign territory or have served in situations warranting special recognition where no other campaign medal was awarded. Many operations have qualified for the award, beginning (retroactively) with operations by Navy and Marine Corps personnel in Honolulu, Hawaii in 1874 and culminating in the operations involving the attack on the *USS Cole* between 2000 and 2002.

The Navy Expeditionary Medal is a circular bronze disc depicting a sailor beaching a boat containing an officer and Marines with a flag of the United States and the word, "EXPEDITIONS." The reverse of the medal shows an American eagle perched atop an anchor and laurel branches. On either side of the eagle are the words, "FOR SERVICE." Above, in a semicircle is a raised inscription, "UNITED STATES NAVY." The ribbon contains the official colors of the Navy with a wide blue center stripe flanked by gold with narrow blue edges. Additional awards are denoted by three-sixteenth inch diameter bronze stars. For those who served in the defense of Wake Island in December, 1941, a one-quarter inch silver "W" is worn on the ribbon bar and a bronze clasp bearing the inscription, "WAKE ISLAND" is affixed to the suspension ribbon of the medal. This represents the last time in the 20th century that a named bar has been issued by any Service to commemorate a specific battle or engagement. The Navy Expeditionary Medal is worn after the Navy Good Conduct Medal and before all other service and campaign awards.

- ★ Cuban Military Operation, Jan. 3, 1961 - Oct. 23, 1962
- ★ Thailand Military Operation, May 16, 1962 - Aug. 10, 1962
- ★ Iranian, Yemen & Indian Ocean Operation, Dec. 8, 1978 - Jun. 6, 1979, Nov. 21, 1979 - Oct. 20, 1981
- ★ Lebanon, Aug. 20, 1982 - May 31, 1983
- ★ Libyan Expedition, Jan. 20, 1986 - Jun. 27, 1986
- ★ Persian Gulf, Feb. 1, 1987 - Jul. 23, 1987
- ★ Panama, Apr. 1, 1988 - Dec. 19, 1989. *(Pre and post invasion)* Feb. 1, 1990 - Jun. 13, 1990
- ★ Operation Sharp Edge - Liberia, Aug. 5, 1990 - Feb. 21, 1991
- ★ Operation Distant Runner - Rwanda, Apr. 7-18, 1994 *(11th Marine Exped. Unit USS Peleliu)*
- ★ Operation Safe Departure - Eritrea, Jun. 6-25, 1998
- ★ Operation Determined Response - USS Cole, Oct. 12, 2000-Dec. 15, 2002

China Service Medal

Service	Navy, Marine Corps, Coast Guard
Instituted	1942
Criteria	Service ashore in China or on-board naval vessels 7 Jul 1937 to Sept. 1939 or between 2 Sept. 1945 and 1 April 1957.
Devices	Bronze Star
Notes	Medal was reinstituted in 1947 for extended service during dates shown above

Bronze

Anodized or Gold-Plated

Miniature Medals

Medal Reverse

Regulation Ribbon Bar

Enamel Lapel Pin

Mini Ribbon (unofficial)

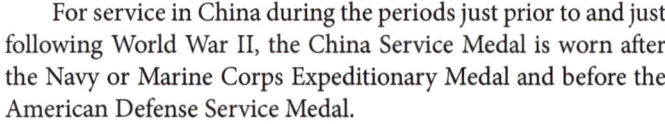

For service in China during the periods just prior to and just following World War II, the China Service Medal is worn after the Navy or Marine Corps Expeditionary Medal and before the American Defense Service Medal.

The China Service Medal was authorized by the Department of the Navy on July, 1 1942 for members of the Navy and Marine Corps who served in China or were attached to ships in the area during the period July 7, 1937 to September 7, 1939. The second period was for those who were present for duty during operations in China, Taiwan and the Formosa Straits during the period September 2, 1945 to April 1, 1957.

The China Service Medal was designed by George Snowden and A.A. Weinman. The medal is a circular bronze disc showing a Chinese junk under full sail with the raised inscribed words, "CHINA" above and "SERVICE" below. The reverse of the medal shows an American eagle perched on an anchor and laurel branches. On either side of the eagle are the words, "FOR SERVICE." Above, in a semicircle is a raised inscription, "UNITED STATES NAVY" or "UNITED STATES MARINE CORPS" depending on the recipient's branch of service. The ribbon is yellow with a narrow red stripe near each edge. If an individual served during both periods, a bronze three-sixteenth inch star is worn.

Did You Know? It sounds like a familiar story: on a bright Sunday in December, nearly 80 years ago, Japanese planes blazed out of the sky to strafe and bomb an American warship while it lay at anchor. The surprise attack caught the crew off-guard, and despite valiant action, the ship was critically damaged, had to be abandoned, and soon sank. If you said December 7th, 1941, Pearl Harbor, you'd be wrong. The date was December 12, 1937, and the place was the Yangtze River in war-torn China. The vessel? The gunboat USS Panay. It was a sudden and deliberate attack that might have led to war, save for swift diplomacy, and luck.

American Defense Service Medal

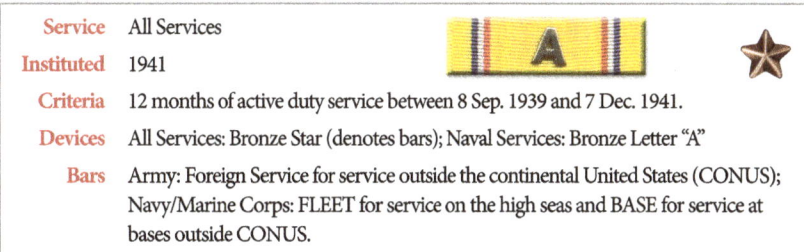

Service	All Services
Instituted	1941
Criteria	12 months of active duty service between 8 Sep. 1939 and 7 Dec. 1941.
Devices	All Services: Bronze Star (denotes bars); Naval Services: Bronze Letter "A"
Bars	Army: Foreign Service for service outside the continental United States (CONUS); Navy/Marine Corps: FLEET for service on the high seas and BASE for service at bases outside CONUS.

Bronze

Anodized or Gold-Plated

Miniature Medals

Medal Reverse

Regulation Ribbon Bar

Enamel Lapel Pin

Authorized on June 28, 1941 for military service during the limited emergency proclaimed by President Roosevelt on Sept. 8, 1939 or during the unlimited emergency proclaimed on May 27, 1941 until December 7, 1941 if under orders to active duty for 12 months or longer. In addition to the bars depicted to the right, a bronze star is worn on the service ribbon to denote receipt of any of the bars. The Navy also authorized the wear of a bronze letter "A" if the recipient served with the Atlantic Fleet during the period of the national emergency. The bronze star was not worn if the letter "A" was awarded.

On the front of the medal is the Grecian figure, Columbia, representing America or Liberty, holding a shield and sword while standing on an oak branch, symbolic of strength. The oak leaves represent the strength of the Army, Navy, Marine Corps and Coast Guard. The inscription, "AMERICAN DEFENSE," is around the outside upper edge. The reverse of the medal carries the inscription, "FOR SERVICE DURING THE LIMITED EMERGENCY PROCLAIMED BY THE PRESIDENT ON SEPTEMBER 8, 1939 OR DURING THE UNLIMITED EMERGENCY PROCLAIMED BY THE PRESIDENT ON MAY 27, 1941."

The golden yellow color of the ribbon symbolizes the golden opportunity of United States youth to serve the nation, represented by the blue, white and red stripes on both sides of the ribbon.

The American Defense Service Medal (ADSM) was authorized with the following devices:

Foreign Service Clasp: Issued by the United States Army for military service outside the continental limits of the United States, including service in Alaska.

Base Clasp: Issued by the U.S. Navy and United States Marine Corps for service outside the continental limits of the United States (service in either Alaska or Hawaii qualified).

Fleet Clasp: Issued by the Navy, Marine Corps and United States Coast Guard for service on the high seas while regularly attached to any vessels of the Atlantic, Pacific, or Asiatic fleets as well as vessels of the Naval Transport Service and vessels operating directly under the Chief of Naval Operations. The Fleet clasp is a bronze bar 1/8 inch in width and 1-1/2 inches in length with the words FLEET inscribed.

The World War II Navy Campaign Medals

Medals and ribbons of the U.S. Navy

American Campaign Medal

Service	All Services
Instituted	1942
Criteria	Service outside the U.S. in the American theater for 30 days, or within the continental United States (CONUS) for one year.
Devices	All Services: Bronze star.

Bronze

Anodized or Gold-Plated

Miniature Medals

Regulation Ribbon Bar

Medal Reverse

Enamel Lapel Pin

Mini Ribbon (unofficial)

Enamel Hat Pin (unofficial)

For service during World War II within the American Theater of Operations. The American Campaign Medal (ANCM) was established by Executive Order on November 6, 1942 and amended on March 15, 1946, which established a closing date. The medal is awarded to any member of the Armed Forces who served in the American Theater of Operations during the period from December 7, 1941 to March 2, 1946 or was awarded a combat decoration while in combat against the enemy. The service must have been an aggregate of one year within the continental United States, or thirty consecutive days outside the continental United States, or sixty nonconsecutive days outside the continental United States, but within the American Theater of Operations. Maps of the three theaters of operations during World War II were drawn on November 6, 1942 to include the American Theater, European- African - Middle Eastern Theater and Asiatic-Pacific Theater.

The American Campaign Medal was designed by the Army's Institute of Heraldry. The medal is a circular bronze disc showing a Navy cruiser, a B-24 bomber and a sinking enemy submarine above three waves. Shown in the background are some buildings representing the United States. Above is the raised inscription, "AMERICAN CAMPAIGN." The reverse of the medal shows an American eagle standing on a rock. On the left of the eagle are the raised inscribed dates, "1941-1945" and on the right, "UNITED STATES OF AMERICA." The ribbon is azure blue with three narrow stripes of red, white and blue *(United States)* in the center and four stripes of white, red *(Japan)*, black and white *(Germany)* near the edges. Three-sixteenth inch bronze stars indicated participation in specialized antisubmarine, escort or special operations. The American Campaign Medal is worn after the Women's Army Corps Service Medal by Army & Air Force personnel and after the American Defense Service Medal by the Naval Services.

Asiatic-Pacific Campaign Medal

Service	All Services
Instituted	1942
Dates	7 December 1941 to 2 March 1946
Criteria	Service in the Asiatic-Pacific theater for 30 days or receipt of any combat decoration.
Devices	Bronze, Silver Star, FMF Bronze Device.

Bronze

Anodized or Gold-Plated

Miniature Medals

Medal Reverse

Regulation Ribbon Bar

Enamel Lapel Pin

Mini Ribbon (unofficial)

Hat Pin (unofficial)

Authorized on November 6, 1942 and amended on March 15, 1946. Awarded to members of the U.S. Navy for at least 30 consecutive *(60 nonconsecutive)* days service *(less if in combat)* within the Asiatic-Pacific Theater between December 7, 1941 and March 2, 1946.

The front of the medal has a palm tree amidst troops with an aircraft overhead and an aircraft carrier, battleship and submarine in the background. The reverse has the American eagle, symbolizing power, on a rock, symbolizing stability, with the inscription, "UNITED STATES OF AMERICA" on the eagle's back. The orange yellow of the ribbon represents Asia while the white and red stripes toward each edge represent Japan. The center blue, white and red thin stripes are taken from the American Defense Service Medal, referring to America's continued defense preparedness after Pearl Harbor.

A bronze star denoted participation in a campaign. A silver star attachment is used to represent five bronze stars. The FMF Device is worn by Navy combat personnel serving with Marine Corps units and is worn centered in the middle of the ribbon. The ribbon is worn with the center blue stripe on the wearer's right.

NOTE: THE EUROPEAN-AFRICAN-MIDDLE EASTERN CAMPAIGN MEDAL COMES BEFORE THE ASIATIC-PACIFIC CAMPAIGN MEDAL BUT IS SHOWN HERE IN ORDER TO HAVE A TWO PAGE FACING SPREAD.

Designated Navy and Marine Corps campaigns for the Asiatic-Pacific Campaign Medal are:

- ★ Pearl Harbor-Midway, 1941
- ★ Wake Island, 1941
- ★ Philippine Islands Operation, 1941-1942
- ★ Netherlands East Indies, 1942
- ★ Pacific Raids, 1942
- ★ Coral Sea, 1942
- ★ Midway, 1942
- ★ Guadalcanal, Tulagi Landings, 1942
- ★ Capture and defense of Guadalcanal, 1942-1943
- ★ Makin Raid, 1942
- ★ Eastern Solomons (Stewart Island), 1942
- ★ Buin-Faisi-Tonolai Raid, 1942
- ★ Cape Esperance (Second Savo), 1942
- ★ Santa Cruz Islands, 1942
- ★ Guadalcanal (Third Savo), 1942
- ★ Tassafaronga (Fourth Savo), 1942
- ★ Eastern New Guinea, 1942-1944
- ★ Rennel Island Operation, 1943
- ★ Solomon Islands Consolidation, 1943-1945
- ★ Aleutians Operations, 1943
- ★ New Georgia Group Operation, 1943
- ★ Bismarck Archipelago, 1943-1944
- ★ Pacific Raids, 1943
- ★ Treasury-Bougainville Operation, 1943
- ★ Gilbert Island Operation, 1943
- ★ Marshall Islands Operation, 1943-1944
- ★ Asiatic-Pacific Raids, 1944
- ★ Western New Guinea, 1944-1945
- ★ Marianas Operation, 1944
- ★ Western Caroline Islands, 1944
- ★ Leyte Operation, 1944
- ★ Luzon Operation, 1944-1945
- ★ Iwo Jima Operation, 1945
- ★ Okinawa Gunto Operation, 1945
- ★ Third Fleet Operations against Japan, 1945
- ★ Kurile Islands Operation, 1944-1945
- ★ Borneo Operation, 1945
- ★ Tinian Capture and Occupation, 1944
- ★ Consolidation of Southern Philippines, 1945
- ★ Hollandia Operation, 1944
- ★ Manila Bay-Bicol Operation, 1945
- ★ Escort, Antisubmarine, etc, 1942-1945
- ★ Minesweeping Operations, 1945-1946
- ★ Submarine War Patrols, 1941-1945

3 Campaign Stars StarsOperation

5 Campaigns = 1 Silver Star

Medals of America Press

European-African-Middle Eastern Campaign Medal

Bronze

Anodized or Gold-Plated

Service	All Services
Instituted	1942
Dates	7 December 1941 to 2 March 1946
Criteria	Service in the European-African-Middle Eastern theater for 30 days or receipt of any combat decoration.
Devices	Bronze, Silver Star; FMF Globe and Anchor

Miniature Medals

Regulation Ribbon Bar

Medal Reverse

Enamel Lapel Pin

Mini Ribbon (unofficial)

Hat Pin (unofficial)

First called the "EAME Ribbon", the European–African–Middle Eastern Campaign Medal (EAMECM) was awarded for service during World War II within the European, African, Middle Eastern Theater of Operations. The European - African - Middle Eastern Campaign Medal is worn after the American Campaign Medal and before the Asiatic - Pacific Campaign Medal. The European - African - Middle Eastern Campaign Medal was established by Executive Order on 6 November 1942 and amended on 15 March 1946, which established a closing date.

The medal is awarded to all members of the Armed Forces who served in the European, African, Middle Eastern Theater of Operations during the period from 7 December 1941 to 2 March 1946. The service must have been as a member of the Armed Forces on permanent assignment in the theater, or within the theater on temporary assignment for thirty consecutive days, or sixty nonconsecutive days, or the award of a combat decoration in the theater. Maps of the three theaters of operations during World War II were drawn on 6 November, 1942 to include the American Theater, the European - African - Middle Eastern Theater and the Asiatic - Pacific Theater.

The medal's obverse was designed by Mr. Thomas Hudson Jones based on General Eisenhower's request that the medal include an invasion scene. The reverse side was designed by Adolph Alexander Weinman and is the same design as used on the reverse of the Asiatic–Pacific and American Campaign Medals. The medal is a circular bronze disc showing troops assaulting a beach. A LST (*Landing Ship Tank*) and an airplane are in the background. Above is the raised inscription EUROPEAN AFRICAN MIDDLE EASTERN CAMPAIGN set in three lines. The reverse of the medal shows an American eagle standing on a rock. On the left of the eagle are the raised inscribed dates 1941 - 1945 and on the right UNITED STATES OF AMERICA. The ribbon has narrow center stripes of red, white and blue (*United States*). These are flanked by wide stripes of green on the left by narrow stripes of green, white and red (*Italy*), and on the right by narrow stripes of white, black and white (*Germany*). The stripes at the edges are brown (*Africa*). Participation in specific combat operations is denoted by three-sixteenth inch bronze stars. A three-sixteenth inch silver star is worn in lieu of five bronze stars.

The nine designated Navy and Marine Corps campaigns for the European-African-Middle Eastern Campaign Medal are as follows:

- ★ Reinforcement of Malta, 1942
- ★ North African Occupation, 1942-1943
- ★ Sicilian Occupation, 1943
- ★ Salerno Landings, 1943
- ★ West Coast of Italy Operations, 1944
- ★ Invasion of Normandy, 1944
- ★ Northeast Greenland Operation, 1944
- ★ Invasion of Southern France, 1944
- ★ Escort, antisubmarine, armed guard special operations, 1941-1944

World War II Victory Medal

Service	All Services
Instituted	1945
Dates	7 December 1941 to 31 December 1946
Criteria	Awarded for service in the U.S. Armed Forces during the above period.
Devices	None

Bronze

Anodized or Gold-Plated

Miniature Medals

Medal Reverse

Regulation Ribbon Bar

Enamel Lapel Pin

Mini Ribbon (unofficial)

Hat Pin (unofficial)

Authorized by an Act of Congress on July 6, 1945 and awarded to all members of the Armed Forces who served at least one day of honorable, active federal service between December 7, 1941 and December 31, 1946, inclusive. The World War II Victory Medal was initially issued as a service ribbon called the "Victory Ribbon." Not until after the war in 1946 was a full medal designed and struck with a new title: World War II Victory Medal (WWIIVM).

The front of the medal depicts the Liberty figure resting her right foot on a war god's helmet with the hilt of a broken sword in her right hand and the broken blade in her left hand. The reverse contains the words, "FREEDOM FROM FEAR AND WANT, FREEDOM OF SPEECH AND RELIGION, and UNITED STATES OF AMERICA 1941-1945." The red center stripe of the ribbon is symbolic of Mars, the God of War, representing both courage and fortitude. The twin rainbow stripes, suggested by the World War I Victory Medal, allude to the peace following a storm. A narrow white stripe separates the center red stripe from each rainbow pattern on both sides of the ribbon. The World War II Victory Medal provides deserving recognition to all of America's veterans who served during World War II.

No attachments are authorized although some veterans received the ribbon with an affixed bronze star which, according to rumors at the time, was to distinguish those who served in combat from those who did not. No official documentation has ever been found to support this supposition. Although eligible for its award, many World War II veterans never actually received the medal since many were discharged prior to the medal's institution.

The reason for this late date is that President Harry S. Truman did not declare an official end of hostilities until the last day of 1946

U.S. Antarctic Expedition Medal

Rear Admiral Richard E. Byrd,

Bronze

Medal Reverse

Service: Navy/Coast Guard

Instituted: 1945 for 1939-41

Criteria: Awarded in gold, silver and bronze to members of the U.S. Antarctic Expedition of 1939-41.

Devices: None

The U.S. Antarctic Expedition Medal was created by an Act of Congress on September 24, 1945 and was awarded in gold, silver and bronze to the participants. 160 medals were authorized, with 60 minted in gold and 50 each in silver and bronze. Rear Admiral Richard E. Byrd, who headed the endeavor, received one of the medals in gold. Unlike previous expeditions headed by Admiral Byrd, this effort was not named for him as it was an official undertaking of the United States Government rather than a privately funded enterprise.

The 1939-1941 expedition was envisioned as the first of a long series of efforts to explore the South Pole but the advent of World War II forced all such plans to be shelved indefinitely.

The medal was designed by John R. Sinnock. The lower half of the obverse shows a partial map with the engraved names, "SOUTH PACIFIC OCEAN, LITTLE AMERICA, SOUTH POLE, ANTARCTICA, AND PALMERLAND." Above this is a three-part scroll inscribed, "SCIENCE, PIONEERING, EXPLORATION." Around the edge is the inscription, "THE UNITED STATES ANTARCTIC EXPEDITION 1939 1941." On the reverse, the inscription, "BY ACT OF CONGRESS OF THE UNITED STATES OF AMERICA TO" is set in four lines over a blank space for the recipient's name. Below is the inscription, "IN RECOGNITION OF INVALUABLE SERVICE TO THIS NATION BY COURAGEOUS PIONEERING IN POLAR EXPLORATION WHICH RESULTED IN IMPORTANT GEOGRAPHICAL AND SCIENTIFIC DISCOVERIES," in seven lines.

The ribbon has three equal stripes - ice blue, white, ice blue - and the white center stripe has two narrow dark red stripes near each edge.

Navy Occupation Service Medal

Bronze

Anodized or Gold-Plated

Miniature Medals

Medal Reverse

Regulation Ribbon Bar

Hat Pin

For thirty consecutive days of service in occupied zones following World War II. The Navy Occupation Service Medal is worn after the World War II Victory Medal and before the Medal for Humane Action.

The Navy Occupation Service Medal was authorized by ALNAV 24 on January 22, 1947 and Navy Department GO on January 28, 1948. The medal was awarded for occupation duty in Japan and Korea from September 2, 1945 to April 27, 1952. The medal was also awarded for occupation service in Germany, Italy, Trieste and Austria.

The Navy Occupation Service Medal was designed by the Army's Institute of Heraldry. The medal is a circular bronze disc showing Neptune, god of the sea, riding a sea serpent with the head and front legs of a horse. Neptune is holding a trident in his right hand and is pointing to an image of land, at the left of the medal, with his left hand. The lower front of the medal depicts the ocean with the words, "OCCUPATION SERVICE" in two lines. The reverse of the medal shows an American eagle perched on an anchor and laurel branches. On either side of the eagle are the words, "FOR SERVICE." Above, in a semicircle is a raised inscription, "UNITED STATES NAVY" or "UNITED STATES MARINE CORPS." The ribbon has two wide stripes of red and black in the center with border stripes of white. Clasps, similar to those used on the World War I Victory Medal, are used to denote service in EUROPE and ASIA, which are authorized for wear with the medal. There are no devices to represent these clasps authorized for wear on the ribbon bar. However, Navy and Marine personnel who served 90 consecutive days in support of the Berlin Airlift (1948-1949) are authorized to wear the Berlin Airlift device, a three-eighths inch gold C-54 airplane, on the ribbon bar and suspension ribbon.

Service	Navy, Marine Corps, Coast Guard
Instituted	1948
Criteria	30 consecutive days of service in occupied territories of former enemies during above period
Devices	Gold Airplane
Bars	"Europe", "Asia"

Europe Clasp   Asia Clasp

Eligibility	Navy, Marine Corps, and Coast Guard personnel
Awarded for	Occupation duty during and/or following World War II
Status	No longer awarded
Clasps	Europe, Asia
Established	January 22, 1947
First awarded	May 8, 1945
Last awarded	October 3, 1990
Next (higher)	U.S. Antarctic Expedition Medal
Equivalent	Army of Occupation Medal
Next (lower)	Medal for Humane Action

★ Italy, May 8, 1945 - Dec. 15, 1947
★ Trieste, May 8, 1945 - Oct. 26, 1954
★ Germany (except West Berlin), May 8, 1945 - May 5, 1955
★ Austria, May 8, 1945 - Oct. 25, 1955
★ Asiatic Pacific, Sep. 2, 1945 - Apr. 27, 1952
★ West Berlin, 1945 - 1990

Medal for Humane Action

Service	All Services
Instituted	1949
Dates	1948-49
Criteria	120 consecutive days of service participating in, or in support of the Berlin Airlift.
Devices	None

Bronze

Anodized or Gold-Plated

Miniature Medals

Regulation Ribbon Bar

Medal Reverse

Enamel Lapel Pin

Mini Ribbon (unofficial)

Hat Pin (unofficial)

Note: This medal was only awarded for Berlin Airlift service and is not to be confused with the Humanitarian Service Medal established in 1997.

Authorized for members of the U.S. Armed Forces on July 20, 1949 for at least 120 days of service while participating in or providing direct support for the Berlin Airlift during the period June 26, 1948 and September 30, 1949. The prescribed boundaries for qualifying service include the area between the north latitudes of the 54th and the 48th parallels and between the 14th east longitude and the 5th west longitude meridians. Posthumous award may be made to any person who lost his/her life while, or as a direct result of, participating in the Berlin Airlift, without regard to the length of such service.

The front of the medal depicts the C-54 aircraft, which was the primary aircraft used during the airlift, above the coat of arms of Berlin which lies in the center of a wreath of wheat. The reverse has the American eagle with shield and arrows and bears the inscriptions, "FOR HUMANE ACTION and TO SUPPLY NECESSITIES OF LIFE TO THE PEOPLE OF BERLIN GERMANY."

On the ribbon, the black and white colors of Prussia refer to Berlin, capital of Prussia and Germany. Blue alludes to the sky and red represents the fortitude and zeal of the personnel who participated in the airlift. The medal was designed by Thomas Hudson Jones of the Army Heraldic Section

No attachments are authorized. However, instances have been noted where the gold C-54 airplane device was incorrectly placed on this award rather than its proper usage, the Occupation Medal.

(USAF Photo)

National Defense Service Medal

Service	All Services
Instituted	1953
Dates	1950-54, 1961-74, 1990-95, 2001-2022
Criteria	120 consecutive days of service participating in, or any honorable active duty service during any of the above periods.
Devices	Bronze Star, Bronze Oak Leaf Cluster (Obsolete)
Notes	Reinstituted in 1966, 1991 and 2001 for Vietnam, Southwest Asia (Gulf War) and Iraq/Afghanistan actions respectively.

Bronze

Anodized or Gold-Plated

Miniature Medals

Regulation Ribbon Bar

Medal Reverse

Enamel Lapel Pin

Mini Ribbon (unofficial)

Hat Pin (unofficial)

Initially authorized by executive order on April 22, 1953. It is awarded to members of the U.S. Armed Forces for any honorable active federal service during the Korean War *(June 27, 1950 - July 27, 1954)*, Vietnam War *(January 1, 1961- August 14, 1974)*, Desert Shield/Desert Storm *(August 2, 1990 - November 30, 1995)* and/or Operations Iraqi Freedom and Enduring Freedom *(Afghanistan) (September 11, 2001 to a date TBD)*. President Bush issued an Executive Order 12776 on October 8, 1991 authorizing award of the medal to all members of the Reserve forces whether or not on active duty during the designated period of the Gulf War.

The latest award of the medal was promulgated in a memo, dated April 2, 2002, from the Office of the Deputy Secretary of Defense, Mr. Paul Wolfowitz who authorized the award to all U.S. Service Members on duty on or after September 11, 2001 to Dec. 31, 2022. Today, there are probably more people authorized this medal than any other award in U.S. history. Circumstances not qualifying as active duty for the purpose of this medal include: *(1)* Members of the Guard and Reserve on short tours of active duty to fulfill training obligations; *(2)* Service members on active duty to serve on boards, courts, commissions, and like organizations; *(3)* Service members on active duty for the sole purpose of undergoing a physical examination; and *(4)* Service members on active duty for purposes other than extended active duty. Reserve personnel who have received the Armed Forces Expeditionary Medal or the Vietnam Service Medal are eligible for this medal. The National Defense Service Medal is also authorized to those individuals serving as cadets or midshipmen at the Air Force, Army or Naval Academies. The front of the medal shows the American bald eagle with inverted wings standing on a sword and palm branch and contains the words, "NATIONAL DEFENSE"; the reverse has the United States shield amidst an oak leaf and laurel spray. Symbolically, the eagle is the national emblem of the United States, the sword represents the Armed Forces and the palm is symbolic of victory. The reverse contains the shield from the great seal of the United States flanked by a wreath of laurel and oak representing achievement and strength. The ribbon has a broad center stripe of yellow representing high ideals. The red, white and blue stripes represent the national flag. Red for hardiness and valor, white for purity of purpose and blue for perseverance and justice. No more than one medal is awarded to a single individual and today a three-sixteenth inch diameter bronze star denotes an additional award of the medal in lieu of the bronze oak leaf used earlier.

Korean Service Medal

Bronze

Anodized or Gold-Plated

Miniature Medals

Regulation Ribbon Bar Medal Reverse

Enamel Lapel Pin

Mini Ribbon (unofficial)

Medal Reverse

Hat Pin (unofficial)

Authorized by executive order on November 8, 1950 and awarded for service between June 27, 1950 and July 27, 1954 in the Korean theater of operations. Members of the U.S. Armed Forces must have participated in combat or served with a combat or service unit in the Korean Theater for 30 consecutive or 60 nonconsecutive days during the designated period. Personnel who served with a unit or headquarters stationed outside the theater but in direct support of Korean military operations are also entitled to this medal. The combat zone designated for qualification for the medal encompassed both North and South Korea, Korean waters and the airspace over these areas.

The first campaign began when North Korea invaded South Korea and the last campaign ended when the Korean Armistice cease-fire became effective. The period of Korean service was extended by one year from the cease fire by the Secretary of Defense; individuals could qualify for the medal during this period if stationed in Korea but would not receive any campaign credit. An award of this medal qualifies personnel for award of the United Nations (Korean) Service Medal and the Republic of Korea War Service Medal (approved 1999)

A Korean gateway is depicted on the front of the medal along with the inscription, "KOREAN SERVICE" and on the reverse are the "Taeguk" symbol from the Korean flag that represents unity and the inscription. "UNITED STATES OF AMERICA." A spray of oak and laurel line the bottom edge. The suspension ribbon and ribbon bar are both blue and white representing the United Nations. Bronze and silver stars are affixed to the suspension drape and ribbon bar to indicate participation in any of the 10 designated campaigns in the Korean War *(see below)*.

Service	All Services
Instituted	1950
Dates	1950-54
Criteria	Participation in military operations within the Korean area during the above period.
Devices	Bronze and Silver Star, FMF Globe and Anchor

The displays to the right are based on the wide variety of service and experiences of Navy Veterans during the Korean War. No display case is alike as no veterans experience or service was identical and each veteran has a different way of displaying what was important to him. The display case in the upper right corner has the new Korean Defense Medal which means the sailor served for aat least 30 days in the Korean waters after the war. Some sailors also added commemorative medals to recognize events important to them.

The ten Navy & Marine Corps campaign designations for the Korean Service Medal are:

- ★ North Korean aggression, 27 June - 2 Nov 1950
- ★ Communist China aggression, 3 Nov 1950 - 24 Jan 1951
- ★ Inchon Landing, 13 September - 17 Sept 1950
- ★ 1st United Nations counteroffensive, 25 Jan - 21 Apr 1951
- ★ Communist China spring offensive, 22 Apr - 8 July 1951
- ★ United Nations summer-fall offensive, 9 July - 27 Nov 1951
- ★ 2nd Korean winter, 28 November 1951 - 30 Apr 1952
- ★ Korean defensive, summer-fall 1952, 1 May - 30 Nov 1952
- ★ 3rd Korean winter, 1 December 1952 - 30 Apr 1953
- ★ Korean summer 1953, 1 May - 27 July 1953

Korean Navy Veterans' Displays

Medals of America Press

Antarctica Service Medal

Service	All Services
Instituted	July 7, 1960
Dates	1946 to Present
Criteria	15 calendar days of service on the Antarctic Continent.
Devices	All Services: Bronze, Gold, Silver disks.
Bars	Wintered Over" in Bronze, Gold, Silver.

For participation in an expedition, operation or support of a U.S. operation in Antarctica after 1 January 1946. The Antarctica Service Medal is worn after the Korean Service Medal and before the Armed Forces Expeditionary Medal. The medal was intended as a military award to replace several commemorative awards which had been issued for previous Antarctica expeditions from 1928 to 1941. With the creation of the Antarctica Service Medal, the following commemorative medals were declared obsolete;

Byrd Antarctic Expedition Medal

Second Byrd Antarctic Expedition Medal

United States Antarctic Expedition Medal

The Antarctica Service Medal (ANTSM) was established by an Act of Congress on 7 July 1960. The ribbon was approved in 1961 and the medal in 1963. The medal is awarded to any American or resident alien who subsequent to 1 January 1946, served on the Antarctic continent on or in support of U.S. operations there. Originally no minimum time was required for the medal; from 1 June 1973 to 31 Aug 2008 a minimum of 30 consecutive days at sea or ashore south of sixty degrees latitude is required. One day on the continent count for two days toward the thirty day eligibility. Effective 1 Sept 2008 the minimum time for award became 15 days.

The Antarctica Service Medal was designed by the U.S. Mint. The medal is a circular green-gold disc showing a man in the center with Antarctic clothing. On either side of the man is the raised inscription ANTARCTICA SERVICE. In the distant background is a mountain range and a line of clouds. The medal's reverse has the words COURAGE, SACRIFICE and DEVOTION set in the lines over a polar projection of the Antarctic continent. Around the edges is a border of penguins and marine life.

The ribbon has a narrow white center stripe flanked on either side by progressively darker shades of blue and borders of black. Individuals who spend the months of March to October are entitled to wear a bronze clasp with the words WINTERED OVER on the suspension ribbon for the first stay, a gold clasp for the second stay and a silver clasp representing a third winter on the Antarctic continent. Five-sixteenth inch discs of the same finish are worn on the ribbon bar to represent the clasps.

Armed Forces Expeditionary Medal and Its' Counterparts

The Armed Forces Expeditionary Medal

Vietnam Service Medal

Navy Expeditionary Medal

Armed Forces Service Medal

Global War on Terrorism Expeditionary Medal

The Armed Forces Expeditionary Medal (AFEM) was first created in 1961 by President John Kennedy. Back dated to July, 1958 it is awarded to members of the U.S. Armed Forces who participated in U.S. military operations, U.S. operations in direct support of the United Nations (UN) or NATO, and U.S. operations of assistance for friendly foreign nations.

Since its establishment the Armed Forces Expeditionary Medal has been authorized for United States participation in over forty five designated military campaigns (see next 2 pages). The first campaign being the Cuban Missile Crisis and between October 1962 and June 1963. The retroactive AFEM was also issued for actions in Lebanon, Taiwan, Republic of the Congo, Quemoy and Matsu, and for duty in Berlin between 1961 and 1963.

During the first years of the Vietnam War, the Armed Forces Expeditionary Medal was issued for operations in South Vietnam, Laos, and Cambodia. In 1965, with the creation of the Vietnam Service Medal, the AFEM was discontinued for Vietnam War service. Personnel who had previously received the AFEM were given the option to exchange the Armed Forces Expeditionary Medal for the Vietnam Service Medal. Most service members did so.

The Armed Forces Expeditionary Medal was intended to replace the Marine Corps Expeditionary Medal and Navy Expeditionary Medal. The Navy Expeditionary Medal was established in 1936. The full-sized medal is one of the oldest medals still issued to active duty personnel.

For award of the Navy Expeditionary Medal, a Sailor must have engaged in a landing on foreign territory, participated in combat operations against an opposing force, or participated in a designated operation for which no other service medal is authorized. In 1968, the AFEM was awarded for Naval operations in defense of the USS Pueblo, seized by North Korea, and for Korean Service, and also in Thailand and Cambodia operations in 1973. Because of these awards were during the Vietnam war period, some military personnel have been awarded both the Armed Forces Expeditionary Medal and the Vietnam Service Medal.

Beginning in 1992, the DOD begun to phase out the AFEM in favor of campaign specific medals and the newly created Armed Forces Service Medal. The Armed Forces Service Medal was originally intended to be a replacement for the Armed Forces Expeditionary Medal, however, the two awards are considered separate awards with different award criteria. The primary difference between the two is that the Armed Forces Expeditionary Medal is normally awarded for combat operations and combat support missions. The Armed Forces Service Medal is the non-combat parallel of the Armed Forces Expeditionary Medal and pretains more to peacekeeping operations and long term humanitarian operations.

The creation of the Global War on Terrorism Expeditionary Medal in 2003, led to the AFEM being discontinued for Iraq, Saudi Arabia, and Kuwait. In March 2003, some personnel became eligible for the Armed Forces Expeditionary Medal, as well as the Global War on Terrorism Expeditionary Medal but only one medal may be awarded.

Armed Forces Expeditionary Medal

Service	All Services
Instituted	1961
Dates	July 1, 1968 to Present
Criteria	Participation in military operations not covered by specific war medal.
Devices	Bronze and Silver Star. FMF Globe and Anchor.
Notes	Authorized for service in Vietnam until establishment of Vietnam Service Medal.

President John F. Kennedy characterized the post World War II period as "*a twilight that is neither peace nor war.*" During the period commonly referred to as the Cold War, the Armed Services agreed to one medal to recognize major actions not otherwise covered by a specific campaign medal.

The Armed Forces Expeditionary Medal (AFEM) was authorized on December 4, 1961 to any member of the United States Armed Forces for U.S. military operations, U.S. operations in direct support of the United Nations and U.S. operations of assistance to friendly foreign nations after July 1, 1958. Operations that qualify for this medal are authorized in specific orders. Participating personnel must have served at least 30 consecutive *(60 nonconsecutive)* days in the qualifying operation or less if the operation was less than 30 days in length. The medal may also be authorized for individuals who do not meet the basic criteria but who do merit special recognition for their service in the designated operation.

The first qualifying operation was Operation Blue Bat, a peacekeeping mission in Lebanon from July 1 to November 1, 1958. This medal was initially awarded for Vietnam service between July 1, 1958 and July 3, 1965; an individual awarded the medal for this period of Vietnam service may elect to keep the award or request the Vietnam Service Medal in its place. However, both awards may not be retained for the same period of Vietnam service. Many personnel received this medal for continuing service in Cambodia after the Vietnam cease-fire. The medal was also authorized for those serving in the Persian Gulf area who previously would have qualified for the Southwest Asia Service Medal and the National Defense Service Medal whose qualification periods for that area terminated on November 30, 1995. Individuals who qualify for both the Southwest Asia Service Medal and the Armed Forces Expeditionary Medal must elect to receive the Expeditionary medal.

The front of the medal depicts an American eagle with wings raised, perched on a sword. Behind this is a compass rose with rays coming from the angles of the compass points. The words "ARMED FORCES EXPEDITIONARY SERVICE" encircle the design. The reverse of the medal depicts the Presidential shield with branches of laurel below and the inscription, "UNITED STATES OF AMERICA." The American national colors are located at the center position or honor point of the ribbon. The light blue sections on either side suggest water and overseas service, while various colors representing areas of the world where American troops may be called upon to serve run outward to the edge.

The qualifying campaigns:

- **Lebanon,** Jul. 1, 1958 - Nov. 1, 1958
- **Taiwan Straits,** Aug. 23, 1958 - Jan. 1, 1959
- **Quemoy & Matsu Islands,** Aug. 23, 1958 - Jun. 1, 1963
- **Vietnam,** Jul. 1, 1958 - Jul. 3, 1965
- **Congo,** Jul. 14, 1960 - Sep. 1, 1962
- **Laos,** Apr. 19, 1961 - Oct. 7, 1962
- **Berlin,** Aug. 14, 1961 - Jun. 1, 1963
- **Cuba,** Oct. 24, 1962 - Jun. 1, 1963
- **Congo,** Nov. 23-27, 1964
- **Dominican Republic,** Apr. 23. 1965 - Sep. 21, 1966
- **Korea,** Oct. 1, 1966 - Jun. 30, 1974
- **Cambodia,** Mar. 29, 1973 - Aug. 15, 1973
- **Thailand,** Mar. 29, 1973 - Aug. 15, 1973 *(Only those in direct support of Cambodia)*
- **Operation Eagle Pull** - Cambodia, Apr. 11-13, 1975 *(Includes evacuation)*
- **Operation Frequent Wind** - Vietnam, Apr. 29-30, 1975
- **Mayaquez Operation,** May 15, 1975
- **El Salvador,** Jan. 1 , 1981 - Feb. 1, 1992
- **Lebanon,** Jun. 1, 1983 - Dec. 1, 1987
- **Operation Urgent Fury-Grenada,** Oct. 23, 1983 - Nov. 21, 1983
- **Eldorado Canyon** - Libya, Apr. 12-17, 1986
- **Operation Earnest Will** - Persian Gulf, Jul. 24, 1987 - Aug. 1, 1990 *(Only those participating in, or in direct support)*
- **Operation Just Cause** - Panama, Dec. 20, 1989 - Jan. 31, 1990 *(USS Vreeland & other SVS-designated aircrew mbrs. outside the Conus in direct support)*
- **United Shield** - Somalia, Dec. 5, 1992 - Mar. 31, 1995
- **Operation Restore Hope** - Somalia, Dec. 5, 1992 - Mar. 31, 1995
- **Operation Uphold Democracy** - Haiti, Sept. 1994 - Mar. 31, 1995
- **Operation Joint Endeavor** - Bosnia, Croatia, the Adriatic Sea & Airspace, Nov. 20, 1995 - Dec. 19, 1996
- **Operation Vigilant Sentinel** - Iraq, Saudi Arabia, Kuwait, & Persian Gulf Dec. 1, 1995 - Sep. 1, 1997
- **Operation Southern Watch** - Iraq, Saudi Arabia, Kuwait, Persian Gulf, Bahrain, Qatar, UAE, Oman, Gulf of Oman W of 62° E Long., Yemen, Egypt, & Jordan
- **Operation Maritime Intercept** - Iraq, Saudi Arabia, Kuwait, Red Sea, Persian Gulf, Gulf of Oman W of 62° E Long., Bahrain, Qatar, UAE, Oman, Yemen, Egypt & Jordan Dec. 1, 1995 - Mar 18, 2003
- **Operation Joint Guard** - Bosnia, Herzegovina, Croatia, Adriatic Sea & Airspace, Dec. 20, 1996 - Jun. 20, 2008
- **Operation Northern Watch** - Iraq, Saudi Arabia, Kuwait, Persian Gulf of W of 56° E Long., and Incirlik AB, Turkey (Only pers. TDY to ONW), Jan. 1, 1997 - 18 March 2003
- **Operation Joint Forge** - Bosnia-Herzegovina, Croatia, Adriatic Sea & Airspace, Jun. 21, 1998 - Dec. 2, 2004
- **Operation Desert Thunder** - Iraq, Saudi Arabia, Kuwait, Bahrain, Qatar, UAE, Omar, Yemen, Egypt, Jordan, Persian Gulf, Gulf of Oman, Red Sea support,Nov. 11, 1998 - Dec. 22, 1998
- **Operation Desert Fox** - Iraq, Saudi Arabia, Kuwait, Bahrain, Qatar, UAE, Oman, Yemen, Egypt, Jordan, Persian Gulf, Gulf of Oman, USN Red Sea support, 16 Dec. -22 Dec. 1998
- **Operation Desert Spring,** Haiti, Southwest Asia, 31 Dec.1998-18 Mar. 2003
- **Operation Secure Tomorrow,** 29 Feb. 2004-15 Jun. 2004
- **Operation Joint Guardian,** , 01 Jan. 2014-TBD
- **Operation Allies Refuge,** 14 Jul. 2021-30 Aug.2021

The Defense Department announced the transition of the Kosovo Campaign Medal to the Armed Forces Expeditionary Medal, effective Jan. 1, 2014.

As smaller contingencies of U.S. forces continue to support Operation Joint Guardian and NATO headquarters in Sarajevo, the AFEM will be awarded to recognize that support of operations in the Balkans.

The AFEM area of eligibility mirrors that of the KCM with the addition of Bosnia-Herzegovina, Croatia and Hungary. The eligible area also encompasses Serbian land and airspace including Vojvodina, Montenegro, Albania, Macedonia.

The Department of Defense Manual 1348.33, Volume 2, "Manual of Military Decorations and Awards" contains specific eligibility criteria.

Vietnam Service Medal

Bronze

Anodized or Gold-Plated

Miniature Medals

Medal Reverse

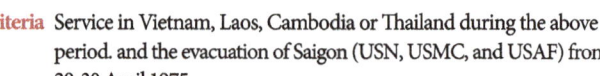

Service	All Services
Instituted	1965
Dates	1958-1973
Criteria	Service in Vietnam, Laos, Cambodia or Thailand during the above period. and the evacuation of Saigon (USN, USMC, and USAF) from 29-30 April 1975.
Devices	Bronze, Silver Star. FMF Globe and Anchor

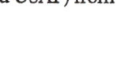

Enamel Lapel Pin

Regulation Ribbon Bar

Mini Ribbon (unofficial)

Hat Pin (unofficial)

Authorized by executive order on July 8, 1965 for U.S. military personnel serving in the Vietnam Theater of Operations after July 3, 1965 through March 28, 1973. Personnel must have served in Vietnam on temporary duty for at least 30 consecutive/60 nonconsecutive days or have served in combat with a unit directly supporting a military operation in Southeast Asia. Military personnel serving in Laos, Cambodia or Thailand in direct support of operations in Vietnam are also eligible for this award. The Armed Forces Expeditionary Medal was awarded for earlier service in Vietnam from July 1, 1958 to July 3, 1965, inclusive; personnel receiving that award may be awarded the Vietnam Service Medal (VSM) but are not authorized both awards for Vietnam service.

The front of the medal depicts an oriental dragon behind a grove of bamboo trees; below the base of the trees is the inscription, "REPUBLIC OF VIETNAM SERVICE." The reverse of the medal depicts a crossbow with a torch through the center and contains the inscription, "UNITED STATES OF AMERICA" along the bottom edge. The colors of the suspension drape and ribbon suggest the flag of the Republic of Vietnam *(the red stripes represent the three ancient Vietnamese empires of Tonkin, Annam, and Cochin China)* and the green represents the Vietnamese jungle. The distinctive design has been attributed to both sculptor Thomas Hudson Jones, a former employee of the Army Institute of Heraldry and Mercedes Lee who created the design. Bronze and silver stars are authorized to signify participation in any of the 17 designated campaigns during the inclusive period.

South Vietnam also issued its own service medal for the Vietnam War, known as the Republic of Vietnam Campaign Medal. This is a separate military award which was accepted by the U.S. Congress and the U.S. military in accordance with DoD 1348 C7. Six months of service in support of South Vietnamese military operations was the general U.S. requirement for the award

★ **Vietnam (VN) Advisory**, 1962 - 1965
★ **VN Defense**, 1965 - 1965
★ **VN Counteroffensive Campaign**, 1965 - 1966
★ **VN Counteroffensive Campaign Phase II**, 1966 -1967
★ **VN Counteroffensive Campaign Phase III**, 1967 - 1968
★ **TET Counteroffensive**, 1968
★ **VN Counteroffensive Campaign Phase IV**, 1968
★ **VN Counteroffensive Campaign Phase V**, 1968
★ **VN Counteroffensive Campaign Phase VI**, 1968 - 1969
★ **TET69 Counteroffensive**, 1969
★ **VN Summer - Fall 1969**, 1969
★ **Vietnam Winter - Spring 1970**, 1969 - 1970
★ **Sanctuary Counteroffensive**, 1970
★ **VN Counteroffensive Campaign Phase VII**, 1970 - 1971
★ **Consolidation I**, 1971
★ **Consolidation II**, 1971 - 1972
★ **Vietnam Cease-Fire Campaign**, 1972 - 1973

Vietnam Navy Veterans Service Displays

This young Seabee was decorated for saving a Navy Base Ammo dump during a rocket attack by moving ammuntion from an area on fire.

This Navy Vietnam Veteran added commorative medals for Vietnam, Cold War Victory, Sea service and Honorable Discharge.

This veteran added three Commorative Medals that represent the Combat Action Ribbon, The Navy Presidential Unit Citation and the Vietnam Gallantry Cross Unit Citation.

This young Navy veteran was with River Assault Division 152 in Vietnam.

Medals of America Press 139

Southwest Asia Service Medal

Bronze

Anodized or Gold-Plated

Miniature Medals

Regulation Ribbon Bar

Medal Reverse

Lapel pin

Mini Ribbon (unofficial)

Hat Pin (unofficial)

Service	All Services
Instituted	1992
Dates	1991-1995
Criteria	Active participation in, or support of, Operations Desert Shield, Desert Storm and follow-on operations in southwest Asia.
Devices	Bronze Star, FMF Globe and Anchor.
Notes	Recipients are usually entitled to the Saudi Arabian Medal for the Liberation of Kuwait and the Emirate of Kuwait Medal for the Liberation of Kuwait.

Awarded to members of the United States Armed Forces who participated in, or directly supported, military operations in Southwest Asia or in surrounding areas between August 2, 1990 and November 30, 1995 (Operations Desert Shield, Desert Storm and follow-up). Naval personnel awarded the Southwest Asia Service Medal must have participated in or supported military operations in Southwest Asia between August 2, 1990 and November 30, 1995. That includes participation in *Operations Desert Shield* or *Desert Storm* in these areas: Iraq, Kuwait, Saudi Arabia, Oman, Bahrain, Qatar, United Arab Emirates, Persian Gulf, Red Sea, Gulf of Oman and the Gulf of Aden.

Sailors serving in Israel, Egypt, Turkey, Syria and Jordan (including the airspace and territorial waters) directly supporting combat operations between January 17, 1991 and April 11, 1991 are also eligible for the medal. To qualify, a marine must be: attached to or regularly serving for one or more days with an organization participating in ground/shore military operations; attached to or regularly serving for one or more days aboard a naval vessel directly supporting military operations; participating as a crew member in aerial flights directly supporting military operations in the designated areas; or serving on temporary duty for 30 consecutive days or 60 nonconsecutive days, except, a waiver is authorized for personnel participating in actual combat. For those service members who performed "home service" during the Persian Gulf War, such as support personnel in the United States, the Southwest Asia Service Medal (SWASM) is not authorized. The award is also not authorized for those who performed support of the Persian Gulf War from European or Pacific bases.

The front of the medal depicts the tools of modern desert warfare, i.e., aircraft, helicopter, tank, armored personnel carrier, tent and troops, battleship, in both desert and sea settings along with the inscription, "SOUTHWEST ASIA SERVICE" in the center. The reverse of the medal contains a sword entwined with a palm leaf representing military preparedness and the maintenance of peace and the inscription "UNITED STATES OF AMERICA" around the periphery. The ribbon is predominately tan, symbolizing the sands of the desert and contains thin stripes of the U.S. national colors towards each edge. The green and black center stripes and the black edges, along with the red and white, suggest the flag colors of most Arab nations in the region of Southwest Asia. ***Each recipient of the medal should wear at least one campaign star.***

The 3 Approved Campaigns are:

Defense of Saudi Arabia	August 2, 1990 January 16, 1991
Liberation and Defense of Kuwait	January 17, 1991 April 11, 1991
Southwest Asia Cease-Fire	April 12, 1991 November 30, 1995

Kosovo Campaign Medal

Service	All Services
Instituted	2000
Dates	1999 - 2013
Criteria	Active participation in, or direct support of, Kosovo operations.
Devices	Bronze Star, FMF Globe and Anchor.

Bronze

Anodized or Gold-Plated

Miniature Medals

Regulation Ribbon Bar

Medal Reverse

Lapel Pins

Mini Ribbon (unofficial)

Hat Pin (unofficial)

For participation in, or in direct support of Kosovo operations. The Kosovo Campaign Medal is worn after the Southwest Asia Service Medal and before the Afghanistan Campaign Medal. The Kosovo Campaign Medal was established by executive order on May 15, 2000. The medal is awarded to all members of the Armed Forces who participated in or provided direct support to Kosovo operations within established areas of eligibility (AOE) from March 24, 1999 to December 31, 2013. The marine must have been a member of a unit participating in, or engaged in support of one or more of the following operations for 30 consecutive days or 60 nonconsecutive days.

Allied Force: 24 March - 10 June 1999
Task Force Hawk: 5 April - 24 June 1999
Joint Guardian: 11 June 1999- 31 Dec. 2013
Task Force Saber: 31 March - 8 July 1999
Allied Harbour: 4 April - 1 Sept 1999
Task Force Falcon: 11 June - 31 Dec. 2013
Sustain Hope/Shining Hope: 4 April - 10 July 1999
Task Force Hunter: 1 April - 1 Nov 1999
Noble Anvil: 24 March - 20 July 1999

One Bronze Service Star is worn on the the Kosovo Campaign Medal suspension and service ribbon for each campaign period (a marine who participated in one campaign would wear the Medal and/or Service Ribbon with one star). Those serving in each of the two campaigns wear the Medal and two Bronze Service Stars. However, if a Sailor's 30 or 60 days began in one campaign and carried over into the 2d campaign, they only qualify for the Kosovo Campaign Medal and one Service Star.

The Kosovo Campaign Medal was designed by the Institute of Heraldry. The medal is a circular bronze disk depicting rocky terrain, a fertile valley and sunrise behind a mountain pass in Kosovo. Above the scene, on two lines, are the words, "KOSOVO CAMPAIGN." At the lower edge is a stylized wreath of grain reflecting the agricultural nature of the area. The reverse shows an outline of the province of Kosovo with the curved inscription, "IN DEFENSE OF HUMANITY" across the top.

To date, there are two bronze service stars authorized for the Kosovo Campaign Medal as follows:

(1) **Kosovo Air Campaign** - 24 March 1999 to 10 June 1999
(2) **Kosovo Defense Campaign** - 11 June, 1999 to 31 December 2013

The Secretary of Defense approved award of the Kosovo Campaign Medal to sailors and Marines on the following Navy vessels for campaign participation as an exception to the 30 consecutive day rule: USS Norfolk; USS Miami, USS Boise; USS Albuquerque, USS Nicholson, USS Philippine Sea, and the USS Gonzalez.

Afghanistan Campaign Medal

Service	All Services
Instituted	2004
Dates	October 24, 2001, to August 31, 2021
Criteria	Active service in direct support of Operation ENDURING FREEDOM, and FREEDOM'S SENTINEL.
Devices	Bronze Star, Silver Star. FMF Globe and Anchor.

Bronze

Anodized or Gold-Plated

Miniature Medals

Regulation Ribbon Bar

Medal Reverse

Enamel Lapel Pin

Mini Ribbon (unofficial)

Enamel Hat Pin (unofficial)

The Afghanistan Campaign Medal (ACM) was signed into law by President George W. Bush, May 28, 2004 and implemented by Executive Order 13363, Nov. 29, 2004. It is awarded to Service members who have served in direct support of Operation Enduring Freedom The ACM is awarded retroactively to those who served in Afghanistan from October 24, 2001, to August 31, 2021. The area of eligibility encompasses all land areas of the country of Afghanistan and all air spaces above the land.

Service members must have been assigned, attached or mobilized to units operating in these areas of eligibility for 30 consecutive days or for 60 non-consecutive days or meet one of the following criteria:

a. Be engaged in combat during an armed engagement, regardless of the time in the area of eligibility; or
b. While participating in an operation or on official duties, is wounded or injured and requires medical evacuation from the area of eligibility; or
c. While participating as a regularly assigned air crewmember flying sorties into, out of, within or over the area of eligibility in direct support of the military operations; each day of operations counts as one day of eligibility.

Service members qualified for the Global War on Terrorism Expeditionary Medal by reasons of service between Oct. 24, 2001, and April 30, 2005, in an area for which the Afghanistan Campaign Medal was subsequently authorized and between March 19, 2003, and Feb. 28, 2005, in an area for which the Iraq Campaign Medal was subsequently authorized remain qualified for the medal.

Upon application, any such service member may be awarded the Afghanistan Campaign Medal in lieu of the Global War on Terrorism Expeditionary Medal for such service. No service member shall be entitled to both medals for the same act, achievement or period of service.

Only one award of the Afghanistan Campaign Medal may be authorized for any individual. A bronze service star is worn on the suspension and campaign ribbon for one or more days of participation in each designated campaign phase. The Afghanistan Campaign Medal shall be positioned below the Kosovo Campaign Medal and above the Iraq Campaign Medal. The medal may be awarded posthumously.

On the front of the medal, above a range of mountains is a map of Afghanistan in the center with the inscription, "AFGHANISTAN CAMPAIGN" around the top. On the reverse side on top is a radiating demi-sun superimposed by an eagle's head. Inscribed on the bottom half of the reverse side are three lines, "FOR SERVICE IN AFGHANISTAN" all enclosed by a laurel wreath symbolizing victory.

Phase
Liberation of Afghanistan	Sept.11, 2001	Nov. 30, 2001
Consolidation I	Dec. 1, 2001	Sept. 30, 2006
Consolidation II	Oct. 1, 2006	Nov. 30, 2009
Consolidation III	Dec. 1, 2009	June 30, 2011
Transition I	July 1, 2011	Dec. 31, 2014
Transition II (Note 1)	Jan. 1, 2015	August 31, 2021

Note 1: For Operation FREEDOM's SENTINEL, USD(P&R) memorandum dated February 13, 2015, titled, "Afghanistan Campaign Medal –Operation FREEDOM's SENTINEL and Transition II Campaign Phase."

142 Medals and Ribbons of the U.S. Navy

Iraq Campaign Medal

Bronze

Anodized or Gold-Plated

Miniature Medals

Medal Reverse

Regulation Ribbon Bar

Enamel Lapel Pin

Mini Ribbon (unofficial)

Enamel Hat Pin (unofficial)

Service	All Services
Instituted	2004
Dates	2003 to 31 December 2011
Criteria	Active service in direct support of Operation IRAQI FREEDOM.
Devices	Bronze Star, Silver Star, FMF Globe and Anchor.

On Nov. 29, 2004, Public Law 108-234 and Executive Order 13363 approved the Iraq Campaign Medal (ICM) to recognize service members who are serving or have served in Iraq and the contiguous water area out to 12 nautical miles, and all air spaces above the land and above the contiguous water area out to 12 nautical miles of Iraq.

Eligibility for the ICM requires Navy personnel to have served in direct support of Operation Iraqi Freedom (OIF). The period of eligibility is on or after March 19, 2003 to 31 December 2011. Service members qualified for the Global War on Terrorism Expeditionary Medal (GWOT-EM) by reasons of service between March 19, 2003 and Feb. 28, 2005, in an area for which the ICM was subsequently authorized, shall remain qualified for that medal. Upon application, any such service members may be awarded the ICM in lieu of the GWOT-EM for such service. No service members shall be entitled to both medals for the same deployment, action, achievement or period of service.

Service members must have been assigned, attached or mobilized to units operating in the area of eligibility for 30 consecutive days or for 60 non-consecutive days or meet one of the following criteria:

1) Be engaged in combat during an armed engagement, regardless of the time in the area of eligibility; 2) While participating in an operation or on official duties, is wounded or injured and requires medical evacuation from the area of eligibility; 3) While participating as a regularly assigned aircrew member flying sorties into, out of, within or over the area of eligibility in direct support of the military operations; each day of operations counts as one day of eligibility. The Iraq Campaign Medal may be awarded posthumously.

Only one award of the ICM may be authorized for any individual. In April 2008, the Dept. of Defense authorized service stars to recognize service members for participating in the different campaigns. The Iraq Campaign Medal is positioned below the Afghanistan Campaign Medal and above the Global War on Terrorism Expeditionary Medal.

The medal's obverse features a relief map of Iraq displaying two irregular lines representing the Tigris and Euphrates Rivers surmounting a palm wreath. Above is the inscription, "IRAQ CAMPAIGN". The Statue of Freedom is shown on the reverse surmounting a sunburst, encircle by two scimitars, points down, crossed at the tips of the blades, all above the inscription, "FOR SERVICE IN IRAQ".

A bronze star is worn on the suspension and campaign ribbon for one or more days of participation in each designated campaign phases. A silver campaign service star device is used for participation in five campaigns. Under most circumstances, no personnel or unit should receive the Iraqi Campaign Medal, the Global War on Terrorism Expeditionary Medal (GWOT-EM), the Global War on Terrorism Service Medal (GWOT-SM), or the Armed Forces Expeditionary Medal (AFEM) for the same deployment, action or period of service.

Campaign phases:

Phase	From	To
Liberation of Iraq	19 March 2003	to 1 May 2003
Transition of Iraq	2 May 2003	to 28 June 2004
Iraqi Governance	29 June 2004	to 15 December 2005
National Resolution	16 Dec., 2005	to 9 January 2007
Iraqi Surge	10 January 2007	to 31 December 2008
Iraqi Sovereignty	1 January 2009	to 31 August 2010
New Dawn	1 September 201015	to December 2011

Inherent Resolve Campaign Medal

Regulation Ribbon Bar

Enamel Lapel Pin

Bronze

Medal Reverse

Service	All Services
Instituted	30 march 2016
Dates	15 June, 2014 to TBD
Criteria	Active service in direct support of Operation Inherent Resolve.
Devices	Bronze and Silver Star., FMF Globe and Anchor.

The Inherent Resolve Campaign Medal was established 30 March, 2016. It provides special recognition for members of the Armed Forces serving, or having served, 30 consecutive days or 60 nonconsecutive days in Iraq, Syria, or contiguous waters or airspace on or after 15 June, 2014 to a future date to be determined by the Secretary of Defense. Personnel are also authorized the medal regardless of the time criteria if they were engaged in combat during an armed engagement or while participating in an operation or official duties and were killed or wounded. Aircrew members accrue one day of eligibility for each day they fly into, out of, within, or over the area of engagement.

Previously the Global War on Terror Expeditionary Medal was authorized for service in Iraq and Syria for operation INHERENT RESOLVE ,however, that award is now terminated. Service members who were awarded a GWOT–EM for their Inherent Resolve Campaign Medal qualifying service in Iraq or Syria during the period of 15 June, 2014 to 30 March, 2016 remain qualified for the GWOT–EM. However, service members, may apply to be awarded the IRCM in lieu of the GWOT–EM. Service members can not be awarded both medals for the same qualifying periods.

The Inherent Resolve Campaign Medal is worn after the Iraq Campaign Medal and before the GWOT–EM. The medal is only presented upon initial award and a separate bronze campaign star is worn on the suspension and campaign ribbon to recognize each designated campaign phase in which a member participated for one or more days.

The scorpion, symbolic for treachery and destruction, is found on most major land masses. The dagger alludes to swiftness and determination. The eagle represents the United States and is symbolic of might and victory. The decorated star panels are common in the Arabian and Moorish styles of ornamentation.

The ribbon is blue, teal, sand and orange. This color combination is inspired by the colors of the Middle East landscape and the Ishtar Gate, the eighth gate leading to the historic inner city of Babylon.

Designated Inherent Resolve campaigns are:

Abeyance 15 June 2014 - 24 November 2015
Intensification: 25 November 2015 - TBD

Did You Know? The award distinctly recognizes service members battling terrorist groups in Iraq and Syria. Service members who were killed or were medically evacuated from those countries due to wounds or injuries immediately qualify for the award, as do members who engaged in combat. Previously, the Global War on Terrorism Expeditionary Medal recognized service in Iraq and Syria, and service members in neighboring countries such as Turkey will continue to receive that award.

The president establishes campaign medals for large-scale and long-duration combat actions or operations. Inherent Resolve meets the criteria, officials said. The entire operational area has been subject to lethal combat operations. U.S. forces are executing an extensive air campaign in the region. A U.S. division-plus force is providing command and control, intelligence, and other advisory services.

The award is separate from the Iraq Campaign Medal awarded for service during operations Iraqi Freedom and New Dawn, officials said and is no longer awarded for service in Iraq.

Global War on Terrorism Expeditionary Medal

Instituted	All Services
Dates	2001 to a date to be determined.
Criteria	Active participation in, or support of, Operations ENDURING FREEDOM, IRAQI FREEDOM, NOMAD SHADOW or follow-on operations while deployed abroad for service in the Global War on Terrorism.
Devices	Bronze and Silver Star.

The medal has been redesigned and is slightly smaller in diameter and word medal has been removed from the reverse. Original first medals are still official.

Bronze

Anodized or Gold-Plated

Miniature Medals

1st Medal Reverse

Regulation Ribbon Bar

Enamel Lapel Pin

Mini Ribbon (unofficial)

Enamel Hat Pin (unofficial)

Awarded for deployed service abroad in support of Global War on Terrorism operations on, or after September 11, 2001. The Global War on Terrorism Expeditionary Medal is worn after the Iraq Campaign Medal and before the Global War on Terrorism Service Medal. The Global War on Terrorism Expeditionary Medal was authorized by executive order. The medal is awarded to any member of the Armed Forces who is deployed in an approved operation, such as ENDURING FREEDOM. The Chairman of the Joint Chiefs of Staff has designated the specific area of deployed eligibly per qualifying operation. To be eligible personnel must have participated in the operation by authority of written order. Qualification includes at least 30 consecutive days or 60 nonconsecutive days, or be engaged in actual combat (hostile weapons fire is exchanged), or duty that is equally as hazardous as combat duty, or wounded or injured requiring evacuation from the operation, or while participating as a regularly assigned air crewmember flying sorties into, out of, within or over the are of eligibility in direct support of the military operations.

Personnel may receive both the Global War on Terrorism Expeditionary Medal and the Global War on Terrorism Service Medal if they meet the requirements of both awards; however, service eligibility for one cannot be used to justify service eligibility for the other. The Global War on Terrorism Expeditionary Medal was designed by the Institute of Heraldry. The medal is a circular bronze disc which displays a shield adapted from the Great Seal of the United States surmounting two sword hilts enclosed within a wreath of laurel; overall an eagle, wings displayed, grasping a serpent in its claws. The reverse of the medal displays the eagle, a serpent and swords from the front of the medal within the encircling inscription, "WAR ON TERRORISM EXPEDITIONARY." The ribbon is scarlet, white and blue representing the United States; light blue refers to worldwide cooperation against terrorism; gold denotes excellence. *Effective 2005, the GWOTEM is no longer authorized to be awarded for service in Afghanistan and/or Iraq.*

To date, the Areas of Eligibility associated with the operations ENDURING FREEDOM, IRAQI FREEDOM and NOMAD SHADOW are:

Afghanistan	Jordan	Syria	Gulf of Aden	**Operations**
Bahrain	Kazakhstan	Tajikistan	Gulf of Aqaba	• Enduring Freedom, Sept. 11, 2001 – to be determined.
Bulgaria	Kenya	Turkey (east of 35 degrees east lat.)	Gulf of Oman	• Iraqi Freedom, March 19, 2003-Aug. 31, 2010.
Crete	Kuwait		Gulf of Suez	• Nomad Shadow, Nov. 5, 2007 – to be determined.
Cyprus	Kyrgyzstan	Turkmenistan	That portion of the Mediterranean Sea east of 28 degrees east longitude	• New Dawn, Sept.1, 2010-Dec. 31, 2011.
Diego Garcia	Lebanon	United Arab Emirates		• Inherent Resolve, June 15, 2014 – to be determined
Djibouti	Oman	Uzbekistan		• Freedom's Sentinel, Jan. 1, 2015 – Aug. 31, 2021.
Egypt	Pakistan	Yemen		• Odyssey Lightning Aug. 1, 2016 – Jan. 17, 2017.
Eritrea	Philippines	That portion of the Arabian Sea north of 10 degrees north latitude and west of 68 degrees longitude	Persian Gulf	• Operation Prosperity Guardian, Dec. 18, 2023 – to be determined.
Ethiopia	Qatar		Red Sea	
Iran	Romania			• Operation Poseidon ArcherJan. 1, 2015 – TBD.
Iraq (Removed)	Saudi Arabia		Strait of Hormuz	• Operation Pandora Throttle, Jan. 18, 2024 – TBD.
Israel	Somalia	Bab el Mandeb	Suez Canal	

Global War on Terrorism Service Medal

Awarded to members of the United States Armed Forces who participated in, or served in support of operations relating to the Global War on Terrorism between September 11, 2001 and a date to be determined at a later date. The medal was established by an executive order signed by President George W. Bush on October 28, 2003. Initial award of the Global War on Terrorism Service Medal was limited to Airport Security Operations from September 27, 2001 until May 31, 2002 and to Service members who supported Operations ENDURING FREEDOM, NOBLE EAGLE and IRAQI FREEDOM.

Qualifying service members must be assigned, attached or mobilized to a unit participating in or service in direct support of designated for 30 consecutive days or 60 nonconsecutive days. It is to be noted that eligibility for the Global War on Terrorism Service Medal is defined as support for the War on Terrorism in a non-deployed status, whether stationed at home or overseas. By contrast, service in an operationally deployed status abroad within a designated area of eligibility merits primary eligibility for the Global War on Terrorism Expeditionary Medal. Personnel may receive both the Global War on Terrorism Service and Expeditionary Medals if they meet the requirements of both awards. However, the qualifying period for one cannot be used to justify eligibility for the other.

Establishing the award of the GWOT-SM for general support of the war on terror makes the medal similar to the award of the National Defense Service Medal. The major difference between the National Defense Service Medal and GWOT-SM is that the NDSM is authorized when an individual joins the Armed Forces and the GWOT-SM is only authorized after 30 days of active service or 60 days non consecutive service for reserve forces. Although qualifying circumstances would be extremely rare, Battle Stars may be applicable for personnel who were engaged in actual combat against the enemy under circumstances involving grave danger of death or serious bodily injury from enemy action.

The Global War on Terrorism Service Medal was designed by the Institute of Heraldry. The medal is a circular bronze disc which displays an eagle, wings displayed, with a stylized shield of thirteen vertical bars on its breast and holding in dexter claw an olive branch and in sinister claw three arrows, all in front of a terrestrial globe with the inscription above, "WAR ON TERRORISM SERVICE." The reverse of the medal displays a laurel wreath on a plain field. The ribbon is scarlet, white and blue representing the United States; gold denoting excellence.

The Original Medal

The new version of the medal has been redesigned and is slightly smaller in diameter and word "medal" has been removed from the front. The original issued medals are still official and are issued until the current stock is exhausted. As it was first it is more desirable than a restrike.

146 Medals and Ribbons of the U.S. Navy

Korea Defense Service Medal

Service	All Services
Instituted	2003
Dates	1954 to date TBD
Criteria	For service in the Republic of Korea, or the waters adjacent thereto, for a qualifying period of time between 28 July, 1954 and a date to be determined.
Devices	None

Bronze

Anodized or Gold-Plated

Miniature Medals

Regulation Ribbon Bar

Medal Reverse

Enamel Lapel Pin

Mini Ribbon (unofficial)

Enamel Hat Pin (unofficial)

The Korea Defense Service Medal is authorized for Armed Forces members who served in support of the defense of the Republic of Korea after the signing of the Korean Armistice Agreement. To qualify a service member must serve at least 30 consecutive days in the Korean theater. The medal is also awarded for 60 non-consecutive days of service to include reservists on annual training in Korea.

Exceptions are made for the time requirement if a service member participated in a combat armed engagement, was wounded or injured in the line of duty requiring medical evacuation, or participated as a regularly assigned aircrew member in flying sorties which totaled more than 30 days of duty in Korean airspace. In such cases, the KDSM is authorized regardless of time served in theater.

The medal is retroactive to the end of the Korean War and is granted for any service performed after July 28, 1954. An official exception to policy entitles military personnel to both the Armed Forces Expeditionary Medal, and the KDSM for being in operations in Korea between October 1, 1966 - June 30, 1974. Only one award of the Korea Defense Service Medal is authorized, regardless of the time served in the Korean theater. The Korea Defense Service Medal is worn after the Global War on Terrorism Service Medal and before the Armed Forces Service Medal.

Designed by John Sproston of the Institute of Heraldry, the medal is a bronze disc with a Korean circle dragon within a scroll inscribed, "KOREA DEFENSE SERVICE" with two sprigs of laurel at the base. The four-clawed dragon is a traditional Korean symbol representing intelligence and strength of purpose. The sprig of laurel denotes honorable endeavor and victory, the bamboo refers to the land of Korea. The reverse displays two swords placed over a map of Korea to signify defense of freedom and the readiness to engage in combat. The enclosing circlet represents the five-petal symbols common in Korean armory.

The dark green ribbon represents the land of Korea, blue indicates overseas service and commitment to achieving peace. Gold denotes excellence, white symbolizes idealism and integrity.

The Original Medal

The Institute of Heraldry changed the specifications for the Korea Defense Service Medal. At first glance you might not notice the change, but the new medals being manufactured have a slightly different look and the word medal has been removed from the front of the medallion. The original medal is still authorized for wear and may still be issued as long as they are in the supply system.

Armed Forces Service Medal

Service	All Services
Instituted	1995
Dates	1995 to Present
Criteria	Participation in military operations not covered by a specific war medal or the Armed Forces Expeditionary Medal.
Devices	Bronze, Silver Star.

Authorized on January 11, 1996 for U.S. military personnel who, on or after June 1, 1992, participate in a U.S. military operation deemed to be a significant activity in which no foreign armed opposition or imminent hostile action is encountered and for which no previous U.S. service medal is authorized. The medal can be awarded to service members in direct support of the United Nations or North Atlantic Treaty Organization and for assistance operations to friendly nations. The initial awards of this medal were for operations that have occurred in the Balkans since 1992. Qualifications include at least one day of participation in the designated area. Direct support of the operation and aircraft flights within the area also qualify for award of this medal as long as at least one day is served within the designated area.

The Chairman, Joint Chiefs of Staff approved the award of the AFSM *(JCF)*:

(1) For operations inthe former Republic of Yugoslavia from 1 June 1992 to a future date. This area includes military forces deployed in operations Provide Promise, Joint Endeavor, Able Sentry, Deny Flight, Maritime Monitor, Sharp Guard and Joint Guard within the total land and air space of the former Republic of Yugoslavia, the country of Italy *(including Sicily)*; and the waters and air space above a portion of the Adriatic Sea north of forty degrees atitude;

(2) Operations: United Nations Missions in Haiti *(UNMIH)*; US Forces Haiti *(USFORHAITI)* and US Support Group-Haiti *(USSPTGP-Haiti)* from 1 April 1995 to a date to be determined. This area includes the total land area, sea and air space along the Haitian/Dominican Republic Border.

The front of the medal contains the torch of liberty within its center and contains the inscription "ARMED FORCES SERVICE" around its periphery. The reverse of the medal depicts the American eagle with the U.S. shield in its chest and spread wings clutching three arrows in its talons encircled by a laurel wreath and the inscription, "IN PURSUIT OF DEMOCRACY." Bronze and silver service stars are worn to denote additional awards.

The Original Medal

The Institute of Heraldry redesigned the Armed Forces Service Medal. The change to the AFSM is one of 4 medals: GWOT-EM, GWOT-SM and the Korea Defense Service Medal that the Institution of Heraldry has made minor modifications to and removed the word "Medal" Unless you compare the original medal first authorized in 1995 with the new ones being struck you might not notice the change. The original medal is still authorized for wear and may still be issued as long as they remain in the supply system.

Did You Know? The **Armed Forces Service Medal** was originally intended to complement the Armed Forces Expeditionary Medal. The primary difference between the two is that the Armed Forces Service Medal is awarded for actions "through which no foreign armed opposition or imminent threat of hostile action was encountered." This definition separates the two medals in that the Armed Forces Expeditionary Medal is normally awarded for combat operations and other combat support missions.

Humanitarian Service Medal

Service	All Services
Instituted	1977
Dates	1975 to Present
Criteria	Direct participation in specific operations of a humanitarian nature.
Devices	Bronze, Silver Star, Bronze Numeral.

Bronze

Anodized or Gold-Plated

Miniature Medals

Regulation Ribbon Bar

Medal Reverse

Enamel Lapel Pin

Mini Ribbon (unofficial)

Enamel Hat Pin (unofficial)

Note: *All branches now use Coast Guard placement of stars.*

Authorized on January 19, 1977 and awarded to Armed Forces personnel *(including Reserve components)* who, after April 1, 1975, distinguish themselves by meritorious direct participation in a DOD-approved significant military act or operation of a humanitarian nature. According to regulations, the participation must be "hands-on" at the site of the operation; personnel assigned to staff functions geographically separated from the operation are not eligible for this medal. Service members must be assigned and/or attached to participating units for specific operations by official orders. Members who were present for duty at specific qualifying locations for the medal but who did not make a direct contribution to the action or operation are specifically excluded from eligibility. It should be noted that some of the earliest recipients of the Humanitarian Service Medal, e.g., for the evacuations of Laos, Cambodia and Vietnam, would more likely be awarded the Armed Forces Service Medal in today's environment.

The medal was designed by Mr. Jim Hammond and sculptured by Mr. Jay Morris of the Institute of Heraldry. The front of the medal depicts a human right hand with open palm within a raised circle. At the top of the medal's reverse is the raised inscription, "FOR HUMANITARIAN SERVICE" set in three lines. In the center is an oak branch with three acorns and leaves and, below this, is the raised circular inscription, "UNITED STATES ARMED FORCES" around the lower edge of the medal. The ribbon is medium blue with a wide center stripe of navy blue. It is edged by a wide stripe of purple which is separated from the light blue field by a narrow white stripe. Bronze and silver stars are authorized for additional awards. This medal may not be presented if either the Armed Forces Service Medal or Armed Forces Expeditionary Medal was presented for the same period of service.

Outstanding Volunteer Service Medal

Bronze

Anodized or Gold-Plated

Miniature Medals

Medal Reverse

Regulation Ribbon Bar

Enamel Lapel Pin

Mini Ribbon (unofficial)

Enamel Hat Pin (unofficial)

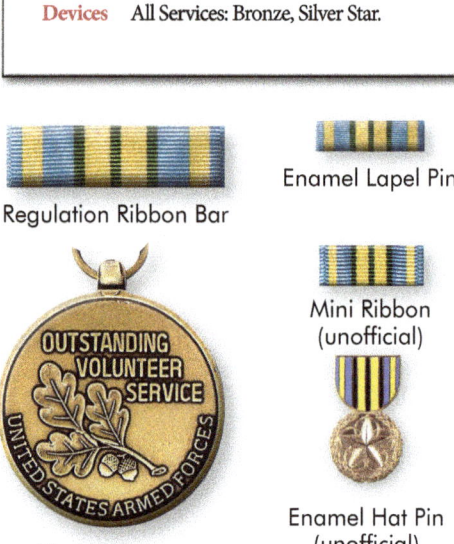

Service	All Services
Instituted	1993
Dates	1993 to Present
Criteria	Awarded for outstanding and sustained voluntary service to the civilian community.
Devices	All Services: Bronze, Silver Star.

The Military Outstanding Volunteer Service Medal was authorized in 1993 to members of the U.S. Armed Forces and reserve components and is awarded for outstanding and sustained voluntary service to the civilian community after December 31, 1992. It may be awarded to active duty and reserve members who perform outstanding volunteer service over time as opposed to a single event. The service performed must have been to the civilian community and must be strictly voluntary and not duty-related.

The volunteerism must be of a sustained and direct nature and must be significant and produce tangible results while reflecting favorably on the Armed Forces and the Department of Defense. There are no specific time requirements as to how many hours must be spent on the volunteer activity, but the activity should consist of significant action and involvement rather than, for example, simply attending meetings as a member of a community service group. The definition of volunteer service is left intentionally vague, allowing for a wide variety of activities and volunteer duties which would qualify a service member for the Military Outstanding Volunteer Service Medal. Since the award is classified as a service medal, there is no citation which accompanies the award, however some commanders present a personal letter to Sailors who receive the Military Outstanding Volunteer Service Medal. Multiple awards of the MOVSM are denoted by service stars An individual would normally be considered for only one award during an assignment.

The front of the bronze medal has a five-pointed star with a circular ring over each point; the star, a symbol of the military and representing outstanding service, is encircled by a laurel wreath which represents honor and achievement. The reverse has an oak leaf branch, symbolic of strength and potential, with three oak leaves and two acorns along with the inscriptions, "OUTSTANDING VOLUNTEER SERVICE," and "UNITED STATES ARMED FORCES." Bronze and silver stars are authorized to denote additional awards.

Navy Sea Service Deployment Ribbon

The Navy Sea Service Deployment Ribbon (SSDR) was approved by the Secretary of the Navy in 1981 and made retroactive to August 15, 1974. The ribbon was created to recognize the unique and demanding nature of sea service and the arduous duty attendant with such service deployments. The award is made to Navy and Marine Corps personnel for twelve months of accumulated sea duty or duty with the Fleet Marine Force, which includes at least one, ninety day deployment.

The ribbon consists of a wide center stripe of light blue, bordered on either side by a narrow stripe of medium blue and equal stripes of gold, red and navy blue. Additional

Service	Navy, Marine Corps
Instituted	1981 (retroactive to 1974)
Criteria	12 months active duty on deployed vessels operating away from their home port for extended periods
Devices	Bronze, Silver Star

awards are denoted by three-sixteenth inch bronze stars. The Sea Service Deployment Ribbon is worn after the Outstanding Volunteer Service Medal and before the Navy Arctic Service Ribbon.

Navy Arctic Service Ribbon

The Navy Arctic Service Ribbon was established by the Secretary of the Navy on May 8, 1986 and authorized for wear on June 3, 1987. The ribbon is awarded to members of the Naval Service who participate in operations in support of the Arctic Warfare Program. To be eligible, the individual must have served 28 days north of, or within 50 miles of the Marginal Ice Zone (MIZ). The MIZ is defined as an area consisting of more than 10% ice concentration. The ribbon is medium blue with a narrow center stripe of navy blue flanked on either side by three thin stripes of gradually lighter shades of blue, a narrow stripe of white, followed again by two thin stripes of gradually darker shades of blue.

Service	Navy, Marine Corps
Instituted	1986
Criteria	28 days of service on naval vessels operating above the Arctic Circle.
Devices	None

There are no provisions for additional awards. The Navy Arctic Service Ribbon is worn after the Navy Sea Service Deployment Ribbon and before the Naval Reserve Sea Service Ribbon. The Ribbon is considered a seperate award from the Artic Service Medal.

Navy Arctic Service Medal

MINIATURE

REVERSE

Service	Navy, Marine Corps
Instituted	1 Jan. 1982
Criteria	28 days of service on naval vessels operating above the Arctic Circle.
Devices	North Star, Compass Rose

Designed by the crew of the USS HARTFORD (SSN 768) during ICEX 2018 to recognize the unique sacrifices and circumstances involved in operating under ice for prolonged periods beyond those experienced by crews operating in arctic areas. Awarded as an extension of the Navy Arctic Service Ribbon to officers and enlisted personnel of the Navy and Marine Corps or civilians of units who have been assigned to a unit that conducted an ice-covered strait transit, such as the Bering Strait or Barrow Strait, or a unit that conducted a transit of the North Pole. It is also awarded for those assigned to a submarine that conducted a vertical surfacing through ice, or a submarine that conducted at least seven days of military operations while under the marginal ice zone or pack ice and those who were assigned to an ice camp or an operations center set up on an ice floe.

The medal is a silver disc, with a representation of the Arctic Circle bearing at center the North Star and at top a scroll bearing the inscriptions "ARCTIC" on the upper portion and "SERVICE" on the lower portion. The reverse inscription "FOR SERVICE INVOLVING SIGNIFICANT OPERATIONS IN HIGH LATITUDE REGIONS ABOVE THE ARCTIC CIRCLE," with three icebergs in the Arctic Sea under the Big Dipper constellation. First award is indicated by a North Star device with up to four North Star/Compass Rose devices are allowed.

Naval Reserve Sea Service Deployment Ribbon

The Naval Reserve Sea Service Deployment Ribbon (NRSSDR) was authorized by the Secretary of the Navy on May 28, 1986. It is awarded to officer and enlisted personnel of the U.S. Navy and Naval Reserve who perform active duty or Selected Reserve service, or any combination of active or Selected Reserve service after August 15, 1974 aboard a Naval Reserve ship or its Reserve unit or an embarked active or Reserve staff, for a cumulative total of 24 months. Qualifying ship duty includes duty in a self-propelled Naval Reserve ship, boat or craft operated under the operational control of fleet or type commanders. Selected Reserve duty with staffs which regularly embark in such Naval Reserve

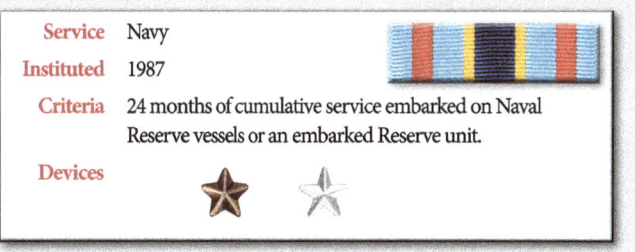

Service	Navy
Instituted	1987
Criteria	24 months of cumulative service embarked on Naval Reserve vessels or an embarked Reserve unit.
Devices	

ships, craft, or boats, is also qualifying provided at least 50 percent of the drills performed for each creditable period have been underway drills. A 3/16 inch bronze star denotes a subsequent award.

Navy and Marine Corps Overseas Service Ribbon

The Navy and Marine Corps Overseas Service Ribbon (OSR) was approved by the Secretary of the Navy on June 3, 1987 and made retroactive to August 15, 1974. The award is made to active duty members of the Naval Service who serve 12 months consecutive or accumulated active duty at an overseas duty station; or 30 consecutive days or 45 cumulative days of active duty for training or temporary active duty.

The ribbon was originally intended to recognize individuals who serve overseas, but are not members of ships, squadrons or detachments of the Fleet Marine Force and do not qualify for the Navy Sea Service Deployment Ribbon. However, as of Dec 1, 1999, members of the U.S. Navy may receive the award for active duty at an overseas sea or shore based duty station. Note that the original award requirement *(shore-based duty only)* remains in place for U.S. Marine Corps personnel. The Navy and Marine Corps Overseas Service Ribbon is worn after the Naval Reserve Sea Service Deployment Ribbon and before the Navy Recruiting Service Ribbon (USN) or Marine Corps Recruiting Ribbon (USMC). Additional awards are denoted by three-sixteenth inch bronze stars.

Service	Navy, Marine Corps
Instituted	1987
Criteria	12 months consecutive or accumulated duty at an overseas duty station. *(Navy: sea or shore base; Marine Corps: shore base only)*
Devices	Bronze, Silver Star

Navy Recruiting Service Ribbon

The Navy Recruiting Service Ribbon (RS) was established in 1986 (retroactive to August 15, 1974) and is awarded for successful completion of three consecutive years of recruiting duty. The ribbon is gold with navy blue stripes near the borders and at the center. The blue center stripe has a thin red stripe and is bordered by stripes of light green on either side. A bronze numeral is worn to denote the total number of Gold Wreath awards for superior productivity. Additional individual awards are denoted by three-sixteenth inch bronze and silver service stars.

Service	Navy
Instituted	1989 retoactive to 1973
Criteria	Successful completion of 3 consecutive years of recruiting duty.
Devices	

Navy Accession Training Service Ribbon

The Navy Acession Training Service Ribbon was established in 1998 (retroactive to 1995) and is awarded for successful service as a Navy Recruit Division Commander (RDC) and training at least nine divisions over a minimum tour of three years. The ribbon has a broad scarlet center with equal-sized blue stripes on either side and gold edges. The Navy Acession Training Service Ribbon is worn after the Navy Recruiting Service Ribbon and before the Ceremonial Duty Ribbon. Additional awards are denoted by three-sixteenth inch bronze and silver stars.

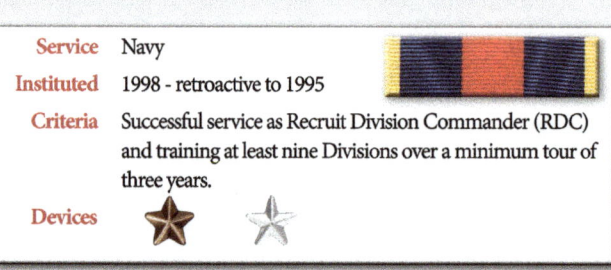

Service	Navy
Instituted	1998 - retroactive to 1995
Criteria	Successful service as Recruit Division Commander (RDC) and training at least nine Divisions over a minimum tour of three years.
Devices	

Navy Ceremonial Duty Ribbon

The Navy Ceremonial Duty Ribbon was established in 2003 and is awarded to Naval personnel who successfully complete a tour of duty as members of a Ceremonial Guard unit. The ribbon has equal stripes of dark blue, golden yellow and white (from outboard to inboard) with a narrow silver-gray center stripe. The Navy Ceremonial Duty Ribbon is worn after the Navy Acession Training Service Ribbon and before the Armed Forces Reserve Medal. Additional awards are denoted by three-sixteenth inch bronze and silver stars.

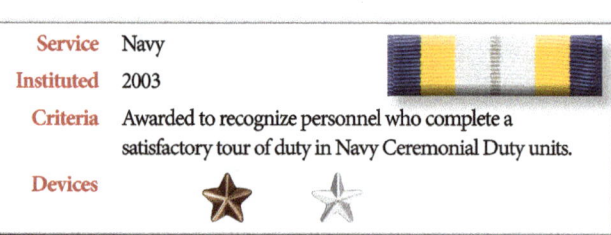

Service	Navy
Instituted	2003
Criteria	Awarded to recognize personnel who complete a satisfactory tour of duty in Navy Ceremonial Duty units.
Devices	

Navy Basic Military Training Honor Graduate Ribbon

The Navy basic Military Training Honor Graduate Ribbon is awarded to recruits for superb performance during basic military training, in academics, physical fitness, recruit leadership and commitment to the Navy core values of honor, courage and commitment. No more than three percent of each training group are designated as honor graduates.

Service	Navy
Instituted	2015
Criteria	Awarded to recruits for superb performance during basic military training.
Devices	None

Armed Forces Reserve Medal

Service	All Services
Instituted	1950
Criteria	10 years of honorable service in any reserve component of the United States Armed Forces Reserve or award of "M" device.
Devices	Bronze, Silver and Gold Hourglass, Bronze Letter "M", Bronze Numeral.

Bronze

Anodized or Gold-Plated

Miniature Medals

Regulation Ribbon Bar

Medal Reverse

Enamel Lapel Pin

Mini Ribbon (unofficial)

Enamel Hat Pin (unofficial)

Authorized in 1950 for 10 years of honorable and satisfactory service within a 12 year period as a member of one or more of the Reserve Components of the Armed Forces of the United States. The medal recognizes service performed by members of the reserve components and is awarded to both officers and enlisted personnel. The medal is considered a successor award to the Naval Reserve Medal and the Marine Corps Reserve Ribbon, which were discontinued in 1958 and 1967 respectively.

An executive order of Aug. 8, 1996 authorized the award of a bronze letter "M" mobilization device to U.S. reserve component members who were called to active-duty service in support of designated operations on or after August 1, 1990 *(the M device was not authorized for any operations prior to August 1, 1990 although it had been previously proposed)*. Units called up in support of Operations Desert Storm/Desert Shield were the first units to be authorized the "M" device. If an "M" is authorized, the medal is awarded even though service might be less than 10 years. Previous to this change, only bronze hourglasses were awarded at each successive 10 year point *(first hourglass at the 20 year point)*.

The front of the medal depicts a flaming torch placed vertically between a crossed bugle and powder horn; thirteen stars and thirteen rays surround the design. The front of the medal is the same for all services; only the reverse design is different *(see designs on next page)*. Bronze numerals beginning with "2" are worn to the right of the bronze "M" on the ribbon bar and below the "M" on the medal, indicating the total number of times the individual was mobilized. Bronze, silver and gold hourglasses are awarded for 10, 20 and 30 years service, respectively.

(Continued on next page)

The different services medal reverses are shown here:

Army
has a Minuteman in front of a circle with 13 stars representing the original colonies.

Navy
has a sailing ship with an anchor on its front with an eagle with wings spread superimposed upon it.

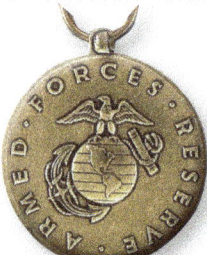
Marine Corps
has the USMC emblem, eagle, globe and anchor.

Coast Guard
has the Coast Guard emblem, crossed anchor with the Coast Guard shield in the center.

National Guard
has the National Guard insignia on the reverse, an eagle with crossed fasces in its center.

The ribbon to the Armed Forces Reserve Medal consists of a buff background bisected by a blue center stripe. There are three additional blue pinstripes at each edge, one of them forming the edge stripes of the ribbon itself. Buff and blue were selected because they are Colonial colors and represent the spirit of the Minutemen who responded to the call to service against the British during the Revolutionary War. If the medal is awarded for periods of service, it is accompanied by an hourglass device. Depending on the length of service, a bronze, silver, gold, or bronze and gold hourglass are worn on the suspension ribbon and service ribbon, indicating 10, 20, 30, or 40 years of service respectively.

If the medal is awarded in connection with a mobilization, it is accompanied by an "M" device. Subsequent mobilizations under an unrelated presidential call-up order result in a numeral device being worn to indicate the number of mobilizations. *See section on ribbon and devices for details on devices.*

For service – the Hourglass device

In the Naval Reserve, members of the Individual Ready Reserve are eligible for the medal after 10 years of service. Periods of service for the Armed Forces Reserve Medal are denoted through the use of the hourglass device. The length of the period for which the Armed Forces Reserve Medal is awarded is indicated using a bronze hourglass, silver hourglass, gold hourglass, or bronze and gold hourglasses together.

The initial presentation of the Armed Forces Reserve Medal is authorized with the bronze hourglass device denoting ten years of reserve service. At twenty years of service, the hourglass is upgraded to silver and at thirty years the hourglass becomes gold. For those who complete forty years of reserve service, a gold and bronze hourglass device are worn simultaneously. This is the only case where hourglasses are worn together; in all other cases the hourglass device is upgraded to the next higher award degree and is worn as a single device.

The left hand medal shows a Navy Reservist mobilized for active service in Operation Desert Storm and Iraq. His Bronze hourglass indicates over 10 years Reserve Service and "M" device with the numeral 2 shows two mobilization. The right hand medal shows a Navy reservist mobilized for active service three times and his silver hour class indicates 20 years Reserve Service. The right hand medal has the devices mounted vertically in order for the devices to be viewable when over lapping medals will cover devices mounted horizontally.

Naval Reserve Medal *(Obsolete)*

This medal was authorized on September 12, 1938, and awarded to officers and enlisted men of the Naval Reserve who had completed ten years of satisfactory federal service in the U.S. Naval Reserve. Eligibility ceased during a time of war or national emergency if called to active duty. After the establishment of the Armed Forces Reserve Medal in 1950, a Naval Reservist who was eligible for the Naval Reserve Medal and the Armed Forces Reserve Medal could elect which award he was to receive. The Naval Reserve Medal was terminated on September 12, 1958 and now only the Armed Forces Reserve Medal is awarded. The obverse of the Naval Reserve Medal shows an eagle in an attitude of defiance, facing left, with wings raised. The eagle is perched on an anchor, flukes down to the left. The reverse of the medal is flat, with the inscription, "UNITED STATES NAVAL RESERVE" encircling the outer edge. At the bottom is a large star and the words, "FAITHFUL SERVICE" centered in two lines. A bronze star was authorized for each additional ten years of qualifying service. However there is little likelihood that a device was ever earned since a potential recipient would have to spend the total life span of the medal *(twenty years)* in the Naval Reserve during both World War II and the Korean Conflict.

Service: Navy
Instituted: 1938
Dates: 1938-58
Criteria: 10 years of honorable service in the U.S. Naval Reserve.
Devices:

Notes: Replaced by the Armed Forces Reserve Medal. Some earlier versions had deep red ("plum") ribbon.

Award of Foreign Military Decorations

Authorized foreign decorations for wear by United States Marines are those military decorations which have been approved for wear by the Department of Defense but whose awarding authority is a foreign government. French and British and other Allies decorations were presented to U.S. service members extensively during World War I and World War II. In World War I and II the French and Belgium Croix de Guerre was the most commonly awarded decoration to United States service members of all ranks.

Republic of Vietnam military awards (South Vietnam decorations) were first awarded to United States service members beginning around 1964. The Vietnamese Gallantry Cross and the Vietnamese Civil Actions Medal were awarded to many U.S. servicemen for heroism and meritorious service.

Foreign campaign medals and unit awards have also been awarded U.S. military personnel. Those that were commonly awarded to all U.S. military personnel and are covered in the following pages.

The French Croix de Guerre was instituted in 1915 and was awarded to Marines, Soldiers and Sailors of all ranks in the French and Allied forces for individual feats of arms mentioned in despatches by the commanding officer of any unit from an Army down to a Regiment.

Republic of Vietnam Personal Decorations

RVN Navy Distinguished Service Order

Hải-Quân Huân-Chương
two classes — June 5, 1964

Purpose: For citations and wounds in combat or line of duty, or exceptional achievements that reflect great credit or benefit to the Navy in any field.

Description: Front: an eight-pointed silver star with a gold wreath underneath, and in the center a gold disk with crossed anchors and a traditional stylized grenade, and around a dark blue ribbon inscribed HẢI-QUÂN HUÂN-CHƯƠNG in gold, 45mm; Back: stamped VIỆT-NAM in a lined circle with HẢI-QUÂN HUÂN-CHƯƠNG around. The suspension ribbon is an odd embroidered design of two pieces that cross each other three times, the one on the left at the top being white, and on the right being blue, ending up with a hanging thread fringe of the colors on the opposite side. The service bar is yellow with an embroidered design like an M on top of a W, with the lines that slope down to the right in blue and those that rise to the right in white.

First Class
Description: There is a rosette on the suspension ribbon and on the service bar.
Second Class
Description: Ribbon is without a rosette.

Background: This was for senior Vietnamese and Allied naval officers and was received by a number of American admirals. The US-made version is entirely gold with a thinner wreath, indented central disk, and larger letters on the ribbon around the disk; the rosette is smaller and placed at the top instead of the middle of the suspension. A Japanese-made version is closely similar to the Vietnamese-made one, but more finely made. The star design is the traditional navy compass rose.

Rarity: First Class R-6; Second Class R-5

Navy DSO 1st Class American made

Navy DSO 2d Class Vietnamese made

RVN Navy Gallantry Cross

Hải-Dũng Bội-Tinh
three grades — June 5, 1964

Purpose: For servicemen of the Navy for coolness and heroism while the vessel was underway and in distress due to a technical failure, foul weather or combat.

Description: Front: cross-like four spear points with smaller pointed and lined rays between, in gold, with central disk of blue with anchor and Vietnamese national flag design shield, surrounded with ribbon with inscription HẢI-DŨNG BỘI-TINH, 37mm. Back: the inscription VIỆTNAM in a lined circle with a rim of thin lines radiating outwards. The ribbon is blue 12mm, white 12mm, blue 12mm.

Gold Anchor or First Class
Description: The device is a gold anchor on both the suspension ribbon and service bar.
Silver Anchor or Second Class
Description: The device is a silver anchor on both the suspension ribbon and service bar.
Bronze Anchor or Third Class
Description: The device is a bronze anchor on both the suspension ribbon and service bar.

Background: The US-made version is flattish and has a fixed suspension, rather large lettering, and neater, if scrawnier looking, enamel work in the center. The US-version sometimes comes with ribbon with unbound edges. The anchors designated the citation level similar to the Gallantry Cross. It was also intended for civilian and allied personnel with the Navy.

Rarity: R-4

RVN Armed Forces Honor Medal *January 7, 1953*

First Class   Second Class

Miniature Medals

Medal Reverse

Purpose: Presented by the Republic of Vietnam for contributions to the formation and organization of the Armed Forces and the training of troops and technical cadres of the various branches. It was intended for non-combat achievements.

Description: Front: a cross formee couped with additional points reflected down the arms and with thin blade points coming between the arms, and in the central disk, a coiled dragon with a ribbon around inscribed, with a wreath of oak leaves around the design of the cross arms, 38mm. Back: plain. Suspension is by a laurel wreath.

First Class
Purpose: For officers.
Description: Gold. The ribbon is yellow 1°mm, red 6mm, yellow 3mm, light blue 3mm, yellow 3mm, light blue 3mm, yellow 3mm, light blue 3mm, yellow 3mm, red 6mm, yellow 1° mm. Device on the service bar is a gold eagle with shield on breast and holding swords.

Second Class
Purpose: For Petty Officers and enlisted men.
Description: Silver. The ribbon is 7°mm, yellow 3mm, light blue 3mm, yellow 3mm, light blue 3mm, yellow 3mm, light blue 3mm, yellow 3mm, red 7°mm. Device on the service bar is a silver eagle with shield on its breast and holding swords. This medal without the ribbon devices was widely presented to U.S. officers and men after six months staff service in combat or non combat units. The award was originally entitled in French as *La Medaille du Merite Vietnamien* and was intended for "French or foreign military men who participate in the capacity of advisors or contribute to organization of the Army."

RVN Staff Service Medal   Two classes — *May 12, 1964*

Purpose: Presented by the Republic of Vietnam for staff service to the Armed Forces evidencing outstanding initiative and devotion to duty.

Description: Front: A square fortress design, with bastions at each point, suspended from one point, with a sword and writing brush crossing underneath, and in the center a blue diamond with gold crossed rifles, wings and anchor symbol of the Armed Forces, 40mm.

First Class Purpose: For officers.
Description: The ribbon is green 3mm, diagonal red 7mm and white 3mm stripes 30mm, green 3mm.

Second Class Purpose: For NCO's and enlisted men.
Description: The ribbon is blue 3mm, diagonal red 7mm and white 3mm stripes 30mm, blue 3mm.

First Class   Second Class

Background: This was widely given to American advisors. The U.S. made version closely resembles the Vietnamese-made ones; one small detail of difference is that the sword and pen of the U.S. made one has a more squarish shape in contrast to the more sculptured shape of the Vietnamese-made one. It normally required at least six months duty with a Vietnamese unit for award to allied personnel. It is also occasionally referred to as the Staff Service Honor Medal.

RVN Technical Service Medal Two classes — *June 5, 1964*

Anodized or Gold-Plated — Miniature Medal

Purpose: Presented by the Republic of Vietnam for military servicemen and civilians working as military technicians who have shown outstanding professional capacity, initiative, and devotion to duty.

Description: Front: gold, four aircraft propeller blades, 50mm across, interspersed with four ship's propeller blades, and between those eight white enameled rays, inside a planchet shaped as a gear, and in the center on a blue-green background—the Armed Forces insignia of wings, crossed rifles, and an anchor.

First Class Purpose: For officers.

Description: The ribbon is silver grey 5mm, red 2mm, silver grey 20mm, red 2mm, silver grey 5mm, and in the center two thread-like red stripes 1mm apart.

Second Class Purpose: For NCO's and enlisted men.

Description: The ribbon is the same except without the two thread-like red stripes in the center.

Background: This was also frequently awarded to American advisors. It is occasionally called the Technical Service Honor Medal.

RVN Training Service Medal Two classes — *May 12, 1964*

First Class — Second Class

Purpose: Presented by the Republic of Vietnam for instructors and cadres at military schools and training centers and civilians and foreigners who contribute significantly to training.

Description: Gold rectangle, 20mm wide and 50mm high. Front: sword surmounted with open book and with inscription at bottom.

First Class Purpose: For officers.

Description: The ribbon is white 3mm, pink 9mm, white 11mm with two thread-like pink stripes 1mm apart in center, pink 9mm, white 3mm.

Second Class Purpose: For NCO's and enlisted men.

Description: The ribbon is the same as the First Class, but without the two thread-like pink stripes in the center.

Background: It is occasionally called the Training Service Honor Medal.

RVN Civil Actions Medal   *Two classes — May 12 1964*

Purpose: Presented by the Republic of Vietnam for outstanding achievements in the field of civil affairs.

Description: Front: eight-pointed gold star, with the points on the diagonal being smooth and long and the points on the horizontal and vertical being a little shorter and with cut lines, and in the center a brown disk with the figure of a soldier, a child, and a farmer with a shovel, surrounded with a white ribbon inscribed above with many short lines between, 30mm. Back: plain.

First Class Purpose: For officers.

Description: The ribbon is green 2mm, red 5mm, green 22mm with two thin thread-like red stripes in center 1mm apart, red 5mm, green 2mm.

Second Class Purpose: For NCO's and enlisted men.

Description: The ribbon is the same but without the two thread-like red stripes in center.

Unit Award Description: The ribbon is the same as for the First Class. It is in a gold frame with a leaf pattern.

Background: Particularly as a unit award, this was widely bestowed on the American forces in Vietnam. One US-made version closely resembles the Vietnamese-made ones except that the central disk is higher, the enamel neater, the gold brighter, and the reverse plain. It is occasionally called the Civic Actions Honor Medal.

Anodized or Gold-Plated

Medal Reverse

Regulation Ribbon Bar

1st Class

2nd Class

Notes: *1st Class for officers is shown; the 2nd Class ribbon has no center red stripes.*

Foreign Unit Awards

Philippine Republic Presidential Unit Citation

Service All Services
Instituted 1948
Devices None
Criteria Awarded to units of the U.S. Armed Forces for service in the war against Japan and/or for 1970 and 1972 disaster relief.

Korean Republic Presidential Unit Citation

Service All Services
Instituted 1951
Devices None
Criteria Awarded to certain units of the U.S. Armed Forces for services rendered during the Korean War.

Republic of Vietnam Presidential Unit Citation

Service Army/Navy/Marine Corps/Coast Guard
Instituted 1954
Devices None
Criteria Awarded to certain units of the U.S. Armed Forces for humanitarian service in the evacuation of civilians from North and Central Vietnam.

Republic of Vietnam Gallantry Cross Unit Citation

Service All Services
Instituted 1966
Devices
Criteria Awarded to certain units of the U.S. Armed Forces for valorous combat achievement during the Vietnam War, 1 March 1961 to 28 March 1974.

Republic of Vietnam Civil Actions Unit Citation

Service All Services
Instituted 1966
Devices
Criteria Awarded to certain units of the U.S. Armed Forces for meritorious service during the Vietnam War, 1 March 1961 to 28 March 1974.

Foreign Campaign Medals

The next section covers approved foreign campaign medals for wear. The period covers from World War II to present and the medals are shown in the Navy order of precedence:

- **Philippine Defense Medal**
- **Philippine Liberation Medal**
- **Philippine Independence Medal**
- **United Nations Medal Korea**
- **United Nations Medals**
- **NATO Medals**
- **Multinational Force & Observers Medal**
- **Inter-American Defense Board Medal**
- **Republic of Vietnam Campaign Medal**
- **Kuwait Liberation Medal (Govt. of Saudi Arabia)**
- **Kuwait Liberation Medal (Govt. of Kuwait)**
- **Republic of Korea War Service Medal**

WW II Sailor Display with Phillipine Liberation Medal

Philippine Defense Medal

Country	Republic of the Philippines
Instituted	1945
Dates	8 December 1941 and 15 June 1942.
Criteria	Service in defense of the Philippines between 8 December 1941 and 15 June 1942.
Devices	Bronze Star.

Anodized or Gold-Plated

Miniature Medal

Medal Reverse

Regulation Ribbon Bar

The Philippine Defense Medal was instituted by the Philippine Commonwealth *(now The Philippine Republic)* in 1944 and authorized for wear on the U.S. uniform by the United States Government in 1945. It is awarded for service in the defense of the Philippine Islands from December 8, 1941 to June 15, 1942.

To qualify, the recipient must: (a) have been assigned or stationed in Philippine territory or in Philippine waters for not less than 30 days during the above period and/or (b) have participated in any engagement against the enemy on Philippine territory, in Philippine waters or in the air over the Philippines or Philippine waters during the above period.

Participation includes members of the defense garrison of the Bataan Peninsula, or of the fortified islands at the entrance to Manila Bay or members of and present with a unit actually under enemy fire or air attack, or crew members or passengers in an airplane which was under enemy aerial or ground fire. Individuals eligible under both (a) and (b) above are entitled to wear a bronze star on the ribbon bar.

The Philippine Defense Medal is classified as a foreign service award. The medal was designed and struck for the Philippine Government by the Manila firm of El Oro and is a circular gold disc with an outer edge of ten scallops. The medal's center depicts a female figure with a sword and shield representing the Philippines. Above the figure are three stars and surrounding it is a green enamel wreath. At the bottom right of the medal is a map of Corregidor and Bataan. The reverse of the medal has the raised inscription, "FOR THE DEFENSE OF THE PHILIPPINES" in English set in four lines. The ribbon is red with a white stripe near each edge and, repeating the starred motif of the medal, three white five-pointed stars in the form of a triangle base down in the center.

Philippine Liberation Medal

Anodized or Gold-Plated | Medal Reverse | Miniature Medal

Country	Republic of the Philippines
Instituted	1945 (Army)
Dates	17 October 1944 and 3 September 1945.
Criteria	Service in the liberation of the Philippines between 17 October 1944 and 3 September 1945.
Devices	Bronze Star.

Awarded by the Philippine Commonwealth (now The Philippine Republic) for service in the liberation of the Philippine Islands from October 17, 1944 to September 3, 1945. In order to qualify, one of the following provisions must be met:

a. Participation in the initial landing operation on Leyte and adjoining islands from 17-20 October 1944.

b. Participation in any engagement against the enemy during the Philippine Liberation Campaign.

c. Service in the Philippine Islands or in ships in Philippine Waters for not less than 30 days during the period from October 17, 1944, to September 2, 1945.

Individuals eligible under any two of the foregoing provisions are authorized to wear one bronze star on the ribbon bar. Personnel eligible under all three provisions are authorized to wear two bronze stars on the ribbon bar.

The Philippine Liberation Medal is classified as a foreign service award. The medal was designed and struck by the Manila firm of El Oro for the Philippine Government. The medal is gold with a Philippine sword, point up, superimposed over a white native shield having three gold stars at the top and the word, "LIBERTY" below. Below are vertical stripes of blue, white and red enamel with the sword being in the center of the white stripe. At the sides of the medal and below the shield are gold arched wings. The reverse of the medal has the raised inscription, "FOR THE LIBERATION OF THE PHILIPPINES" set in four lines *(all inscriptions are in English)*. The ribbon is red with a narrow blue stripe and a narrow white stripe in the center.

Philippine Independence Medal

Anodized or Gold-Plated | Medal Reverse | Miniature Medal

Country	Republic of the Philippines		
Instituted	1946 *(Army)*	Dates	4 July 1946
Criteria	Receipt of both the Philippine Defense and Liberation Medals/Ribbons. Originally presented to those present for duty in the Philippines on 4 July 1946.		
Devices	None		

Awarded by the Philippine Commonwealth to those members of the Armed Forces who received both the Philippine Defense Medal and the Philippine Liberation Medal. The Philippine Independence Medal was authorized in 1946 by the United States and the Philippine Commonwealth. It is one of the more unusual awards presented to U.S. Service personnel since it has two independent and totally applicable sets of award criteria. As originally promulgated, the ribbon was presented to those members of the United States Armed Forces who were actually serving in the Philippine Islands or in Philippine territorial waters on 4 July 1946. In 1954, the criteria was changed to grant the Medal to all those who were previously awarded both the Philippine Defense Medal and the Philippine Liberation Medal.

Although the award qualifications established in 1946 were removed from applicable regulations, no attempt was made to rescind the previous awards made under those earlier criteria. The Philippine Independence Medal is classified as a foreign service award. The medal was designed and struck for the Philippine Government by the Manila firm of El Oro. The medal is a circular gold disc with a female figure in the center, dressed in native garb and holding the Philippine flag. There are flags on either side of the figure and she is surrounded by a circular border. Inside the border is a raised inscription, "PHILIPPINE INDEPENDENCE" *(in English)* around the top and July 4, 1946 at the bottom. The reverse contains the inscription, "GRANTED PHILIPPINE INDEPENDENCE BY THE UNITED STATES OF AMERICA" set in six lines *(also in English)*. The ribbon is derived from the colors of the Philippine flag and consists of a medium blue base with a narrow white center stripe bordered by thin red stripes. There are thin, golden yellow stripes at each edge.

United Nations Military Medals for the U.S. Armed Forces

Originally, U.S. military personnel serving with United Nations Missions were permitted to wear only two UN medals, the United Nations Korean Service Medal and the United Nations Medal *(shown to the right)*. However, changes in Department of Defense policy in 1996 authorized the wear of the ribbons of 11 missions on the U.S. military uniform.

In 2011 sixteen more missions were added to the list, which, along with the United Nations Special Service Medal, brought the total to 28. However, only one ribbon (or medal) may be worn on the U.S. military uniform and awards for any subsequent missions are denoted by the three-sixteenth inch bronze stars.

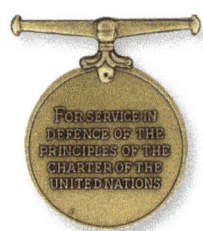

United Nations Service Medal (Korea)

Service: All Services
Instituted: 1951
Criteria: Service on behalf of the United Nations in Korea between 27 June 1950 and 27 July 1954.
Devices: None

Notes: Above date denotes when award was authorized for wear by U.S. military personnel.

United Nations Medal

Service: All Services
Instituted: 1964
Criteria: 6 months service with any authorized UN mission.
Devices:

Notes: Medal worn with appropriate mission ribbon. (See below for complete list).

UNTSO
United Nations Truce Supervision Organization
Country/Location: **Israel, Egypt**
Dates: **1948 - Present**

UNMOGIP
United Nations Military Observer Group in India/Pakistan
Country/Location: **India, Pakistan**
Dates: **1949 - Present**

UNOGIL
United Nations Observer Group in Lebanon
Country/Location: **Lebanon**
Dates: **1958**

UNSF/UNTEA
United Nations Security Force in West Guinea (West Irian)
Country/Location: **West New Guinea (West Irian)**
Dates: **1962 - 1963**

UNIKOM
United Nations Iraq/Kuwait Observation Mission
Country/Location: **Iraq/Kuwait**
Dates: **1991 - 2003**

MINURSO
United Nations Mission for the Referendum in Western Sahara
Country/Location: **Morocco**
Dates: **1991 to Present**

UNAMIC
United Nations Advance Mission in Cambodia
Country/Location: **Cambodia**
Dates: **1991 -1992**

UNPROFOR
United Nations Protection Force
Country/Location: **Former Yoguslavia, (Bosnia, Herzegovina, Croatia, Serbia, Montenegro, Macedonia)**
Dates: **1992 - 1995**

UNTAC
United Nations Transitional Authority in Cambodia
Country/Location: **Cambodia**
Dates: **1992 - 1993**

ONUMOZ
United Nations Operation in Mozambique
Country/Location: **Mozambique**
Dates: **1992 - 1994**

UNOSOM II
United Nations Operation in Somalia II
Country/Location: **Somalia**
Dates: **1993 - 1995**

UNOMIG
United Nations Observer Mission in Georgia
Country/Location: **Georgia (Russia)**
Dates: **1993 - 2009**

UNMIH
United Nations Mission in Haiti
Country/Location: **Haiti**
Dates: **1993 - 1996**

UNPREDEP
United Nations Prevention Deployment Force
Country/Location: **Former Yugoslavia; Republic of Macedonia**
Dates: **1995 - 1999**

UNTAES
United Nations Transitional Administration for Eastern Slavonia, Baranja and Western Sirmium
Country/Location: **Croatia**
Dates: **1996 - 1998**

UNSMIH
United Nations Support Mission in Haiti
Country/Location: **Haiti**
Dates: **1996 - 1997**

MINUGUA
United Nations Verification Mission in Guatemala
Country/Location: **Guatemala**
Dates: **1997-1997**

UNMIK
United Nations Interim Administration Mission in Kosovo
Country/Location: **Kosovo**
Dates: **1999 - Present**

UNTAET
United Nations Transitional Administration in East Timor
Country/Location: **Timor (New Guinea)**
Dates: **1999 - 2002**

MONUC
United Nations Organization Mission in the Democratic Republic of the Congo
Country/Location: **Congo**
Dates: **1999 - 2010**

UNMEE
United Nations Mission to Ethiopia and Eritrea
Country/Location: **Ethiopia, Eritrea**
Dates: **2000 - 2008**

UNMISET
United Nations Mission of Support in East Timor
Country/Location: **Timor (New Guinea)**
Dates: **2002 - 2005**

UNMIL
United Nations Mission in Liberia
Country/Location: **Liberia (West Africa)**
Dates: **2003 - 2018**

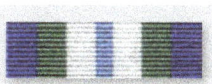
MINUSTAH
United Nations Stabilization Mission in Haiti
Country/Location: **Haiti**
Dates: **2004 - 2017**

UNAMID
United Nations / African Union Hybrid Operation in Darfur
Country/Location: **Darfur (East Africa)**
Dates: **2007 - 2020**

MINURCAT
United Nations Mission in the Central African Republic and Chad
Country/Location: **Central African Republic, Chad (Central Africa)**
Dates: **2007 - 2010**

MONUSCO
United Nations Organization Stabilization Mission in the Democratic Republic of the Congo
Country/Location: **Congo**
Dates: **2010 - Present**

 **United Nations Special Service Medal UNSSM**

Background: Established in 1994 by the Secretary General of the United Nations, the UNSSM is awarded to military and civilian personnel service in capacities other than established peace-keeping missions or those permanently assigned to UN Headquarters. The UNSSM may be awarded to eligible personnel service for a minimum of ninety (90) consecutive days under the control of the UN in operations or offices for which no other United Nations award is authorized. Posthumous awards may be granted to personnel otherwise eligible for the medal who died while serving under the United Nations before completing the required 90 days of service.

Clasps: Clasps engraved with the name of the country or United Nations organization (e.g.: UNHCR, UNSCOM, UNAMI, etc.) may be added to the medal suspension ribbon and ribbon bar.

NATO Medal

Awarded to U.S. military personnel for service under the NATO command and in direct support of NATO operations. Recipients may qualify for such NATO operations as:
(1) Former Yugoslavia: 30 days service inside or 90 days outside the former Republic of Yugoslavia after July 1, 1992 to Oct. 12, 1998.
(2) Kosovo: 30 continuous/accumulated days in or around the former Yugoslavian province of Kosovo from October 13, 1998 to Dec. 31, 2002.

Multiple rotations or tours in either operational area will only qualify for a single award of that medal.

The NATO Medal, like the United Nations Medal, has a common planchet/pendant but comes with unique ribbons for each operation. As in the case of the United Nations, U.S. Service personnel who qualify for both NATO Medals will wear the first medal/ribbon awarded and a bronze service star on the ribbon bar and suspension ribbon to denote the second award. As before however, the two medal clasps which may accompany the medal. i.e., "FORMER YUGOSLAVIA and KOSOVO" may not be worn on the U.S. military uniform.

The medal is a bronze disk featuring the NATO symbol in the center surrounded by olive branches around the periphery. The reverse contains the inscription, "NORTH ATLANTIC TREATY ORGANIZATION" in English around the top edge and the same wording in French along the lower edge. A horizontal olive branch separates the central area into two areas. Atop this, set in three lines, is the inscription, "IN SERVICE OF PEACE AND FREEDOM" in English. The same text in French on four lines is inscribed in the lower half.

In November, 2002, the NATO Military Committee issued a new NATO Medal Policy in which two classes of service awards will now be issued, namely "Article 5" and "Non-Article 5". The reference is to Article 5 of the original NATO Charter Treaty in which the member nations agreed that an armed attack against any one of them in Europe or North America shall be considered an attack against them all and if such an armed attack occurs, each of them will take such action, including the use of armed force, to restore and maintain the security of the North Atlantic area. Non-Article 5 operations are those conducted as a peace support or crisis operation authorized by the North Atlantic Council.

To date, two Article 5 Medals have been issued by NATO, the first being for Operation "Eagle Assist". Following the 9-11 attacks, NATO Early Warning (NAEW&C) aircraft were deployed from October 12, 2001 to May 16, 2002, to monitor the airspace over the United States to protect against further airborne attack by terrorists.

The second award, is awarded to personnel who took part in Operation "Active Endeavor", the deployment of a NATO Standing Naval Force to patrol the Eastern Mediterranean against hostile forces. That effort began on October 26, 2001 and will be terminated at a date to be announced in the future. In addition, two Non-Article 5 NATO have been authorized for U.S. military personnel. The qualification period for the NATO Balkans Medal is 30 days of continuous or accumulated service from January 1, 2003 to a date to be determined. The NATO medals for Afghanistan and Iraq are also awarded for 30 days of service in country.

The medal designs are the same as all previous NATO Medals. As in the past, only one NATO Medal may be worn on the uniform with subsequent operations and/or tours indicated by bronze stars affixed to the center of the ribbon bar or suspension ribbons. Also as before, the mission bars depicted above may not be worn on the U.S. military uniform.

NATO Medal
Service: All Services
Instituted: 1992
Criteria: 30 days service in or 90 days outside the former Republic of Yugoslavia and the Adriatic Sea under NATO command in direct support of NATO operations.
Devices:

Notes: *Above date denotes when award was authorized for wear by U.S. military personnel. "Former Yugoslavia" and "Kosovo" Bars not authorized for wear by U.S. Military personnel.*

Article 5 NATO Medal
Service: All Services
Instituted: 2002
Criteria: 30 days service as part of Operation "Eagle Assist" (Medal 1) or Operation Active Endeavor (Medal 2).
Devices:

Notes: *As per a memorandum issued by the Deputy Secretary of Defense dated 2 March 2006, the above medals are now authorized for wear on the uniform by U.S. military personnel.*

Non-Article 5 NATO Medal and ISAF Medal
Service: All Services
Instituted: 2002
Criteria: 30 days service as part of NATO operations in the Balkans (Medal 3) of Afghanistan (Medal 4).
Devices:

Notes: *As per a memorandum issued by the Deputy Secretary of Defense dated 2 March 2006, the above medals are now authorized for wear on the uniform by U.S. military personnel.*

The NATO Meritorious Service Medal

The NATO Meritorious Service Medal

The **NATO Meritorious Service Medal** was established in 2003 for military and civilian personnel commended for providing exceptional or remarkable service to NATO. The Medal is the personal Award of The Secretary General of NATO, who signs each citation. Generally fewer than 50 medals are awarded each year and it is the only significant award for individual effort on the NATO staff. It can be awarded to both Military and Civilian staff. The criteria for the award reflects: the performance of acts of courage in difficult or dangerous circumstances; showing exceptional leadership or personal example; making an outstanding individual contribution to a NATO sponsored program or activity; or enduring particular hardship or deprivation in the interest of NATO.

The ribbon and medal fabric is NATO Blue with white edges, with silver and gold threads centered on the white. The medal disc is of silver color, occasional you will see copies being sold with the regular brass medallion. The NATO Meritorious Service Medal is now authorized for wear on U.S. Military uniforms.

Multinational Force & Observers Medal

Multinational Force and Observers Medal

Service: All Services
Instituted: 1982
Criteria: 6 months service with the Multinational Force & Observers peacekeeping force in the Sinai Desert.
Devices:

The international peacekeeping force known as The Multinational Force and Observers *(MFO)* was established following the ratification of the Camp David Accords and the 1979 peace treaty between Israel and Egypt. Its sole purpose was to monitor the withdrawal of Israeli forces from the occupied portions of the Sinai Peninsula and the return of that territory to the sovereignty of Egypt.

The MFO Medal was established by the Director General on March 24, 1982 to recognize those personnel who served at least 90 days with the Multinational Force and Observers after August 3,1981 *(the requirement was changed to 170 days after March 15, 1985)*. Periods of service on behalf of the MFO outside the Sinai are also counted towards medal eligibility.

The medal is a bronze disk depicting a stylized dove of peace surrounded by olive branches in its center. Around the edge of the medallion are the raised inscriptions, "MULTINATIONAL FORCE" at the top and "OBSERVERS" on the lower half. The reverse is plain with the inscription, "UNITED IN SERVICE FOR PEACE" set on 5 lines *(all inscriptions are in English)*.

Inter-American Defense Board Medal

Inter-American Defense Board Medal

Service: All Services
Instituted: 1981
Criteria: Service with the Inter-American Defense Board for at least 1 year.
Devices:

Notes: *Above date denotes when award was authorized for wear by U.S. military personnel.*

The medal and ribbon were authorized on December 11, 1945 by the Inter-American Defense Board, *(IADB)* and were approved by the U.S. Department of Defense for wear by U.S. military personnel on May 12, 1981. The IADB Medal is classified as a foreign service award and is awarded for permanent wear to military personnel who have served on the Inter-American Defense Board for at least one year, either as chairman of the board, delegates, advisors, officers of the staff, as officers of the secretariat or officers of the Inter-American Defense College. The medal is a golden-bronze circular disk with a representation of the globe of the world in the center depicting the Western Hemisphere. Around the periphery of the globe are the arrayed the flags of the member nations of the IADB. The reverse of the medal is plain. A five-sixteenth inch diameter gold star device is worn on the ribbon bar and the suspension ribbon for each five years of service to the IADB.

Republic of Vietnam Campaign Medal

Anodized or Gold-Plated

Regulation Ribbon Bar

Medal Reverse

Miniature Medal

Service	All Services
Instituted	1966
Devices	Date Bar "1960"
Criteria	6 months service in the Republic of Vietnam between 1965 and 1973 or if wounded, captured or killed in action during the above period.
Notes	Bar inscribed "1960-" is the only authorized version.

The Republic of Vietnam Campaign Medal was established by the Government of the Republic of Vietnam on May 12, 1964 and authorized for award to members of the United States Armed Forces by the Department of Defense on June 20, 1966. To qualify for award, personnel must meet one of the following requirements:

(1) Have served in the Republic of Vietnam for 6 months during the period from March 1, 1961 to March 28, 1973.

(2) Have served outside the geographical limits of the Republic of Vietnam and contributed direct combat support to the Republic of Vietnam and Armed Forces for six months. Such individuals must meet the criteria established for the Armed Forces Expeditionary Medal *(Vietnam)* or the Vietnam Service Medal, during the period of service required to qualify for the Republic of Vietnam Campaign Medal.

(3) Have served for less than six months and have been wounded by hostile forces, captured by hostile forces, but later escaped, was rescued or released or killed in action.

Special eligibility rules were established for personnel assigned in the Republic of Vietnam on January 28, 1973. To be eligible for the medal, an individual must have served a minimum of 60 days in the Republic of Vietnam as of that date or have completed a minimum of 60 days service in the Republic of Vietnam during the period from January 28, 1973 to March 28, 1973, inclusive.

The Republic of Vietnam Campaign Medal is a white six-pointed star with cut lined, broad gold star points between and a central green disk with a map of Vietnam in silver surmounted with three painted flames in red, signifying the three regions of Vietnam. The reverse contains the inscription, "VIET-NAM" in a lined circle in the center with the name of the medal inscribed in Vietnamese text at the upper and lower edges separated by many short lines. The device, an integral part of the award, is a silver ribbon 28mm long on the suspension ribbon and 15mm long on the service bar inscribed, "1960-" and was evidently intended to include a terminal date for the hostilities. Many examples of this medal are found with devices inscribed with other dates but this is only version authorized for U.S. personnel.

Saudi Arabian Medal for the Liberation of Kuwait

Anodized or Gold-Plated

Miniature Medals

Regulation Ribbon Bar

Medal Reverse

Service	All Services
Instituted	1991
Criteria	Participation in, or support of, Operation Desert Storm. (17Jan.- 28 Feb. 1991).
Devices	

Established in 1991 by the Government of Saudi Arabia for members of the Coalition Forces who participated in Operation DESERT STORM and the liberation of Kuwait. In the same year, the U.S. Defense Department authorized the acceptance and wearing of the Kuwait Liberation Medal by members of the Armed Forces of the United States.

To be eligible, U.S. military personnel must have served for at least one day in support of Operation DESERT STORM between January 17 and February 28, 1991 in The Persian Gulf, Red Sea, Gulf of Oman, portions of the Arabian Sea, The Gulf of Aden or the total land areas of Iraq, Kuwait, Saudi Arabia, Oman, Bahrain, Qatar and the United Arab Emirates. The recipient must have been attached to or regularly serving for one or more days with an organization participating in ground and/or shore operations, aboard a naval vessel directly supporting military operations, actually participating as a crew member in one or more aerial flights supporting military operations in the areas designated above or serving on temporary duty for 30 consecutive days during this period. That time limitation may be waived for people participating in actual combat operations.

The medal depicts the map of Kuwait in the center with a crown at its top between two encircling palm branches, all of which is fashioned in gold. Above this is a gold palm tree surmounted by two crossed swords. Surrounding the entire design is a representation of an exploding bomb in silver. The reverse is plain. The ribbon bar is issued with a replica of the palm tree with crossed swords found on the medal and is the only authorized attachment.

Kuwait Liberation Medal (Emirate of Kuwait)

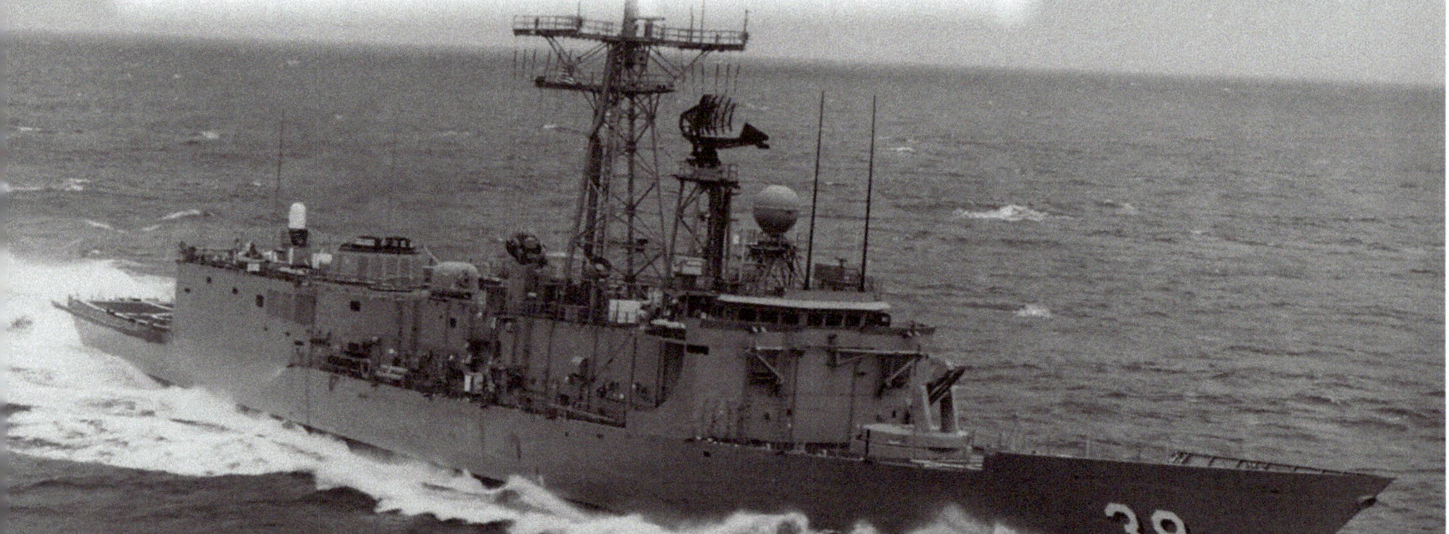

Service	All Services
Instituted	1995
Devices	None
Criteria	Participation in, or support of, Operations Desert Shield and/ or Desert Storm (1990-93).
Notes	Above date denotes when award was authorized for wear by U.S. military personnel.

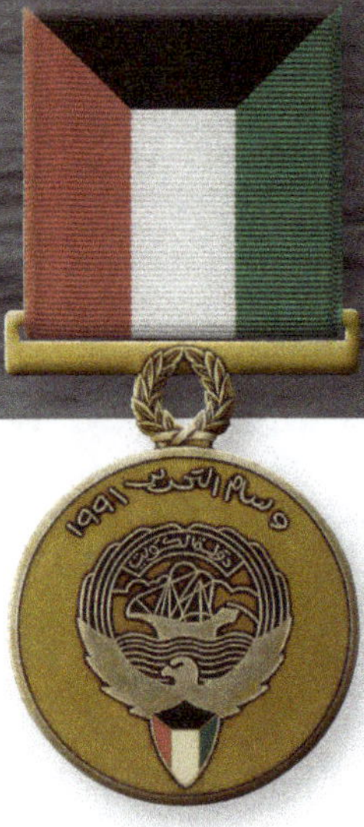

Bronze

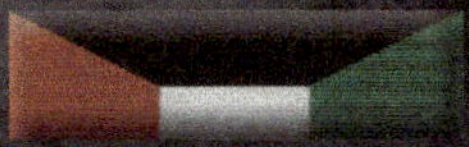

Regulation Ribbon Bar

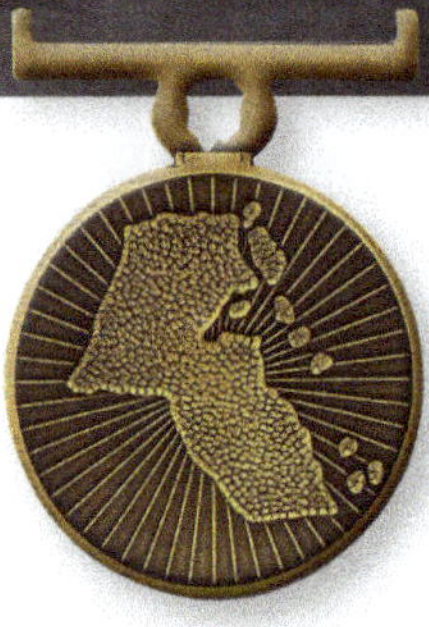

Medal Reverse

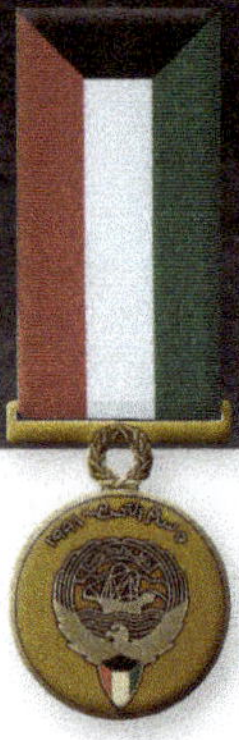

Miniature Medal

Established in July, 1994 by the Government of Kuwait for members of the United States military who participated in Operations DESERT SHIELD or DESERT STORM. On March 16, 1995, the Secretary of Defense authorized the acceptance and wearing of the Kuwait Liberation Medal (Kuwait) by members of the Armed Forces of the United States. To be eligible, U.S. military personnel must have served in support of Operations DESERT SHIELD or DESERT STORM between August 2, 1990 and August 31, 1993, in The Arabian Gulf, Red Sea, Gulf of Oman, portions of the Arabian Sea , The Gulf of Aden or the total land areas of Iraq, Kuwait, Saudi Arabia, Oman, Bahrain, Qatar and the United Arab Emirates. The recipient must have been attached to or regularly serving for one or more days with an organization participating in ground and/or shore operations, aboard a naval vessel directly supporting military operations, actually participating as a crew member in one or more aerial flights directly supporting military operations in the areas designated above or serving on temporary duty for 30 consecutive days or 60 nonconsecutive days during this period. That time limitation may be waived for people participating in actual combat operations. The Kuwait Liberation Medal (Kuwait) follows the Kuwait Liberation Medal from the government of Saudi Arabia in the order of precedence. The medal is a bronze disk which depicts the Kuwaiti Coat of Arms with the Arabic inscription, "1991 - Liberation Medal." The reverse contains a map of Kuwait with a series of rays emanating from the center out to the edge of the medal - all in bas-relief. The ribbon bar may be one of the most unusual ever displayed on the American military uniform. It consists of three equal stripes of red, white and green with a black, trapezoidal-shaped section silk-screened across the entire upper half. No attachments are authorized for the medal or ribbon.

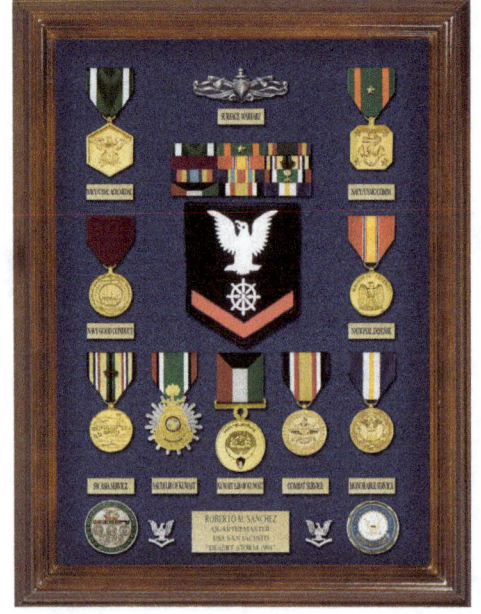

Republic of Korea War Service Medal

Service	All Services
Instituted	1953
Devices	Ancient oriental symbol called a taeguk
Criteria	Service on the Korean Peninsula between 1950 and 1953
Notes	Not accepted by the United States Government for wear on the military uniform until 1999. *Some original 1953 medals had a taeguk in the center of the drape like the ribbon bar.

Bronze

Anodized or Gold-Plated

Miniature Medals

Regulation Ribbon Bar

Medal Reverse

The Republic of Korea War Service Medal was established in 1951 by the Government of the Republic of Korea for presentation to the foreign military personnel who served on or over the Korean Peninsula or in its territorial waters between June 27, 1950 and July 27, 1953. However, it was not approved for acceptance and wear until 1999. To be eligible for this award, U.S. military personnel must have been on permanent assignment or on temporary duty for 30 consecutive days or 60 non-consecutive days. The duty must have been performed within the territorial limits of Korea, in the waters immediately adjacent thereto or in aerial flight over Korea participating in actual combat operations or in support of combat operations. The 48 year interval between establishment and its formal acceptance represents the second longest period of time in U.S. history between an event of significant national and military importance and the establishment of an appropriate commemorative medal.

The medal is a bronze disk containing a map of the Korean Peninsula at top center over a grid of the world and olive branches on either side of the design. Below the map are two crossed bullets. In the center of the ribbon and earlier medal drapes (1950's), is an ancient oriental symbol called a taeguk (the top half is red and the bottom half is blue). The reverse contains the inscription, "FOR SERVICE IN KOREA" in English embossed on two lines with two small blank plaques on which the recipient's name may be engraved.

Marksmanship Medals

The Marksmanship Medal is a United States Navy and U.S. Coast Guard military award and is the highest award one may receive for weapons qualification. The Marksmanship Medal is the equivalent of the U.S. Army and U.S. Marine Corps Expert Marksmanship Badge.

The Marksmanship Medal is awarded for qualifying as an expert marksman on either the Beretta M9 (Navy or Coast Guard), SIG P229 DAK *(Coast Guard only)*, or M16 rifle. To qualify at the expert level, a superior score must be obtained on an approved weapons qualification course. The standard Navy weapons qualification course for pistol consists of several courses of fire from standing and supported kneeling positions. For the rifle, the Navy qualification course consists of firing from a sitting and prone positions.

Personnel qualifying as an expert marksman are authorized to wear the Marksmanship Medal, awarded as a separate decorations for rifle or pistol qualifications. Service members qualifying on both pistol and rifle receive both medals for wear. The Marksmanship Medal is worn as a full-sized medal on dress uniforms. On a duty uniform all qualifiers wear the award as the standard Marksmanship Ribbon. Those qualifying as an expert are authorized to wear the "Expert" device on the ribbon and those qualifying as a sharpshooter are authorized a "S" device.

For a decade, from 1910 to 1920, the U.S. Navy awarded a marksmanship badge, called the Navy Sharpshooter's Badge, to Sailors who qualified with the service rifle and/or service pistol.

The Navy Sharpshooter's Badge 1912

Today, Sailors are awarded marksmanship ribbons and medals to denote service weapon qualification.

The Navy Sharpshooter's Badge was awarded at two qualification levels, expert and sharpshooter. The Navy Sharpshooter's Badge was made of antique bronze with a rectangular brooch that had the word "SHARPSHOOTER" embossed in its center with circling serpent bookends. The badge's pendant hung from two types of clasps, an Expert Qualification Clasp and a Qualification Year Clasp. The Expert Qualification Clasp is identical in design to the brooch but with the word(s) "EXPERT," for the service rifle, or "EXPERT PISTOL SHOT," for the service pistol. Each time a shooter requalified as expert, another Expert Qualification Clasp was hung from the badge. If no Expert Qualification Clasp was suspended from the badge, then the shooter qualified as a sharpshooter *(see example)*. The Qualification Year Clasp is different in design from the brooch which incorporated three ovals along its access for the placement of Year Disks. The Year Disk was made of silver and embossed with the year the shooter qualified/requalified. On the fourth requalification year, another Qualification Year Clasp was hung from the badge with a fourth Year Disk embossed with the year of requalification. There was no limit to the number of clasps that could be hung from the badge. The badge's pendant is the design basis for today's U.S. Navy marksmanship medals. The only difference between the pendant of the Navy Sharpshooter's Badge and the Navy Expert Rifleman Medal or Expert Pistol Shot Medal is the metal color *(from antique bronze to gold)*, the deletion of the crossed rifles from behind a replica of a rifle target, and the addition of the words "EXPERT RIFLEMAN" or "EXPERT PISTOL SHOT" embossed above the rifle target.

Starting in 1920, U.S. Navy marksmanship ribbons replaced the Navy Sharpshooter's Badge. There are two types of U.S. Navy marksmanship ribbons, the U.S. Navy Rifle Marksmanship Ribbon and one for the U.S. Navy Pistol Marksmanship Ribbon. Each can be embellished with a marksmanship device to denote the shooter's qualification level. A silver "E" Device is awarded

Expert Rifleman Medal 1941

to those who qualify as an expert *(the highest qualification level)* while a bronze "S" Device is awarded to those who qualify as a sharpshooter (second highest qualification). If no marksmanship device is displayed, the shooter qualified as a marksman *(lowest qualification level)*. For an unknown period of time, a bronze "E" Device was awarded to those who initially qualified as expert; after three consecutive expert qualifications, the device turned to silver with a permanent award status. Starting in 1969, the Expert Rifleman Medal and Expert Pistol Shot

Medal were introduced and are awarded to Sailors who qualify as expert along with the U.S. Navy marksmanship ribbon with silver "E" Device.

A silver "E" Device is awarded for qualification as an expert (the highest qualification level).

A bronze "S" Device is awarded for qualification as a sharpshooter (second highest qualification).

Expert Pistol shot 1955

Navy Expert Rifleman Medal

The Navy Expert Rifleman Medal was designed by the U.S. Mint and is awarded to members of the U.S. Navy and Naval Reserve who qualify as Expert with a rifle on a prescribed military rifle course. The medallion is a bronze disc bordered with a rope edge. The ribbon hangs from a smaller disc superimposed at the top containing the figure of an eagle clutching an anchor in its talons, taken from the seal of the U.S. Navy. The larger disc has a raised "bull's eye" *(rifle target)* in the center. Above the bull's eye is the raised inscription, "EXPERT RIFLEMAN" and on the lower edge, the curved inscription, "UNITED STATES NAVY." The reverse of the medallion is blank for engraving. The ribbon is navy blue with three thin light green stripes. Although originally intended as a single, one class award, the concept was extended during the Vietnam War to provide for two additional levels of achievement with the creation of the Navy Rifle Marksmanship Ribbon.

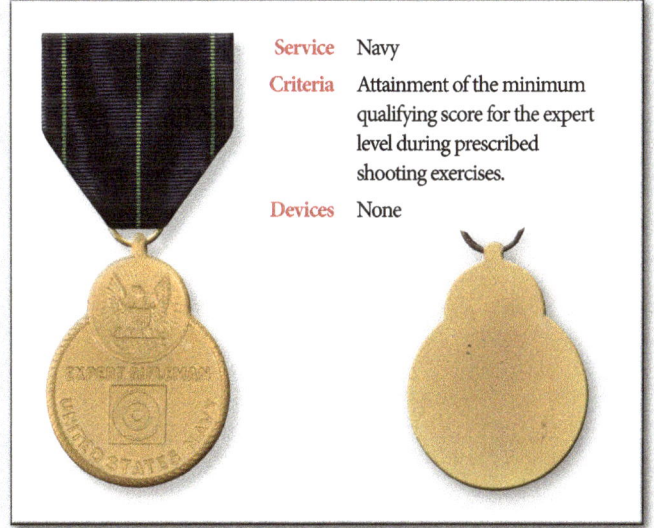

Service Navy
Criteria Attainment of the minimum qualifying score for the expert level during prescribed shooting exercises.
Devices None

Navy Expert Pisto Shot Medal

The Navy Expert Pistol Shot Medal was created at the same time as the Navy Expert Rifleman Medal and is awarded to Naval Personnel who qualify as experts with the pistol on a prescribed military course. The medallion is the same as the Expert Rifleman Medal except for the raised inscription, "EXPERT PISTOL SHOT." The ribbon is navy blue with a narrow light green stripe at each edge. Also like its rifle counterpart, the concept was later extended to provide for two additional levels of achievement with the creation of the Navy Pistol Marksmanship Ribbon.

Service Navy
Criteria Attainment of the minimum qualifying score for the expert level during prescribed shooting exercises.
Devices None

Navy Rifle Marksmanship Ribbon

The Navy Rifle Marksmanship Ribbon was established by the Secretary of the Navy on October 14, 1969 to extend the range of marksmanship awards below the Expert level. To create this "ribbon-only" award, the ribbon of the Navy Expert Rifleman Medal was retained and redesignated as the Navy Rifle Marksmanship Ribbon with devices to denote the Marksman and Sharpshooter levels. To indicate the various levels, the ribbon for the Marksman level is unadorned and the Sharpshooter level uses a bronze letter "S". To reward the attainment of the Expert level, the medal is retained unadorned but a silver letter "E," is placed on the ribbon bar. The ribbon is navy blue with three thin stripes of light green. Attachment letters are affixed to the center

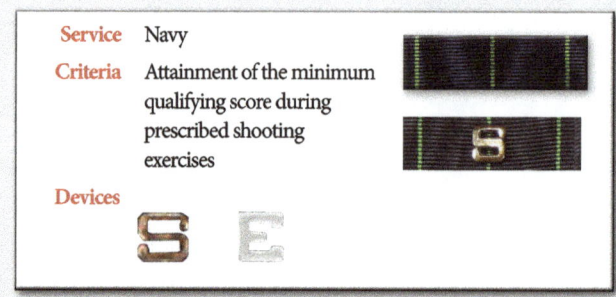

of the ribbon. Earlier regulations provided for a bronze letter "E" to denote to first qualification at the Expert level and the silver "E" to indicate the "final" achievement of Expert status but this was soon discontinued in favor of the silver "E".

Navy Pistol Marksmanship Ribbon

The Navy Pistol Marksmanship Ribbon was established by the Secretary of the Navy on October 14, 1969 to extend the range of marksmanship awards below the Expert level. To create this "ribbon-only" award, the ribbon of the Navy Expert Pistol Shot Medal was retained and redesignated as the Navy Pistol Marksmanship Ribbon with devices to denote the various levels. To indicate the Marksman level, the ribbon is unadorned while the Sharpshooter level uses a bronze letter "S". To reward the attainment of the Expert level, the medal is retained unadorned but a silver letter "E," is placed on the ribbon bar. The ribbon is navy blue with two thin stripes of light green. Attachment letters are affixed to the center of the ribbon. Earlier regulations provided for a bronze letter "E" to

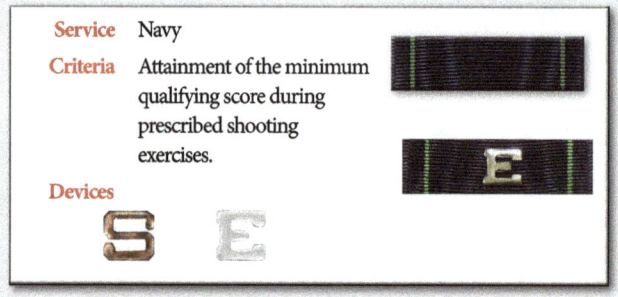

denote to first qualification at the Expert level and the silver "E" to indicate the "final" achievement of Expert status but this was soon discontinued in favor of the silver "E".

Commemorative and Society Medals

The United States Government, State Governments, Veterans Organizations, private mints and individuals have a long history of striking Commemorative and Society Medals to recognize and honor specify military victories, historical events and military service to the United States.

The tradition of honoring U.S. military heroes began when the Continental Congress awarded gold and silver medals to our victorious commanders during the Revolutionary War. While these medals were struck as table display medals, General Gates, the victor of Saratoga, chose to wear his medal hanging from a neck ribbon for his official portrait.

Naval heroes were also honored. Captain John Paul Jones received this gold medal for his victorious engagement with HMS Serapes in 1779.

Grand Army of the Republic Reunion Medal | General Society of the War of 1812 | Military Order of the Loyal Legion of the United States | Military Order of the Dragon 1900

These first Congressionally authorized medals were the forerunners of modern combat decorations.

Veteran's organizations have also issued medals to their members commemorating their service. Some of the more significant examples are the War of 1812 Society, Grand Army of the Republic medals worn by Union veterans at reunions following the Civil War and the Aztec Club Medal struck by veterans of the war with Mexico.

A subject that often comes up is a question of wearing certain military society medals on military uniforms. Title X of United States code, section 1123 (a) states:

"A member of the Army, Navy, Air Force or Marine Corps who is a member of a military society originally composed of men who served in the Armed Forces of the United States during the Revolutionary War, the War of 1812, the Mexican War, the Civil War, the Spanish-American War, the Philippine insurrection, or the Chinese Relief Expedition may wear, on certain occasions of ceremony, the distinctive badges adopted by that society."

Basically this can be interpreted that a member of the Navy who is a member of one of the societies listed below can be wear these medals on their uniform. The Society of the Cincinnatus, the General Society of the War of 1812, the Aztec Club, the Military Order of the Loyola Legion of the United States, the Naval order of the United States and the medals of the Veterans of Foreign Wars since the original founders of the VFW were veterans of the Spanish – American war, the Philippine insurrection and the Chinese relief expedition of 1900.

There may be an occasion when one would wear Society medals or ribbons on their active duty uniform but it is seldom actually done. However, the occasion does occur, that veterans wearing miniature medals on formal occasions could wear their society medals after *(at the end)* of their military decorations and service medals.

The U.S. Mint regularly produces commemorative medals to celebrate and honor individuals, places, events. The Vietnam Veterans National Medal commemorates the courage and dedication of the men and women who served in the Vietnam War. The Missing in Action Medal is a miniature replica of the 3-inch medal authorized for presentation to the next-of-kin of American personnel missing or otherwise unaccounted for in Southeast Asia.

The 200th anniversaries of the U.S. Army, Navy, Marine Corps, and Coast Guard were also celebrated with the striking of medals. The Persian Gulf National Medal honors Persian Gulf War veterans. A complete listing of all commemorative medals available from the U.S. Mint can be obtained by calling (202) 283-2646.

While the Federal Government issues commemorative medals from the U.S. Mint, state and county governments use private mints and contractors to strike medals honoring veterans. Veterans associations such as the American Legion and Veterans of Foreign Wars, have issued commemorative medals.

Commemorative medals reflect the American spirit. The 75th Anniversary of World War I and the 50th Anniversary celebrations of both World War II and the Korean War have occasioned the need for commemorative medals to honor the veterans of those conflicts. The most recent example is the Cold War Victory Commemorative Medal struck to fill the void created when Congress authorized a Cold War Victory Recognition Certificate but elected not to fund a medal.

Although unofficial in nature and not sanctioned by the U.S. Government, commemorative medals represent very tangible mementos for all veterans and honor their service and sacrifice. Commemorative Medals are designed for display and not worn on military uniforms. The commemorative medals shown on page 174-175 are representative of high quality, well designed commemoratives struck to honor veterans for service during the past sixty years.

Medals of America Press

Examples of Current Naval Commemorative Medals

Combat Action Commemorative Medal

Qualifying Dates: 1941-TBD

Criteria: Struck to honor all, Naval Personnel who served in Comat Action

Navy Marine Presidential Unit Citation Commemorative Medal

Qualifying Dates: 1941-TBD

Criteria: Struck to honor all, sailors and Marines who have been award the Presidential Unit Citation..

Navy Marine Unit Commemorative Medal

Criteria: Honors all Sailors and Marines awarded the Navy and Marine Unit Commendation Ribbon.

Republic of Vietnam Service

Qualifying Dates: 1960-1975

Criteria: Struck to honor all soldiers, sailors, marines and airmen who served in or supported the Vietnam Theater.

World War II Commemorative Medal

Qualifying Dates: 1941 - 1946

Criteria: Struck to honor all who served in the United States Armed Forces During WWII and those who worked in war industry.

Korean Defense Commemorative Medal

Qualifying Dates: 1950 - Present

Criteria: Commemorates 50 years in defense of South Korea and is for all military personnel who have served in South Korea or in direct support anytime between 1950 and Present.

RVN Gallantry Cross Unit Citation Commemorative Medal

Qualifying Dates: 1965-1973

Criteria: Struck to honor all soldiers, sailors, marines and airmen who were awarded the RVN Gallantry Cross Unit Citation.

Sea Service Commemorative Medal

Qualifying Dates: 1941-TBD

Criteria: Struck to honor all sailors, or marines who have serviced more than 30 days at sea.

Cold War Victory Commemorative Medal

Qualifying Dates: 1945 - 1991

Criteria: Struck to recognize any honorable military service between 2 Sept 1945 and 26 December 1991.

U.S. Navy Service Commemorative Medal

Instituted: 1939

Qualifying Dates: 1939 - Present

Criteria: Struck to honor all who honorably served in the U.S. Navy between 1939 and the present.

Foreign Expeditionary Service Commemorative Medal

Criteria: Honors all U.S. Armed Forces personnel who have been have deployed overseas as part of an expeditionary forces.

Operation Iraqi Freedom Commemorative Medal

Qualifying Dates: 2003-2011

Criteria: Designed to honor the devotion, loyalty and achievement of all who served in tthe Iraq Campaigns.

American Defense Commemorative Medal

Qualifying Dates: 1775 to Present

Criteria: To honor those who served at least 30 days in the United States Armed Forces during any period of service.

Liberation of Kuwait Commemorative Medal

Instituted: 1990-

Qualifying Dates: 1990-2000

Criteria: To honor all US Navy members who served in combat operations and combat support in Desert Storm.

Overseas Service Commemorative Medal

Qualifying Dates: 1918 to present.

Criteria: Struck to honor all Soldiers, Sailors, Marines and Airmen who served in an overseas theater or expeditionary operation outside the United States for 30 days or more.

Honorable Discharge Commemorative Medal

Qualifying Dates: 1918 to present.

Criteria: Struck to honor all Soldiers, Sailors, Marines, Airmen and Coast Guardmen who recieved an Honorable Discharge for service in Armed Forces of the United States.

Notes and Comments

An artist once told me it took two people to do a painting. One to paint and one to tell the artist when to stop. This book is like that. Where do you stop? It maybe a little heavy on Vietnamese awards but maybe not.

It may have missed some foreign awards that have been presented lately and if you notice that please let me know. A book like this is always a work in progress.

Bibliography

Baldwin, H.W. - *What You Should Know About The Navy*

Belden, B.L. - *United States War Medals*, 1916

Borthwick, D. and Britton, J. - *Medals, Military and Civilian of the United States*, 1984

Department of the Navy - *United States Navy Uniform Regulations*, 1998

Dorling, H.T. - *Ribbons and Medals*, 1983

Foster, F.C. *Military Medals of America*, 2019

Foster, F.C. *Medals and Insignia of the Republic of Vietnam and Her Allies 1950-1975*, 2020

Foster, F.C - *United Nations Medals and Ribbons for Peacekeeping*, 2020

Fowler, W. and Kerrigan, E. - *American Military Insignia and Decorations*, 1995

Gleim, A.F. - *United States Medals of Honor, 1862-1989*, 1989

Kerrigan, E. - *American Medals and Decorations*, 1990

Kerrigan, E. - *Guidebook of U.S. Medals*, 1994

McDowell, C.P. - *Military and Naval Decorations of the United States*

Morgan, J.L. - *Military Patch Guide*, 2018

National Geographic Society - *Insignia and Decorations of the United States*, 1944

Rankin, R.H. - *Uniforms of the Sea Services*

Rosignoli, G. - *Badges and Insignia of World War II*

Rosignoli, G. - *The Illustrated Encyclopedia of Military Insignia of the 20th Century*

Smith, Richard W. - *Shoulder Sleeve Insignia of the U.S. Armed Forces 1941-1945*, 1981

Stacey, John A. - *U. S. Navy Rating Badges 1885 - 1996*, 1986 and 1996

Standberg, J.E. and Bender, R.J. - *The Call to Duty*, 1994

Thompson, James G. - *Decorations, Medals, Ribbons, Badges and Insignia of the United States Navy*, 1998

Thompson, James G. - *Decorations, Medals, Ribbons, Badges and Insignia of the United States Marine Corps*, 1999

United States Naval Institute - *The Blue Jackets Manual United States Navy*, Tenth Edition

U.S. Navy Instruction SECNAVINST 1650.1F - *Navy and Marine Corps Awards Manual*, 2020

U.S. Navy Manual NAVPERS 15,790 - *Decorations, Medals, Ribbons and Badges of the United States Navy, Marine Corps and Coast Guard, 1861-1948*, 1 July 1950

U. S. Navy - *United States Navy Uniform Regulations*

U. S. Navy - *All Hands*

Vietnam Council on Foreign Relations - *Awards and Decorations of Vietnam*, 1972

Windas, Cedric W. - *Traditions of the Navy*, 1942 and 1954

Abbreviations for Awards

AF AIR MEDAL-INDIVIDUAL ACTION
AH AIR MEDAL-INDIVIDUAL ACTION (WITH COMBAT V)
AS AIR MEDAL-STRIKE/FLIGHT
FM AIRMAN'S MEDAL
AR ANTARTICA SERVICE MEDAL
AE ARMED FORCES EXPEDITIONARY MEDAL
BS BRONZE STAR MEDAL
BV BRONZE STAR MEDAL (WITH COMBAT 'V')
ZC CANCELLED
ZU CANCELLED AND UPGRADED OR DOWNGRADED
5C CHIEF OF NAVAL EDUCATION AND TRAINING LETTER OF COMMENDATION
CL CHIEF OF NAVAL OPERATIONS LETTER OF COMMENDATION
CR COMBAT ACTION RIBBON
EC COMMANDER IN CHIEF, U.S. NAVAL FORCES, EUROPE LETTER OF COMMENDATION
PC COMMANDER IN CHIEF, U.S. PACIFIC FLEET LETTER OF COMMENDATION
TL COMMANDER NAVAL TELECOMMUNICATIONS COMMAND LETTER OF COMMENDATION
CT COMMANDER OF THE MARINE CORPS CERTIFICATE OF COMMENDATION
MC COMMANDER, NAVAL MEDICAL COMMAND LETTER OF COMMENDATION
1C COMMANDER, NAVAL RESERVE FORCE LETTER OF COMMENDATION
2C COMMANDER, NAVAL SURFACE RESERVE FORCE LETTER OF COMMENDATION
LC COMMANER IN CHIEF, U.S. ATLANTIC FLEET CERTIFICATE OF COMMENDATION
DS DEFENCE SUPERIOR SERVICE MEDAL
DD DEFENSE DISTINGUISHED SERVICE MEDAL
MR DEFENSE MERITORIOUS SERVICE MEDAL
DX DISTINGUISHED FLYING CROSS
DV DISTINGUISHED FLYING CROSS (WITH COMBAT V)
DM DISTINGUISHED SERVICE MEDAL
GL GOLD LIFE SAVING MEDAL
GC GRAND CRUZ
HO HELD OVER
HS HUMANITARIAN SERVICE MEDAL
JU JOINT MERITORIOUS UNIT AWARD
JA JOINT SERVICE ACHIEVEMENT MEDAL
JC JOINT SERVICE COMMENDATION MEDAL
JV JOINT SERVICE COMMENDATION MEDAL (WITH COMBAT V)
LM LEGION OF MERIT
LV LEGION OF MERIT (WITH COMBAT V)
XX LETTER OF COMMENDATION
ME MARINE CORPS EXPEDITIONARY MEDAL
MH MEDAL OF HONOR
MM MERITORIOUS SERVICE MEDAL
MU MERITORIOUS UNIT COMMENDATION
NE NAVY "E" RIBBON
NA NAVY ACHIEVEMENT MEDAL
NV NAVY ACHIEVEMENT MEDAL (WITH COMBAT V)
NM NAVY AND MARINE CORPS MEDAL
AT NAVY ARCTIC SERVICE RIBBON
NC NAVY COMMENDATION MEDAL
CV NAVY COMMENDATION MEDAL (WITH COMBAT V)
NX NAVY CROSS
EM NAVY EXPEDITIONARY SERVICE MEDAL
NU NAVY UNIT COMMENDATION
ZZ NO AWARD
OM ORDER OF MERIT
OT OTHER
PU PRESIDENTIAL UNIT CITATION
PH PURPLE HEART
RC REPUBLIC OF VIETNAM MERITORIOUS UNIT CITATION
RG REPUBLIC OF VIETNAM MERITORIOUS UNIT CITATION - GALLANTRY
RT RETURNED
ZR REVOKED
SD SEA SERVICE DEPLOYMENT RIBBON
SC SECRETARY OF THE NAVY LETTER OF COMMENDATION
SL SILVER LIFE SAVING MEDAL
SS SILVER STAR MEDAL
SA SOUTHWEST ASIA SERVICE MEDAL
VS VIETNAM SERVICE MEDAL

INDEX

A

Abbreviations for Awards 177

Admiral Dewey 12

Afghanistan Campaign Medal 142

Air Medal 106-107

American Campaign Medal 18, 123

American Defense Service Medal 18

Antarctica Service Medal 134

Armada Medal 5

Armed Forces Expeditionary Medal 136

Armed Forces Reserve Medal 153

Armed Forces Service Medal 148, 139

Army Certificate of Merit 78

Army Civil War Campaign Medal 11, 79

Army Occupation Medal 18

Asiatic-Pacific Campaign Medal 18, 124-125

Attachments and Devices 32

Aztec Club of 1847 14

B

Badge of Military Merit 78, 102

Battle Clasp 82

Benjamin Franklin 6

Bibliography 176

Brian Brakke, Rear Admiral 97

Bronze Star Medal 101

C

Campaign Stars on Ribbons 36, 37, 41

Captain Joel T. Boone 90

Charles-Henri du Ché, French Vice Admir 98

Chief Petty Officers 1941 19

China Relief Expedition Medal (Navy) 15, 81

China Service Medal 120

Civilian Dress 76

Civil War Campaign Medal (Army) 79,11

Civil War Medals of Honor 11, 90

Civil War Service Medal (Navy) 79

Cold War 1947-1991 62

Cold War Recognition Certificate 22, 55

Cold War Victory Commemorative Medal 22, 175

Commemorative and Society Medals 173

Congressional Medal of Honor 87

Crackerjack Dress Blues and Whites 19

Cuban Pacification Medal (Navy) 15

Current Commemorative Medals 174, 175

D

DD214 54

Defense Distinguished Service Medal 93

Defense Meritorious Service Medal 104

Defense Superior Service Medal 96

Denise Romeo, Lt. 104

Derek Richey, HM3, 3rd Class (FMF) 103

Devices on Ribbons 37

Device Usage on the Navy Air Medal 41

Display Medals 64

Distinguished Flying Cross 99

Dominican Campaign (Navy) 15 81

E

EAME Ribbon 126

Esse D. Elliott, Capt. 9

European African Middle Eastern Campaign Medal 18

Examples of Navy Ribbons and Devices 40

F

Female Full Size Medal Wear 48

Female Miniature Size Medal 49

Female Officer and CPO Ribbon Wear 47

Foreign Campaign Medals 160

Foreign Military Decorations 155

Foreign Unit Awards 159

Formal Civilian Wear 76

G

General Society of the War of 1812 14

Global War on Terrorism Expeditionary Medal 27, 145

Global War on Terrorism Service Medal 146

Gordon Smith, Captain 103

Grand Army of the Republic Society Medal 14

Gulf War (Desert Storm) Medals 26

H

Haitian Campaign Medal (Navy) 15, 81

History of United States Armed Forces Decorations, Unit Awards & Service Ribbons 30

Huber, Lt. Gen. Keith M. 104

Humanitarian Service Medal 149

I

Inherent Resolve Campaign Medal 144, 27, 62

Inter-American Defense Board Medal 165

Iraq Campaign Medal 143, 27, 62

J

John F. Kennedy, Lieutenant 100

John Paul Jone's Medal 7

Joint Service Achievement Medal 110

Joint Service Commendation Medal 108

Juan M. Rubio, HM2 FMF 95

Justin Wilson, HMC 92

K

Korea Defense Service Medal 147, 23

Korean Campaign Medals 1950-1954 60, 23

Korean Service Medal 132, 60, 23

Kosovo Campaign Medal 141, 60, 23

Kuwait Liberation Medal 168, 26,62

L

Legion of Merit 97, 98

Lisa M. Franchetti, Vice Admiral 98

Luis E. Fonseca, Jr.HN, FMF 92

M

Male & Female Dress Blues and Whites 50

Male Officer and CPO Ribbon Wear 44

Male Officer, CPO and E6-E1 Medal Wear 45

Male Officer, CPO and E6-E1 Miniature Medal Wear 46

Manila Bay ("Dewey") Medal 12

Mark Brouker, Captain 103

Marksmanship Medals 170

Martin E. Dempsey 93

Medal for Humane Action 130

Medal for the Liberation of Kuwait 167, 26,62

Merchant Marine Officer 75

Meritorious Service Medal 105

Mexican Service Medal (Navy) 15, 81

Michael "Mob" Tremel, Lt. Commander 99

Michael Thornton, Ensign 91

Military Medals Records 56

Military Order of the Dragon 1900 14

Military Order of the Loyal Legion 14

Military Outstanding Volunteer Service Medal 150

Multinational Force & Observers Medal 165

N

National Defense Service Medal 131, 23

NATO Medals 26, 164

Naval Reserve Medal (Obsolete) 155

Naval Reserve Meritorious Service Medal 118

Naval Reserve Sea Service Deployment Ribbon 151

Navy and Marine Corps Campaigns 125

Navy And Marine Corps Medal 100

Navy and Marine Corps Overseas Service Ribbon 152

Navy Cross 16, 92

Navy Distinguished Service Medal 16, 94

Navy Expeditionary Medal 119. 135

Navy Expert Rifleman Medal 171

Navy Good Conduct Badge of 1869 12, 78

Navy Good Conduct Medal 116, 115,117

Navy Korean War Displays 69

Navy Medal of Honor 89, 91, 11

Navy Order of Precedence Ribbon Chart 33

Navy Basic Military Training Honor Graduate Ribbon 153

Navy Recruiting Service Ribbon 152, 25

Navy Recruit Training Service Ribbon 152, 25

Navy Ribbons 33Navy Rifle Marksmanship Ribbon 172

Navy Unit Commendation 113

Navy Achievement Medal 111

Navy Commendation Medal 109

Neckerchiefs 8

Nicaraguan Campaign (Navy) 15, 81

O

Officer, CPO and E1-E6 Ribbons with Medals 43

Officers 1941 Full Dress 19

Oliver Hazard Perry 9

Outstanding Volunteer Service Medal 150

P

Philippine Campaign Medal (Navy) 15

Philippine Defense Medal 18, 160

Philippine Liberation Medal 161

Philippine Medals 161

Placement of Bronze and Silver Campaign Stars 41, 37

Placement of Devices on the Armed Forces Reserve Medal 40, 37,154

Placement of Oak Leaf Cluster Devices on the Ribbon 41

Prisoner of War Medal 114

Pyramid of Honor 84, 75

R

Republic of Korea War Service Medal 169, 60, 23

Republic of Vietnam Campaign Medal 166, 24, 61

Ribbons With Medals 43

Richard E. Byrd, Rear Admiral 128

Right Breast Displays 42

RVN Armed Forces Honor Medal 157

RVN Civil Actions Medal 159

RVN Navy Distinguished Service Order 156

RVN Navy Gallantry Cross 156

RVN Staff Service Medal 157

RVN Technical Service Medal 158

RVN Training Service Medal 158

S

Sea Service Deployment Ribbon 151

Service Clasp 82

Silver Star 95, 16, 95, 82

Society of the Cincinnatus 14

Southwest Asia, Bosnia/Kosovo, Afghanistan & Iraq Campaign Medals 62

Southwest Asia Service Medal 140, 26

Spanish Campaign Medal (Navy) 80, 13

Spanish Campaign Medal Navy, Marines 13, 80

Specially Meritorious Medal, Navy 13, 80

T

The Korean War Medals (1950-1954) 23, 60

Thomas Jefferson 6

Thomas Truxtun's Gold Medal 8

Tiffany Cross 90

Tim Brewer, Captain 105

Types of Medals, Ribbons and Attachments 32

U

Unit Awards & Ribbon Only 32

United Nations Medal 162, 163

United Nations Special Service Medal 163

United States and Foreign Awards 85

United States Merchant Marine Medals 75

United States Navy Multi Service Decorations, Unit Awards & Service Ribbons 35

UN Ribbons for Wear on the U.S. Navy Uniform 36

U.S. Navy Desert Storm (SWA) Award Displays 72

US Navy Regular Brass Miniature Medals 29

US Navy Regulations Medals 29

U.S. Navy Ribbon Devices 38

U.S. Navy Ribbons & Devices 33

U.S. Navy Vietnam Award Displays 71

U.S. Navy World War II Award Displays 67

USS Mississippi 10

USS Olympia 13

V

Variations of a United States Military Medal 29

Veteran's Medals 14

Vietnam Campaign Medals 61

Vietnamese Navy Cross of Gallantry 25, 156

Vietnam Service Medal 138

Vietnam War (1965-1973) 24

Vietnam War Navy Ribbons 25

Volunteer Palmetto Regiment 10

W

West Indies Campaign Medal (Navy) 80, 13

West Indies Campaign Medal Navy and Marines 13

West Indies Naval Campaign (Sampson) Medal (Navy) 13

World War II Navy Campaign Medals 58

World War II Navy Veterans's Medals 20

World War II Victory Medal 127, 18

World War I Navy Uniforms 17

World War I Victory Medal 82

World War I Victory Medal with Campaign Clasps 16, 82

WW I, Greenville, S.C. Commemorative 17

WW II Navy Good Conduct Medal 117

WW II Victory Medal 18, 127

Medals of America Press 181

Press

Other Great Medals and Insignia Books All Available at WWW.MOAPress.com or on Amazon

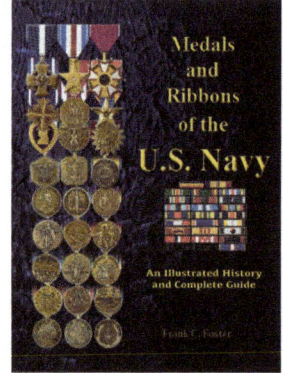
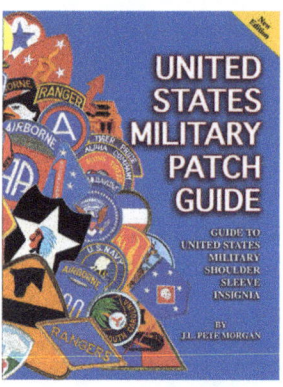

America's Best Medal and Ribbon Wear Guides All Available at WWW.MOAPress.com or on Amazon

Use this space to record some of the memories of your personal service experience for future generations to enjoy.

Use this space to record some of the memories of your personal service experience for future generations to enjoy.

www.ingramcontent.com/pod-product-compliance
Lightning Source LLC
Chambersburg PA
CBHW051246110526
44588CB00025B/2901